1940

8 MARCH In Finland, Viipuri falls to Red Army, but Stalin refuses an armistice.

9–11 APRIL German troops invade Norway and Denmark. Denmark surrenders. First British troops dispatched to Norway.

10 MAY Hitler launches invasion of the Low Countries and France, engaging French and British forces.

4 JUNE Last British evacuation ship leaves Dunkirk.

4 AUGUST Italians invade British Somaliland in East Africa.

20 SEPTEMBER – 29 OCTOBER Chinese attack Japanese lines, repelling them into Indochina.

25 OCTOBER Hostilities end in German-occupied France.

28 OCTOBER Italian troops invade Greece from occupied Albania.

---

5 APRIL Allies inform Norway and Sweden that they will begin mining Norwegian waters.

10 APRIL Major naval engagements between British and German ships. German cruiser *Königsberg* sunk by British dive-bombing attack.

17 JUNE Japan starts a blockade to stop military supplies reaching China.

3 JULY The Royal Navy attacks French fleet at Oran and Mers-el-Kebir to prevent ships from falling into German hands.

6 JULY First U-boat base in France opens at Lorient on the Atlantic coast.

9 JULY First battle between British and Italian naval forces in Mediterranean.

17–20 OCTOBER U-boats sink 32 ships from convoys SC-7 and HX-79.

---

31 JANUARY RAF Coastal Command planes enter service with ASV (Air to Surface Vessel) radar, which could detect surfaced submarines at a range of up to 36 miles (58km).

11 JUNE Italian aircraft bomb British bases at Malta, Aden and Port Sudan.

30 JULY First phase of Battle of Britain ends.

7 SEPTEMBER London subjected to massive bombing as *Luftwaffe* begins move to night *Blitz* attacks.

14/15 NOVEMBER Air raid on Coventry causes severe damage and marks commencement of heavy attacks on British industrial cities.

4/5 DECEMBER The RAF bombs Turin and Dusseldorf.

---

12 MARCH Peace agreement between USSR and Finland signed in Moscow.

27 APRIL Germany declares war on Norway.

8 MAY Neville Chamberlain resigns as British Prime Minister. Winston Churchill replaces him.

28 MAY King Leopold of Belgium orders his army to surrender to Germany.

10 JUNE Norway surrenders to Germany.

22 JUNE Armistice signed between France and Germany.

16 SEPTEMBER US introduces conscription.

27 SEPTEMBER Japan signs tripartite pact with Germany and Italy.

1941

22 JANUARY Tobruk falls to the [...]

7 MARCH British and Com[...] Within two months they h[...]

6 APRIL Axis forces invade Yugoslavia.

22 JUNE Germans launch Operation Barbarossa, the invasion of the USSR.

26–27 JUNE Finland and Hungary declare war on the USSR.

4 SEPTEMBER Leningrad comes under German siege.

23 NOVEMBER German troops advance to within 30 miles (48km) of Moscow.

7 DECEMBER Japanese troops invade British Malaya.

15 DECEMBER Japanese troops enter Burma.

---

19 MARCH Churchill forms Battle of the Atlantic Committee to coordinate British efforts against U-boats.

27 MAY First convoy to enjoy protection of continuous escort sails from Canada. *Bismarck* sunk by the battleships *King George V* and *Rodney*.

4 SEPTEMBER A German U-boat is engaged by US destroyer USS *Greer*.

26 SEPTEMBER First Arctic convoy carrying war material to the USSR leaves Britain.

31 OCTOBER Torpedo attack by U-boat sinks destroyer USS *Reuben James*.

10/11 MAY Last night of *Blitz* on Britain sees heaviest attack of the war on London.

1 AUGUST Soviet TB-3 bomber successfully employs dive-bombing technique in attack on German forces in Romania.

14 SEPTEMBER German heavy transport gliders are used for first time in assault on Baltic islands.

07 DECEMBER Japanese aircraft from aircraft carriers attack the US fleet and airfields at Pearl Harbor, Hawaii, destroying hundreds of planes, but failing to sink any aircraft carriers.

10 DECEMBER British warships HMS *Repulse* and *Prince of Wales* sunk by Japanese air attack off the coast of Malaya.

---

13 APRIL Japanese-Soviet non-aggression treaty signed.

17 APRIL Yugoslavia surrenders.

9–12 AUGUST Churchill and Roosevelt produce the Atlantic Charter.

2 SEPTEMBER Through the Lend-Lease Act, the US begins to send aid to the USSR and supplies 50 destroyers to the UK.

13 NOVEMBER USA repeals Neutrality Act.

5 DECEMBER Britain declares war on Finland, Hungary and Romania.

11 DECEMBER Germany declares war on US.

FOR 1942–45 SEE INSIDE BACK COVER

GREAT BATTLES OF WORLD WAR II

GREAT BATTLES OF WORLD WAR II

DECISIVE CONFLICTS THAT HAVE SHAPED HISTORY

General Editor: Dr. Chris Mann

Bath • New York • Singapore • Hong Kong • Cologne • Delhi
Melbourne • Amsterdam • Johannesburg • Auckland • Shenzhen

This edition published by Parragon in 2011
Parragon
Queen Street House
4 Queen Street
Bath BA1 1HE, UK

ISBN: 978-1-4454-3964-8

Editorial and design by
Amber Books Ltd
Bradley's Close
74–77 White Lion Street
London N1 9PF
United Kingdom
www.amberbooks.co.uk

Project Editor: Michael Spilling
Design: Graham Beehag
Cover and updated edition: Ummagumma Creative
Picture Research: Terry Forshaw
Text: Rupert Butler, Martin J. Dougherty,
Michael E. Haskew, Christer Jorgensen,
Chris Mann, and Chris McNab

Printed in China

PICTURE CREDITS

CONTENTS

INTRODUCTION

World War II was the most destructive conflict in human history. We tend to trace its progress through the milestones of the major engagements between the combatants. This is perfectly understandable, as the course of military history is marked by decisive battles.

This conforms to Western military philosophy, as propounded by Karl von Clausewitz (1780–1831), that it is the job of the military commander to seek out and attack that which will defeat the enemy, his 'centre of gravity'. At the operational level, this centre is the army, and thus it is important to bring an opponent to battle and to win decisively.

Yet in the twentieth century's two world wars, decisive victory proved elusive. Many of the battles or campaigns examined in this work were the result of seeking the decisive blow. Pearl Harbor, the Battle of Britain, Operation *Barbarossa*, Monte Cassino and *Market Garden* are good examples. Yet the knock-out blow was rarely achieved. The breakthrough at Sedan is perhaps the only case where a campaign was virtually decided in a single battle. Rather,

LEADERS IN VICTORY: British Prime Minister Winston Churchill (left), US President Franklin Roosevelt (centre) and Soviet premier Joseph Stalin (right) meet at the Yalta Conference, February 1945. At this tripartite conference, the fate of millions of people was decided by agreements made about the post-war reorganization of Europe.

these battles mark significant moments or turning points over longer, drawn-out campaigns. The battles were building blocks on the way to final victory or defeat. They moved front lines, wore down the enemy's strength and set up the next major clash. Such was the nature of Total War between industrialized nations.

Thus, the battles examined in this collection follow the process as the Allies and Axis sought to impose their will on each over the course of six long years of war. The myth of early German invincibility is challenged by some of the battles from the early period of the war. Whilst Sedan, Dunkirk, Crete and the opening phases of Barbarossa demonstrate the German mastery of combined arms warfare, Westerplatte, Narvik and Leningrad show that the Allies were capable of checking the *Wehrmacht*.

As the prospect of immediate victory faded, the battles of the middle phase of the war took on a more attritional aspect. El Alamein, Stalingrad, Kursk, Imphal and Cassino were all grinding, drawn-out and costly struggles, in which Allied grit and material strength were key to victory. Naval and amphibious warfare was similarly attritional and the battles of Midway and Guadalcanal were more about wearing down Japanese strength than achieving rapid victory. Yet the Germans and Japanese were remarkably skilled and resilient opponents, and even as the tide turned irrevocably they put extraordinary resistance in Normandy and Arnhem and on the islands of Iwo Jima and Okinawa.

It is the job of armies and their commanders to fight these battles and campaigns. The nature of the political leaderships of the major protagonists goes some way to explain the ferocity and longevity of the conflict. This is particularly the case with regards to the rulers of the totalitarian states, Nazi Germany's Adolf Hitler, the Soviet Union's Joseph Stalin and the military leaders of Japan, whose expansionist goals and uncompromising war aims did much to prolong the fighting. Yet they were also matched in determination by the leaders of democracies, such as Britain's Winston Churchill and the United States's Franklin Roosevelt.

The determination of the political leaders to fight to the bitter end was made possible only by the efforts of ordinary people. In a long, drawn-out war of attrition, the willingness of the populations to produce the matériel necessary, provide the manpower and endure, for the first time in history, the deliberate, large-scale targeting of civilians by aerial bombardment was absolutely crucial.

Ultimately, the 'Total War' of World War II was brought to a close only by the capture of the German capital, Berlin, and the use of a new and terrible weapon, the atomic bomb, against Japan.

Dr. Chris Mann, General Editor

THREE CHILDREN WAIT amongst the wreckage of a bomb-damaged street in London following a German air raid, September 1940.

THE GERMAN FÜHRER Adolf Hitler shares words with his Italian counterpart, Benito Mussolini, in a cavalcade through Munich, June 1940.

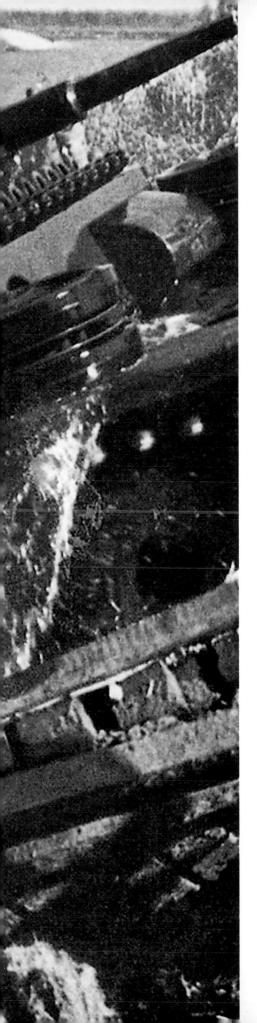

THE EARLY YEARS

The opening campaigns of World War II were marked by German victory after German victory. Superior use of modern weapons systems such as tanks and aircraft, sound doctrine and bold leadership swept aside more minor powers and even lead to impressive victories against broadly numerically, technologically equal and, sometimes, superior powers such as Britain, France and the Soviet Union.

Yet despite the achievements of the German military, the final crushing victory proved elusive and Allied victories in the skies of southern England and outside the gates of Moscow meant Germany was committed to a long-term attritional struggle.

A GERMAN PANZER III *tank crosses a river in Belorussia following the invasion of the Soviet Union in June 1941. German armour proved invincible in the early years of the war, primarily due to superior tactics.*

WESTERPLATTE

1939

Gdansk's Westerplatte peninsula was the site of the official start of World War II. A small forested island separated from Gdansk by the harbour channel, Westerplatte was established as a Polish military outpost during the interwar period.

The Poles were equipped with one 75mm (3in) field gun, two 37mm (1.5in) antitank guns, four mortars and several medium machine guns, but lacked any true fortifications. By the autumn of 1939, the Polish garrison occupying Westerplatte comprised 182 soldiers, who were expected to withstand any attack for 12 hours. The Versailles treaty made the city of Danzig (Gdansk) a free city state under the protection of the League of Nations, where Poland had a post office, special harbour rights and from 1924 the right to have a 'protected' depot. The site of the railway depot was the small, flat sandy peninsula of Westerplatte, which covered about half a square kilometre of land.

When Hitler took power in January 1933, the Poles set out to reinforce their defences at Westerplatte. They built bunkers, officially designated as

WESTERPLATTE FACTS

Who: Major Henryk Sucharski (1898–1946) led the small Polish garrison's resistance during a week of fighting against superior German naval and military police forces under the respective commands of Rear-Admiral Gustav Kleikamp and Police General Friedrich Eberhardt.

What: Westerplatte's unexpectedly fierce resistance delayed the German occupation of the narrow Polish coastline, thereby indirectly saving the Polish Navy and embarrassing the Germans.

Where: The semi-fortified supply depot on the Westerplatte peninsula at the mouth of the Vistula river north of Danzig (Gdansk).

When: 1–7 September 1939

Why: Hitler was determined, despite the existence of a non-aggression pact from 1934, to destroy Poland.

Outcome: The attack on Westerplatte on the morning of 1 September unleashed World War II.

JUST BEFORE THE GERMAN ONSLAUGHT: Polish troops with a light field piece on army manoeuvres, led by an officer wearing the characteristic four-cornered peaked cap.

11

'Guardhouses', while making concrete reinforced shelters at the bottom of the barracks and the NCOs' villa. In addition, the Poles created seven field works (*placówka*), two of which blocked access across the vulnerable land-bridge to the mainland. From March 1939, when Hitler made his demands on Poland, the garrison was on full alert and had completed the construction of the fieldworks by late August. The number of troops was also increased from the stipulated 88 men to 210 by 31 August. The commandant was Henryk Sucharski (1898–1946) and his deputy Captain Dabrowski.

PREPARATIONS

On the German side, the fighting would be done by the *SS-Heimwehr* force of 1500 men led by Police General Friedrich Eberhardt. He had some 225 crack German Marines, under Lieutenant Henningsen, to spearhead any attack on the depot. Overall command would rest with Rear-Admiral Gustav Kleikamp whose flagship *Schleswig-Holstein*, built in 1908, was officially on a

LEFT: A GERMAN MARINE in full white summer uniform as war breaks out in September 1939.

courtesy visit in Danzig. It had anchored on the southern embankment of the Harbour canal at Neufahrwasser during the morning of 25 August – only 150m (164 yards) away. Sucharski put his garrison on heightened alert and ordered that all defensive work was to be conducted during the night, since the Germans could use the tall warehouses along the quays to observe the peninsula during daytime. Kleikamp moved his ship further upstream on 26 August, to be in a better position to open fire on Westerplatte.

FRIDAY 1 SEPTEMBER

At 4.48 a.m. on Friday 1 September, the massive guns of the *Schleswig-Holstein* fired eight grenades at the southeast sector of Westerplatte. World War II had erupted and Sucharski radioed to Hel Peninsula, 'SOS: I'm under fire.'

Three large holes had been created in the perimeter wall while warehouses with oil were blazing away. Eight minutes later, Henningsen's marines attacked in formation of three platoons while his pioneers managed to blow up the railway gate in the perimeter fence cutting across the land bridge. But then things went wrong for the Germans.

First the Poles counterattacked, knocking out the machine-gun nest at the German *Schupo* (security police) post, for the loss of three men. Then Polish commander Lieutenant Leon Pajak opened intense howitzer fire on the advancing Germans, who faltered and stopped their attack. Sucharski ordered his artillery to fire on the German sniper machine-gun nests on top of the warehouses across the canal. It had the desired effect: there was no more shooting from that direction. Then the same battery almost knocked out *Schleswig-Holstein*'s command post, but finally the ship's guns managed to knock out the battery.

BELOW: AS THE FIGHTING INTENSIFIES, Westerplatte's oil tanks and buildings burn fiercely in the darkness of the night.

STILL PULLING A FIERCE PUNCH for an old lady: the Schleswig-Holstein opens fire with her main guns.

At 6.22 a.m., the Marines radioed frantically to the ship: *'Verluste zu gross, gehen zurück'* ('Heavy losses, we're leaving'). At the other end of the Westerplatte, the Danzig police had tried to seize control of the harbour but armed civilians and the garrison had defeated this surprise attack. A total of 50 Germans lay dead while the Poles had lost only eight men. Kleikamp, who had expected to take the depot through a lightning strike, now had a real battle on his hands. Reinforced by 60 *SS-Heimwehr* troops, the marines attacked again at 8.55 a.m., led by Henningsen. They got through the perimeter wall, which lay in ruins, but they were halted by mines, fallen trees, barbed wire and intense Polish fire. By noon, the fighting was still continuing, but the demoralized SS men fled. Henningsen was mortally wounded, and half an hour later the marines had had enough as well.

The fighting had cost the Germans 82 lives and Westerplatte was still holding out. The only consolation for the Germans was that they had massacred the Polish defenders of the post office in Danzig city. The German strike against Westerplatte had been an utter fiasco.

THE LULL: 2–5 SEPTEMBER

In the ensuing days, the Germans claimed they were not making any serious moves on the armed depot, while to the tired, hungry and harassed defenders there seemed to be no end to the German attacks.

Eberhardt convinced the German Commander General Fedor von Bock (1880–1945) that a land attack was not possible. Bock agreed, having witnessed the fiasco of 1 September. The following day, the *Luftwaffe* attacked the garrison with 60 bombers, dropping more than 100 bombs. No 5 bunker sustained a direct hit, killing all but three of its occupants while the kitchen, food supplies and the radio station were knocked out.

urged that Westerplatte was to surrender. An angered Dabrowski adamantly opposed such defeatism and stormed out. Sucharski ordered his men to fight on with the same dogged and brave fashion as before.

FIRETRAIN ATTACK: 6 SEPTEMBER

The Germans had no inkling that the Poles were contemplating capitulation. Every day that Westerplatte held out was superb propaganda for Poland and a humiliation for Hitler who fumed at the setbacks. A Polish agent working for the Germans pointed out that Westerplatte had no deep bunker defences.

At 3 a.m. on 6 September, the Germans sent a fire-train against the land-bridge but it was de-coupled too early by the terrified engine driver and failed to reach the oil cistern inside the Polish perimeter. If it had succeeded, it would have set the forest alight and destroyed its valuable cover for the defenders. The blazing wagons gave the

LEFT: TESTED IN SPAIN IN 1938, the Stuka was used to terrorize both military and civilians in dive bombing operations in Poland.

Now the garrison faced hunger, total isolation and the prospect of renewed attacks. Westerplatte had no anti-aircraft (AA) defences at all and this made the aerial attack on 2 September destructive to the troops' plummeting morale.

During the night of 3–4 September, the Germans attacked the Polish outposts but these were repelled. On 4 September, a German torpedo boat (T-196) made a surprise attack on the peninsula from the sea side. At the same time, the forward post of 'Wal' had been abandoned and this seemed to invite a German attack along the northern side of Westerplatte – only the 'Fort' position prevented this. At the same time, there was no hot food and the number of wounded was piling up.

On 5 September, Sucharski called a war council in the food stores where he

RIGHT: FINALLY, AFTER A WEEK of fierce fighting, the German Reichsflagge is raised above Westerplatte following the capture of the outpost.

THE SCHLESWIG-HOLSTEIN

Built between 1905 and 1908, the old battlecruiser was retained in service after 1919, when most of the German Navy was sunk, and modernized in 1925–26, 1930–31 and 1936. She was used as a cadet training ship and a floating battery. Her displacement was 13,454 tonnes (14,830 tons), her dimensions 126m (413ft) long and 22.2m (73ft) broad, while her draught (the depth of water needed in order to float) was 8.25m (27ft). The *Schleswig-Holstein* was armed with four 280mm (11in), ten 150mm (6in) and four 88mm (3.46in) naval guns, as well as four 200mm (8in) AA guns. Her crew was reinforced with 225 Marines and 60 AA artillery troops when facing the indomitable Poles of Westerplatte. The ordinary crew numbered 907 men, but with all the troops this had grown to a total of 1197 by 25 August 1939.

Poles a perfect field of fire and the Germans suffered heavy casualties as a consequence. A second fire-train attack came in the afternoon but it failed too.

7 SEPTEMBER: THE LAST ASSAULT

Sucharski held a second council of war in the evening and he had by then made up his mind not to continue fighting. After all, the German Army was now outside Warsaw and the first cases of gangrene had appeared among the wounded.

At 4.30 a.m., the Germans opened intense fire upon Westerplatte, which continued until 7 a.m., when there was a final rolling barrage followed by German storm columns. Despite the use of flamethrowers, the Poles repelled the assault. But Bunker 2 was now destroyed and Numbers 1 and 4 badly damaged.

At 9.45 a.m. the white flag appeared, and at 11.00 a.m. Sucharski surrendered the post to Kleikamp who allowed the valiant commandant to keep his sword. The German troops paraded in full order when the haggard and exhausted Polish garrison marched out of Westerplatte at 11.33 a.m.

The White Eagle of Poland had surrendered at last but not without a truly heroic struggle.

LED BY THEIR OFFICER, Polish soldiers are escorted from the fighting – still erect and proud despite their defeat.

WESTERPLATTE

1 A mere 200 Polish troops sheltering on a shallow riverine peninsula faced the awesome might of the German *Wehrmacht*.

WESTERPLATTE

DANZIG POLICE

2 The first German attack on 1 September against the perimeter wall was a resounding failure, leaving 80 Germans dead.

4 During the night of 3–4 September, a German night attack against Westerplatte's perimeter upset some of the defenders.

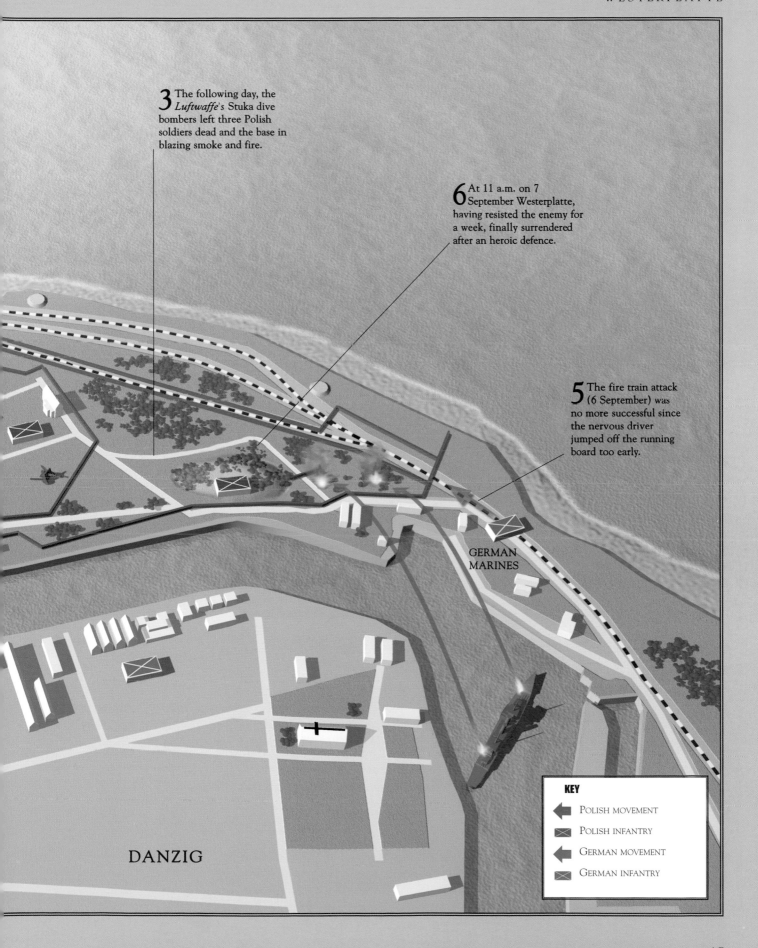

3 The following day, the *Luftwaffe's* Stuka dive bombers left three Polish soldiers dead and the base in blazing smoke and fire.

6 At 11 a.m. on 7 September Westerplatte, having resisted the enemy for a week, finally surrendered after an heroic defence.

5 The fire train attack (6 September) was no more successful since the nervous driver jumped off the running board too early.

GERMAN MARINES

DANZIG

KEY

⬅ POLISH MOVEMENT

⊠ POLISH INFANTRY

⬅ GERMAN MOVEMENT

⊠ GERMAN INFANTRY

NARVIK 1940

In early April 1940, the race was on to see which of the warring powers – Britain or Germany – would be first to seize the strategically vital port of Narvik in northern Norway. General Eduard Dietl, the commander of the German expeditionary force of 2000 mountain troops, made an unopposed landing at Narvik on 9 April.

The Germans' entry onboard 10 modern German cruisers had been blocked by two ancient Norwegian ironclads that were promptly sunk by torpedoes. Berlin had told Dietl and his men that they would be treated as 'liberators' by the Norwegians. To give credence to this fantasy, the local commander Colonel Konrad Sundlo (1881–1965) promptly capitulated. His deputy, Major Spjeldnes, took his 209 troops out of town right under the noses of the puzzled Germans whom he greeted with a cheerful *'Guten Morgen'* (Good Morning). Upon hearing this, Dietl gave orders that all Norwegians were to be disarmed. Otherwise, Narvik fell without a shot being fired in anger.

NARVIK FACTS

Who: The German and Austrian mountain troopers were led by Hitler's favourite general, Eduard Dietl (1890–1944). He faced a superior allied force commanded first by General Pierse Mackesy (1883–1956) and General Field-Marshal Claude Auchinleck (1884–1981). The French were under the command of General Antoine Béthouart (1889–1982).

What: Narvik, recaptured by the Allies by 28 May, was Germany's first military defeat in World War II.

Where: The iron-ore port of Narvik in the semi-Arctic north of Norway.

When: 9 April–7 June 1940

Why: Hitler wanted Norway's strategically valuable coastline, ports and airfields in his war against Britain.

Outcome: The belated Allied recapture of Narvik could not change the outcome of the battle for Norway or the catastrophic fortunes of the Allies on the continent after Hitler's invasion of the Low Countries on 10 May 1940.

A VILLAGE OUTSIDE NARVIK *is swept up in the fighting as it burns after an Allied naval bombardment in May 1940.*

LEFT: MERCHANT SHIPS IN NARVIK HARBOUR in various stages of burning and sinking after the unexpected Allied attack.

At dawn the following day, four British destroyers led by RN Commander Bernard Warburton-Lee (1895–1940) steamed into the port. Lee's ships sank two German destroyers, the captain of one of which was thrown up in the air with the ship but survived. Lee's own ship went straight into a nearby cliff, earning him a posthumous VC.

Three days later, Lee was avenged when the RN returned and sank the remaining eight destroyers. The First Lord of the Admiralty, Churchill, was delighted but in Berlin Hitler was apoplectic at the news. Dietl's force was now completely cut off and Hitler wanted to pull him back.

Dietl had not been idle. He equipped the redundant 2500 sailors with captured Norwegian arms and built a powerful defensive perimeter around Narvik and along the Ofoten railway into Sweden. The 'neutral' Swedes were to keep him generously supplied and informed.

LOST OPPORTUNITY

On 16 April, the lacklustre British commander, General Pierse Mackesy (1883–1956), wired London telling the Cabinet that he could not advance on Narvik. The following day, Hitler cancelled the order to evacuate Dietl, and the Allies concentrated on holding southern Norway

BELOW: GERMANS AND AUSTRIANS served in the Gebirgs or mountain troops, shown here being flown in a German transport plane (Junkers Ju-52) to Narvik.

instead of throwing Dietl's isolated garrison out of Narvik. Thanks to the 'neutral' Swedes, Dietl received 24 wagon-loads of supplies (including much needed ammunition) and three troops disguised as 'medical' staff.

Nevertheless, by late April the Allied Expeditionary Force (AEF) under Admiral Lord Cork (1873–1967) numbered 30,000, including four battalions of *Chasseurs Alpins* (Alpine Hunters) and Polish mountain troops and two battalions of Foreign legionnaires.

FIRST ALLIED OFFENSIVE: 12 MAY

On 28 April, General Antoine Béthouart (1889–1982) landed at Harstad – the Allied GHQ – to be told by Mackesy that Narvik should be taken by a three-pronged attack. Béthouart wanted none of that. His *Chasseurs Alpins*, together with Norwegian ski troops, would seize the Oyjord peninsula as a bridgehead for the final assault upon Narvik.

At midnight on 12 May, in brilliant sunshine and glittering snow, the Allied flotilla opened fire on Bjerkvik, north of Narvik and held by the *Windisch* Group. The Foreign legionnaires landed and advanced in the face of heavy enemy fire. Bjerkvik was an inferno, in which the civilian population was massacred in the crossfire. It took two hours to clear the village.

At Meby, the German resistance was crushed by the guns of HMS *Effingham*, two French Renault tanks and the 2nd Battalion of the Legion. By 7.30 a.m., after three hours of intense fighting, the Legion captured Elvegaardsmoen and a mountain of German supplies, including Dietl's correspondence, fell into French hands. Béthouart sent the Poles and his tanks to chase down the Oyjord peninsula. The Germans fled.

The German army had invaded the Low

ABOVE: A GERMAN NAVAL OFFICER *of the* Kriegsmarine *addresses naval marines and mountain troops on board a German transport ship following operations at Narvik.*

LEFT: THE Chasseurs Alpins *were specially trained and equipped for fighting in mountainous, cold and snowy terrain.*

Countries on 10 May, the same day Churchill was made British Prime Minister. They also controlled the whole of Norway south of Mosjoen, with the aim of relieving Dietl at Narvik. Time was not on the Allies' side. On 20 May, Churchill complained that the AEF was tying up much needed resources in a sideshow campaign.

HOLLOW VICTORY

The British commander Field-Marshal Claude Auchinleck (1884–1981) and Béthouart agreed to take Narvik in a four-pronged attack on the Germans.

At 11.45 p.m. on 27 May, the Allied Fleet opened up a withering bombardment of the landing beaches. Shells plastered Narvik town, Ankenes, Fagernes and the entire shoreline until wooden houses along the shore were burning like torches and the coastline was enveloped in thick smoke.

At 12.15 a.m., the legionnaires landed right into the lap of Naval Artillery Company Nöller, numbering 50 troops, and engaged them in savage hand-to-hand fighting. The heavily outnumbered sailors retreated to the railway embankment, closely followed up the slope by the legionnaires who took control of the railway area despite fierce resistance. A German gun was firing out of the nearby tunnel. The legionnaires pulled up by hand a French gun and fired at the mouth of the tunnel until the German battery was silenced for good.

A Norwegian battalion landed at Orneset and combined with the legionnaires to attack Hill 457, where the German *Gebirgsjägers* and sailors had entrenched themselves. They offered heavy resistance and the advancing Allied troops suffered heavy casualties. By four in the morning, the Poles were under heavy German fire at Ankenes while the Legion's 2nd Battalion had not landed across Rombaksfjord.

Half an hour later, German bombers attacked the Allied Fleet, forcing it back and denying the AEF supportive fire.

Two German companies immediately attacked down the slope of Hill 457, forcing the faltering Allies back and putting their precarious bridgehead in peril. At Ankenes, the Polish left flank was under threat. At sea, Béthouart's chief of staff was killed by German fire while two landing craft were sunk. Things were not looking good.

At 6 a.m., British Hurricanes flew over the battlefield, chasing away the *Luftwaffe* while the 2nd Battalion finally landed at Taraldsvik. The legionnaires and the Norwegians drove back the enemy. They gained the upper hand at Hill 457, which was now pockmarked with craters and littered with corpses.

Meanwhile the 2nd Battalion and the Norwegians pushed back the Germans along the Ofoten railway, while on the northern side of Rombaksfjord the *Chasseurs Alpins* and Norwegians drove back the Germans towards Hundal. The 2nd Polish Battalion took Nybord, from where it could fire on Ankenes.

ESCORTED BY A ROYAL NAVY DESTROYER, British troops in life vests are transported to the far north in April 1940.

At Narvik, Major Häussel and his mixed force of 400 sailors and mountain troops had no reserves, were running low on ammunition and had no communications with Dietl's HQ. Häussel decided to evacuate Narvik, taking his force along the still open Beisfjord road. That left small pockets of Germans still fighting at Hill 457 and Fagernes. By the afternoon, the Allied troops led by Béthouart made a triumphant entry into the newly liberated Narvik.

FRENCH TROOPS DISEMBARK somewhere in the vicinity of Narvik, prior to their successful capture of the port.

It did not last. On 7 June, the Allies sailed out of Narvik, taking the Norwegian King and Government to Britain in exile. By 1941, Narvik was supplying the Germans with 612,000 tonnes (674,615 tons) of iron ore. It had all been in vain.

THE NORWEGIAN ARMED FORCES (1940)

On paper, the mobilized Norwegian army was to number 100,000 men organized in six territorial divisions, one of which was to be under the command of General Carl Fleischer (1883–1942) at Harstad. The troops were equipped with green uniforms dating from 1912 and armed with 1894 Krag-Jorgensen rifles.

The army had no tanks, a handful of armoured cars, few heavy machine-guns and no real professional core. The tiny Norwegian airforce numbered 76 planes (mostly Gloucester Gladiators) and 940 men – it was knocked out on 9 April. The Navy had 113 vessels including two armoured cruisers, *Eidsvold* and *Norge*.

GLUM NORWEGIAN SOLDIERS surrender to the Germans knowing a harsh occupation awaits their country.

NARVIK

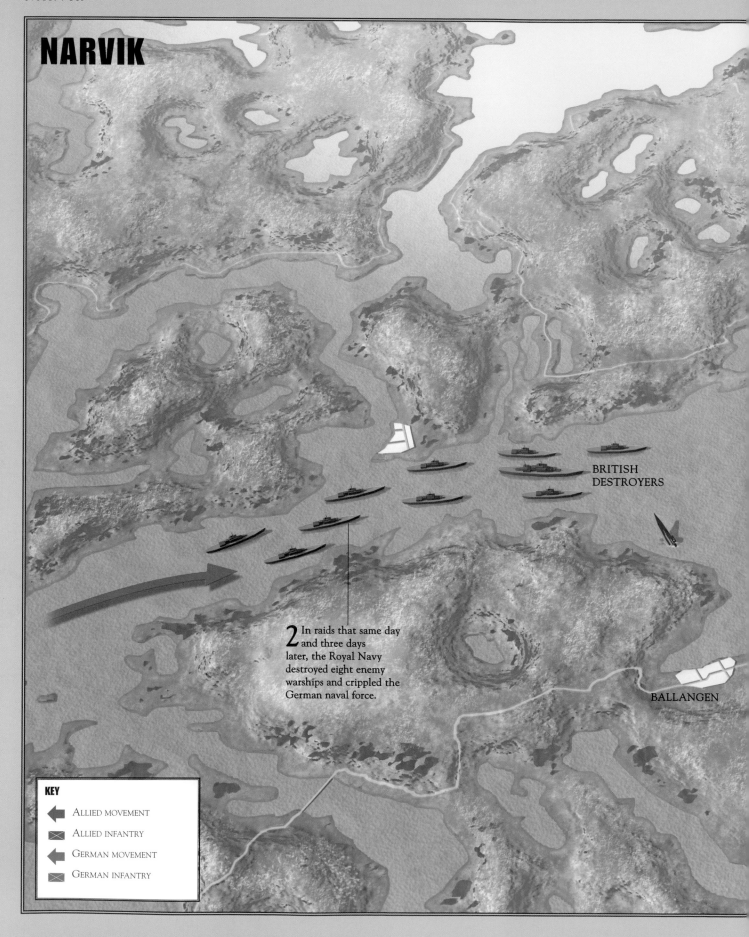

BRITISH
DESTROYERS

2 In raids that same day and three days later, the Royal Navy destroyed eight enemy warships and crippled the German naval force.

BALLANGEN

KEY

ALLIED MOVEMENT

ALLIED INFANTRY

GERMAN MOVEMENT

GERMAN INFANTRY

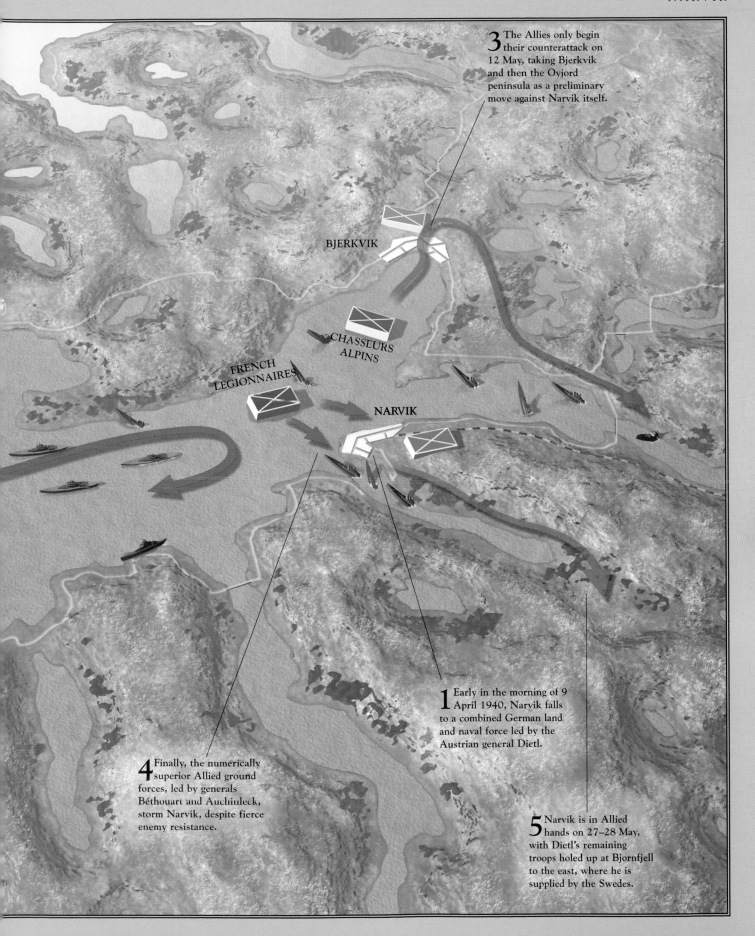

3 The Allies only begin their counterattack on 12 May, taking Bjerkvik and then the Oyjord peninsula as a preliminary move against Narvik itself.

BJERKVIK

CHASSEURS ALPINS

FRENCH LEGIONNAIRES

NARVIK

1 Early in the morning of 9 April 1940, Narvik falls to a combined German land and naval force led by the Austrian general Dietl.

4 Finally, the numerically superior Allied ground forces, led by generals Béthouart and Auchinleck, storm Narvik, despite fierce enemy resistance.

5 Narvik is in Allied hands on 27–28 May, with Dietl's remaining troops holed up at Bjornfjell to the east, where he is supplied by the Swedes.

INVASION OF FRANCE – SEDAN
1940

The conquest of France and the Netherlands during the summer of 1940 was a conspicuous triumph for Germany's Army and Air Force, leading to the defeat of the French, Dutch and Belgian armies. After the successful Polish campaign the previous September, Hitler relished the the triumph of his original Blitzkrieg (Lightning War), codenamed Fall Gelb (Case Yellow), with its emphasis on mobility and fluidity.

However, bad weather, equipment deficiencies and the need for fresh training led to further postponements. Major General Erich von Manstein (1887–1973), Chief-of-Staff in Field-Marshal Gerd von Rundstedt's (1875–1953) Army Group A, urged a giant armoured sweep through the thickly

INVASION OF FRANCE – SEDAN FACTS

Who: Gerd von Rundstedt (1875–1953) and his Chief-of-Staff Erich von Manstein (1887–1973) commanded Army Group A. Heinz Guderian (1888–1954), key in developing the concept of mass tank divisions, versus General Maurice Gamelin (1872–1958), French Commander-in-Chief, and his eventual successor Maxime Weygand (1867–1965).

What: The tactics of *Blitzkrieg* – panzers working in close coordination with artillery and dive bombers (Stukas) – achieved conspicuous successes.

Where: Germany's area of victories extended from the 'impregnable' French Maginot line to Belgium, the edge of the English Channel and the Netherlands to the north.

When: 10–28 May 1940

Why: Hitler wished to turn his attentions to a decisive assault on the Soviet Union.

Outcome: French forces in the Allied line's vital centre were shattered. In the north, Dutch armed forces were all but destroyed.

MAY 1940: A GERMAN ARMOURED COLUMN *of Panzer II tanks passes French anti-tank barriers in Sedan, following the evacuation of the town by the French Army.*

A YOUNG GERMAN SOLDIER POSES for the camera in the advance towards Dunkirk. He is armed with a Kar-98 rifle and has a grenade tucked in his belt.

was considered impregnable. The Belgians shared the belief in the Maginot Line, the elaborate system of fortifications running along France's eastern frontier. Fast-moving German armies had no trouble in outflanking it. Seven panzer divisions totalling 2270 tanks, self-propelling guns and armoured vehicles drove unopposed through Luxembourg and into the wooded hills and densely forested plateau of the Belgian Ardennes. The area was only lightly screened by French cavalry, in the belief that the narrow roads of the region could not accommodate a large armoured force.

In the early hours, the tanks of General Erwin Rommel (1891–1944), the recently appointed commander of 7th Panzer Division, crossed the southern end of the Belgian frontier, heading for the Meuse at Dinant 105km (65 miles) away. Simultaneously Hitler's panzers rolled over the Luxembourg frontier.

General Heinz Guderian (1888–1954), the spearhead commander, had spelt out to his men the prime objective – the Channel. His superior, General Ewald von Kleist (1881–1954), had command of the principal panzer forces in the *Sichelschnitt* (Sickle Stroke) plan, scything through the Allied front's centre to the English Channel, trapping the British Expeditionary Force and the First and Seventh French Armies against the sea. A gigantic phalanx of armour and vehicles, enjoying the added protection of the *Luftwaffe*, stretched back for 160km (100 miles), with its rear rank lying 80km (50 miles) east of the Rhine. Due to intelligence disregarded by the *Deuxième Bureau*, all areas were virtually undefended.

PANZER THRUST

French forces, many on leave, were hastily recalled following an order from General Maurice Gamelin (1872–1958), the Commander-in-Chief. Two Corps on the left of the Ninth Army under France's General André Corap (1873–1953) took up positions on the Meuse between

wooded Ardennes, which the French considered impassable. It was planned that the Germans would then cross the river Meuse just north of the French frontier town of Sedan and break out into the open country, with a race to the Channel at Abbeville. After slicing through the French at Sedan, there would be a heading west along the Somme's north bank to the Channel, entrapping the bulk of major Anglo-French forces.

ATTACK ON THE LOW COUNTRIES

As dawn broke on 10 May, a special force of 424 men and a swarm of gliders swooped down to destroy the heavily armoured fort of Eben Emael, a key Belgian defence, which

THE THICK ARMOURED French Char B1 bis tank required costly maintenance and constant refuelling and faced frequent breakdowns.

Namur and Givet, crossing the water to clash with von Rundstedt, approaching through the Ardennes.

On 12 May, Guderian's corps had captured Bouillon in the western part of the Belgian province of Luxembourg, crossing the French frontier just north of Sedan, where the Belgians had left many road blocks undefended. Keen to press his advantage, Guderian persuaded von Kleist to let him unleash

his three panzer divisions across the Meuse near Sedan without waiting for rear guard infantry protection. Howling Junkers JU 87 Stuka bombers rained down on the French artillery while high velocity 88mm (3.46in) 'ack-ack'

A BREAK ON THE GERMAN advance through the Ardennes – triumphant despite the Allied belief that swift movement was impossible in such terrain.

guns sprayed the enemy bunkers. Infantry of the crack Infantry regiment *Grossdeutschland*, thrusting through Luxembourg into Belgium towards the Meuse, were ferried over to attack the French positions. Within hours, *Grossdeutschland* gained a river line that the French believed would hold. A gap was smashed between Second and Ninth French armies; Guderian's Panzer Corps, driving through the breach, wheeled and positioned on line direct to the English Channel.

Further German advances revealed insufficient coordination between French tanks and infantry. Nevertheless 6th and 8th Panzer Divisions had to contend with ripostes of machine-gun fire, which also hampered the work of engineers building pontoons across the river at the village of Monthermé, within some of the most rugged territory in the Ardennes. Regrouped German armour secured the position after a fierce engagement. Two French

Divisions, 55th and 71st, faced annihilation. Rommel's 7th Panzer Division had reached the Meuse below the city of Dinant but encountered French heavy artillery shelling and small arms fire from troops on the left bank. Rommel's attention fastened on the plight of his motorized infantry attempting to cross the river in its inflatable boats. To screen the crossings, he ordered buildings on the German side to be set alight. The resulting smoke drifted across the river. Rommel's assault troops were able to establish a bridgehead; French reservists were too stunned to fight back.

At Sedan, the entire 1st Panzer Brigade crossed the Meuse on a hastily constructed pontoon bridge. *Luftwaffe* fighters fended off enemy assaults while to the south Guderian's forces deepened their bridgehead, by evening 48km (30 miles) wide. On 14 May also, Allied forces had their first encounter with the Germans sweeping through Belgium. Guderian's rapid advance caused anxiety in Berlin that, deprived of infantry, he could be cut off by any counterattack. But, in fact, the Allies were in danger of being outflanked.

ROAD TO PARIS

The British Prime Minister Winston Churchill (1874–1965) next day received a despairing telephone call from the French premier Paul Reynaud (1878–1966) declaring, 'We are beaten … The road to Paris is open'. With forces hastily assembled near the town of Montcornet, north of Paris, Colonel Charles de Gaulle (1890–1970) launched three

LEFT: *THIS CORPORAL SERVED with 1st Panzer Regiment, one of the many Panzer units involved in the breakthrough at Sedan.*

BELOW: *AN EFFECTIVE LIGHT medium tank with mounted assault, antitank and anti-aircraft armament, the Pz 38t was Czech manufactured throughout the war. This example fought with the 2nd Panzer Division.*

offensive actions, all but reaching Guderian's advanced headquarters, only to be repulsed. A shaky defensive perimeter, to where the British and French could retreat, was assembled around Dunkirk. The situation in Europe deteriorated still further. The concern was how British and French forces could escape annihilation at Dunkirk. Nevertheless, on 21 May, four battalions clashed with the 7th Panzer and Waffen SS *Totenkopf* Division, near Arras, costing the Germans 700 casualties and the loss of 20 tanks. But two days later the German armoured divisions had penetrated to the coast. The BEF was cut off, communications severed and ammunition short. To make matters worse, on 28 May the Belgian army capitulated.

AFTERMATH

Many reasons have been cited for Hitler's order to Guderian to halt his forces at Dunkirk. It might have been advice that the boggy terrain near the coast was unsuitable for tanks, or maybe it was the setback at Arras – or perhaps von Rundstedt's wish to regroup forces for the assault on Paris. Churchill was determined to keep France in the war and sent what reinforcements he could, landing at Cherbourg and Brest, but progress in all areas was hopeless in the face of the panzers and Stukas. On 14 June, the unstoppable juggernaut of the *Wehrmacht* entered the undefended French capital. Within months, Hitler's interest was turning to the east.

PANZER IIIS AND IVS roll down the main street of a town somewhere in northern France. Notably, Panzer IV was the sturdy warhorse throughout, more than holding its own against Allied opponents.

ERICH VON MANSTEIN

Erich von Manstein (1887–1973), the architect of *Blitzkreig*, achieved promotion to general field marshal on 19 July 1940, after France fell. In 1941–42, he conducted Eleventh Army's conquest of the Crimea, while his Caucasian counteroffensive saved Army Group Don from destruction after Germany's devastating defeat at Stalingrad at the end of 1942. He clashed increasingly with Hitler as the military situation on the Eastern Front declined. This served to fuel Hitler's distrust – probably influenced by Manstein's Jewish origins. Hitler sacked him in 1944, but he proved a tough survivor despite a flirtation with the anti-Nazi resistance movement. In 1948, he was arraigned as a war criminal, imprisoned and then released in 1953. He was subsequently consultant to the West German government on military matters, dying near Munich on 1 June 1973, aged 85.

THE INVASION OF FRANCE – SEDAN

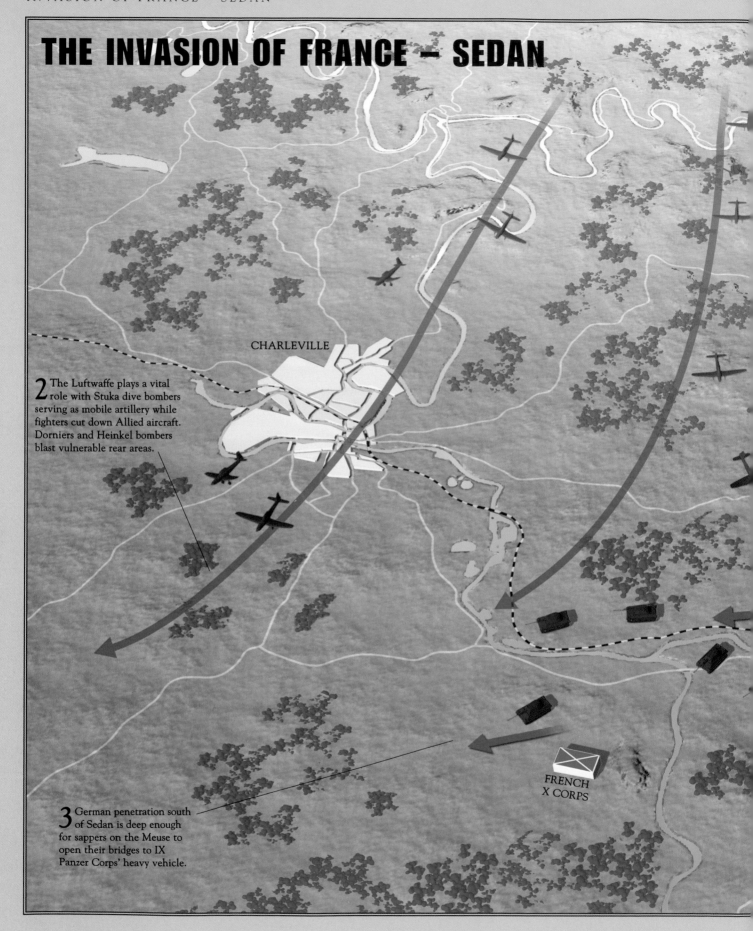

CHARLEVILLE

2 The Luftwaffe plays a vital role with Stuka dive bombers serving as mobile artillery while fighters cut down Allied aircraft. Dorniers and Heinkel bombers blast vulnerable rear areas.

3 German penetration south of Sedan is deep enough for sappers on the Meuse to open their bridges to IX Panzer Corps' heavy vehicle.

FRENCH X CORPS

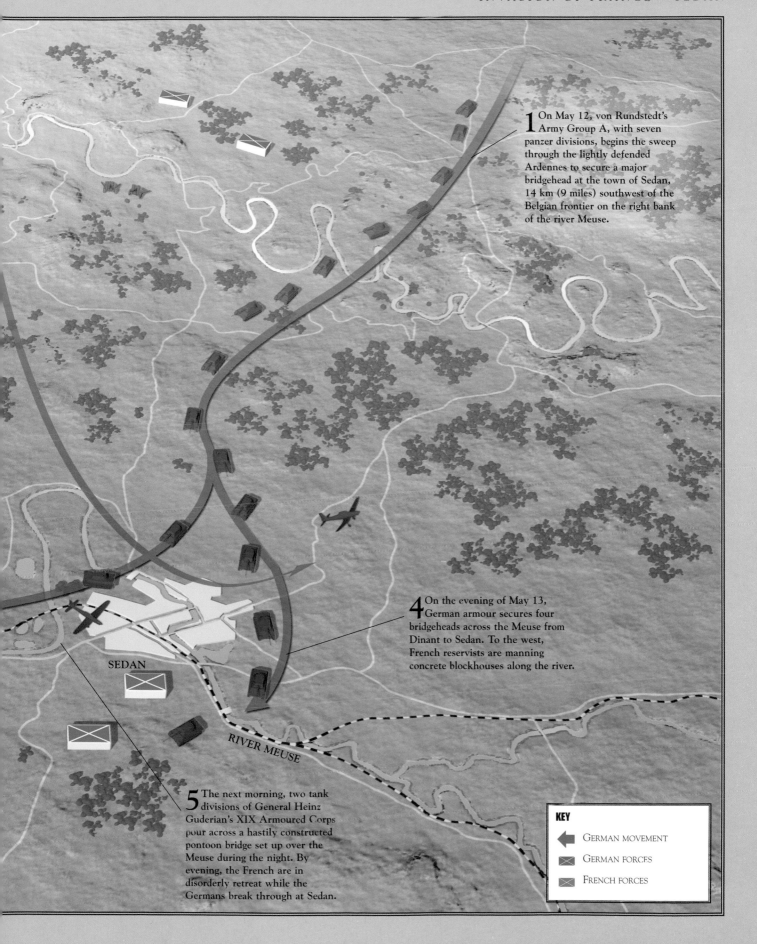

1 On May 12, von Rundstedt's Army Group A, with seven panzer divisions, begins the sweep through the lightly defended Ardennes to secure a major bridgehead at the town of Sedan, 14 km (9 miles) southwest of the Belgian frontier on the right bank of the river Meuse.

4 On the evening of May 13, German armour secures four bridgeheads across the Meuse from Dinant to Sedan. To the west, French reservists are manning concrete blockhouses along the river.

SEDAN

RIVER MEUSE

5 The next morning, two tank divisions of General Heinz Guderian's XIX Armoured Corps pour across a hastily constructed pontoon bridge set up over the Meuse during the night. By evening, the French are in disorderly retreat while the Germans break through at Sedan.

KEY

← GERMAN MOVEMENT

⊠ GERMAN FORCES

⊠ FRENCH FORCES

DUNKIRK

1940

During the opening weeks of World War II in the West, thousands of soldiers of the British Expeditionary Force and the French First Army, with their backs to the sea, were evacuated from the European continent in nine desperate days of fighting on the coast of the English Channel.

The rescue itself was deemed a 'miracle' as a hastily assembled flotilla of military and civilian vessels of every description ran a gauntlet of air attacks by the German *Luftwaffe* to ferry the troops to safety.

For eight months, the opposing armies had only watched one another warily. Then, on 10 May 1940, the *Sitzkrieg* ('Phoney War') was shattered with the German invasion of France and the Low Countries. In the north, 30 divisions of Army Group B advanced across the frontiers of The Netherlands and Belgium on a 322km (200-mile) front. Further south, 45 divisions of Army Group A slashed through the Ardennes Forest and skirted the defences of the Maginot Line. Led by one of the world's foremost proponents of mobile warfare, General Heinz Guderian

DUNKIRK FACTS

Who: The British Expeditionary Force, French, Belgian and Dutch armed forces, with the British under Field-Marshal John, Lord Gort (1886–1946) versus German Army Group A under General Gerd von Rundstedt (1875–1953).

What: The Germans forced the evacuation of the British and other Allied troops from the European Continent but failed to deliver the devastating blow that might have altered the course of World War II inexorably in their favour.

Where: The port city of Dunkirk and environs on the coast of the English Channel in northwest France.

When: 26 May– 4 June 1940

Why: The Germans sought to occupy Western Europe with the conquest of France and the Low Countries.

Outcome: The Allied forces lost thousands of prisoners along with vast quantities of war matériel; however, 338,226 soldiers were evacuated to England.

WOUNDED BRITISH AND FRENCH *soldiers file from the beach at Dunkirk. Within days of the German offensive launched on 10 May 1940, the British Expeditionary Force and remnants of the French Army were forced to evacuate the European continent.*

(1888–1954), German tanks and motorized infantry swept relentlessly northwest in a great arc, reaching the coast in only 10 days.

BLITZKRIEG

The startling swiftness of the German offensive threatened to trap all Allied troops north of the thrust by Army Group A as Guderian sent three panzer divisions racing towards the Channel ports of Boulogne, Calais and Dunkirk. Three key positions, the French at Lille, Belgian Army units along the Lys river and the British at Calais, offered resistance to the German onslaught. Within 72 hours of reaching Abbeville, the Germans captured both Boulogne and Calais, and elements of the 1st Panzer Division had advanced to within 19km (12 miles) of Dunkirk, the sole remaining avenue of

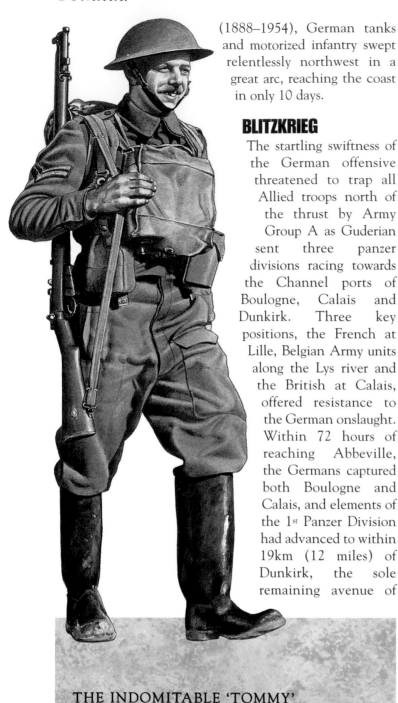

THE INDOMITABLE 'TOMMY'

His trusty Lee-Enfield rifle slung across his shoulder and the distinctive helmet secured by its sturdy chinstrap, a soldier of the British Expeditionary Force (BEF), affectionately known as a 'Tommy', manages a cheerful expression during the dark days of 1940. As the threat of war with Nazi Germany increased, conscription rapidly raised the strength of the British Army, and in 1939 alone the size of the force grew by a million men.

At the time of the German spring offensive in 1940, the BEF comprised 10 divisions deployed on the European continent. During the evacuation of the BEF from Dunkirk, codenamed Operation *Dynamo*, more than 218,000 British and 120,000 French soldiers were evacuated to safety in Britain by a seaborne effort that included many civilian craft.

escape for Allied forces in northern France and Belgium. Although he had been ordered to mount a counterattack in support of the French, Field-Marshal John, Lord Gort (1886–1946), commander of the British Expeditionary Force, chose instead to concentrate his troops in the vicinity of Dunkirk in order to evacuate as many soldiers as possible to the relative safety of England. The heroic defence of Lille by the French, of Boulogne by the 2nd Battalion Irish Guards and a battalion of the Welsh Guards, and Calais by the British 30th Infantry Brigade, bought precious time for Gort to prepare a defensive perimeter around Dunkirk. But the effort appeared to be in vain as German tank commanders peered at the town's church spires through binoculars.

THE PANZERS PAUSE

Quite unexpectedly, the greatest assistance to the Allied evacuation plan came from Hitler himself. On 24 May the *Führer* visited the headquarters of General Gerd von Rundstedt (1875–1953), commander of Army Group A, at Charleville. Influenced by *Reichsmarschall* Hermann Göring (1893–1946) to allow his *Luftwaffe* to deliver the death blow to the enemy at Dunkirk, Hitler directed Rundstedt to halt the tanks of six panzer divisions along the Aa canal.

ABOVE: THOUSANDS OF ALLIED SOLDIERS *waiting for rescue at Dunkirk while German armour and infantry continue to pressure a shrinking perimeter.*

Guderian was rendered 'utterly speechless' by the order. For nearly 48 hours the German ground assault abated and the Allied troops around Dunkirk were pummelled by screeching Stukas and strafed by *Luftwaffe* fighters. On 26 May, the ground attack resumed but the reprieve allowed Gort to patch together the tenuous defence of a 48km (30-mile) stretch of beach from Gravelines in the south to Nieuport, Belgium, in the north. Two days later, Belgian King Léopold III (1901–1983) ordered his forces to surrender, and the Allied defensive perimeter continued to contract. Eventually the Allies were squeezed into a pocket only 11km (7 miles) wide.

OPERATION DYNAMO

As early as 20 May, while the Allied debacle on the Continent was unfolding, British Prime Minister Winston Churchill (1874–1965) authorized the preparation of

RIGHT: UNDER CONSTANT THREAT *of* Luftwaffe *air attack, soldiers of the British Expeditionary Force queue up for the next watercraft that will transport them from Dunkirk to safety.*

Operation *Dynamo*, the evacuation of the British Expeditionary Force from France.

The hard-pressed Royal Navy could not possibly supply the number of vessels needed for the rescue, and Vice-Admiral Bertram Ramsay (1883–1945) called for boats in excess of 9.3m (30ft) in length to assemble at ports in England. Cabin cruisers, ferries, sailing schooners and their civilian crews joined Royal Navy destroyers in the treacherous 88km (55-mile) journey through a maze of German contact mines sown in the Channel, under continuous air attack and often within range of fire from German heavy artillery.

AIR RAIDS

Luftwaffe bombing had set the town of Dunkirk ablaze and wrecked the port facilities. Rescue vessels were compelled to risk running aground in the shoals along the beaches or to tie up at one of two 'moles' – rocky breakwaters covered with planking wide enough for men to stand three abreast – in order to take soldiers aboard. Countless acts of heroism occurred as vessels made numerous shuttle runs. One 19m

As a pall of smoke from a Luftwaffe air strike rises in the background, a British soldier lying on his back takes aim at a low flying German plane.

(60ft) yacht, the *Sundowner*, carried 130 soldiers to safety, while close to a hundred perished aboard the paddlewheel steamer *Fenella* when a German bomb ripped through its deck and detonated. Nearly one-third of the 693 boats involved were destroyed, but from 26 May until the final rescue run in the pre-dawn hours of 4 June, a total of 338,226 Allied soldiers reached England.

When the battered and exhausted Allied troops arrived, they were welcomed as heroes. Townspeople poured out of their homes with food and drink for the famished soldiers. Virtually all of their heavy equipment had been abandoned on the Dunkirk beaches, thousands of their comrades were killed or captured, and the armed forces of Britain and France had suffered one of the greatest military defeats in their history.

Yet these men had survived. Amid the celebration Churchill groused, 'Wars are not won by evacuation.' He later wrote, 'There was a white glow, overpowering, sublime,

RIGHT: THEIR VESSEL SUNK by German aircraft, dazed French soldiers and sailors of the Royal Navy are plucked from the waters of the English Channel during Operation Dynamo.

which ran through our Island from end to end … and the tale of the Dunkirk beaches will shine in whatever records are preserved of our affairs.'

AFTERMATH

Historians have debated Hitler's reasons for halting the panzers. Some assert that the focus of the Germans was already on the complete defeat of France and the capture of Paris. Others say that Hitler was concerned about the marshy terrain in Flanders, which was less than ideal for the manoeuvring of tanks. The tanks themselves had been driven rapidly and engaged for some time. Many of them undoubtedly needed refitting and some of their precious number would have been lost in an all-out attack on the Allied defences. Göring had argued that the *Luftwaffe* was certainly more loyal and fervently Nazi than the leadership of the German Army; therefore, his air arm should be given the honour of annihilating the enemy.

In the end, the *Luftwaffe* had failed to force an Allied capitulation. Thousands of Allied soldiers had escaped death or capture. The miracle of Dunkirk stands as a stirring moment in military history, and Hitler's decision to halt his panzers as one of the great 'what ifs' of World War II.

BELOW: CAPTURED BRITISH AND FRENCH soldiers await disposition following the German occupation of Dunkirk. The Luftwaffe had failed to annihilate the Allied force, and those who were rescued fought another day.

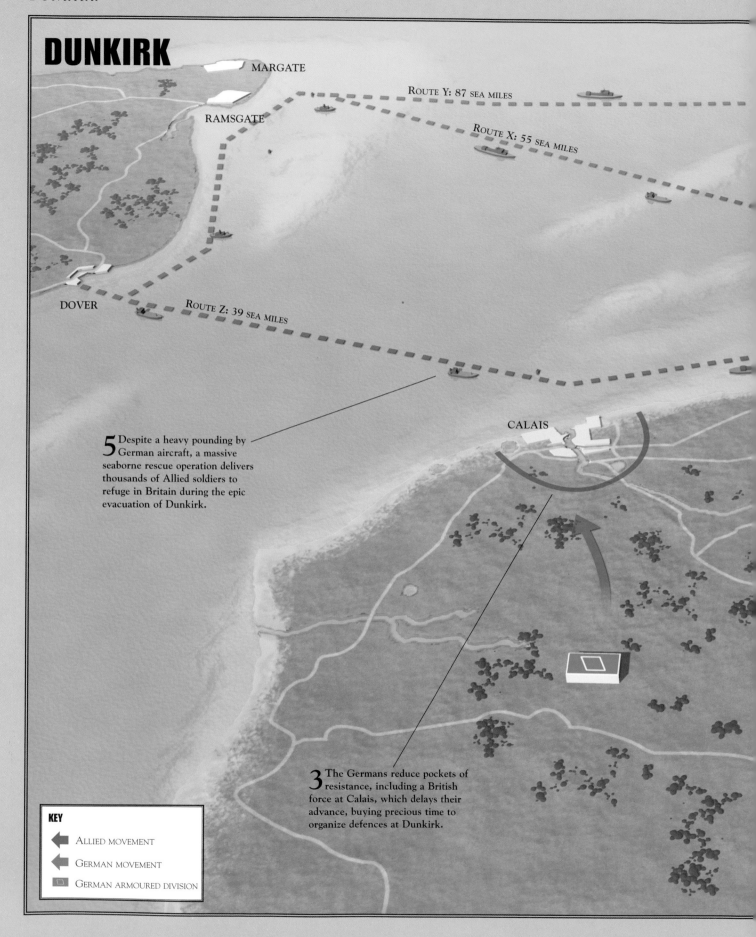

DUNKIRK

MARGATE

RAMSGATE

ROUTE Y: 87 SEA MILES

ROUTE X: 55 SEA MILES

DOVER

ROUTE Z: 39 SEA MILES

5 Despite a heavy pounding by German aircraft, a massive seaborne rescue operation delivers thousands of Allied soldiers to refuge in Britain during the epic evacuation of Dunkirk.

CALAIS

3 The Germans reduce pockets of resistance, including a British force at Calais, which delays their advance, buying precious time to organize defences at Dunkirk.

KEY

← ALLIED MOVEMENT

← GERMAN MOVEMENT

▭ GERMAN ARMOURED DIVISION

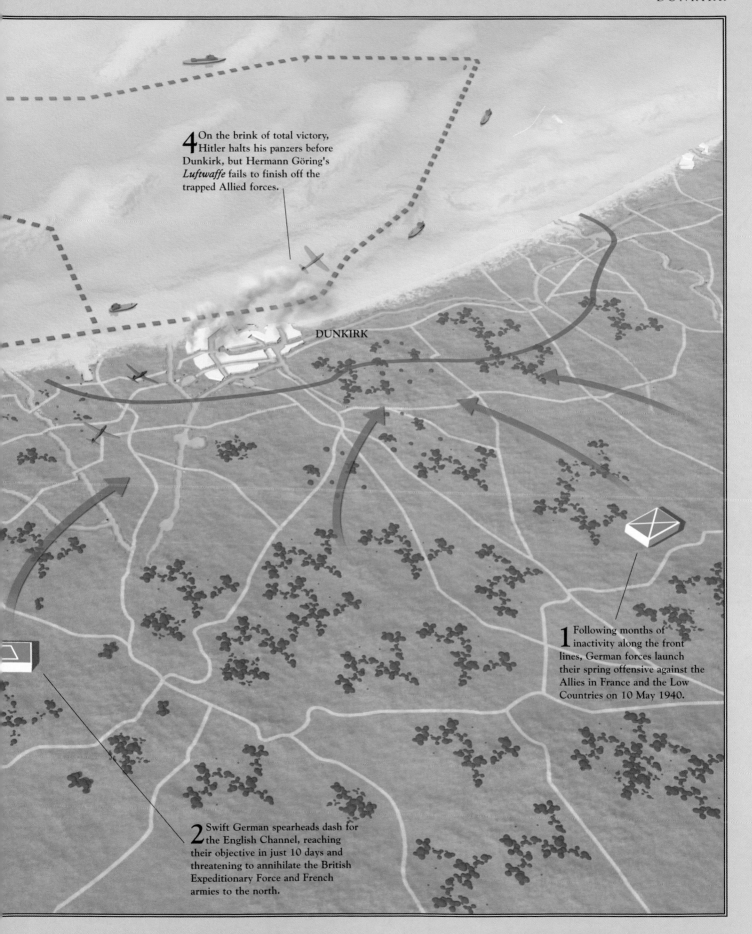

4 On the brink of total victory, Hitler halts his panzers before Dunkirk, but Hermann Göring's *Luftwaffe* fails to finish off the trapped Allied forces.

DUNKIRK

1 Following months of inactivity along the front lines, German forces launch their spring offensive against the Allies in France and the Low Countries on 10 May 1940.

2 Swift German spearheads dash for the English Channel, reaching their objective in just 10 days and threatening to annihilate the British Expeditionary Force and French armies to the north.

BATTLE OF BRITAIN

The German conquest of France and the Low Countries had been accomplished with astonishing speed. During the opening months of World War II in Europe, Nazi Germany had emerged victorious across the Continent. As German troops paraded down the Champs Elysées, Führer Adolf Hitler and his generals planned for the invasion of Great Britain.

German officers and soldiers had gazed from the French coastline across the 32km (20 miles) of the English Channel which separated them from their enemy. To a man, they knew that the conquest of Great Britain would be their greatest challenge to date. However, they were brimming with confidence

BATTLE OF BRITAIN FACTS

Who: The German *Luftwaffe* commanded by *Reichsmarschall* Hermann Göring (1893–1946) versus Royal Air Force Fighter Command under Air Chief Marshal Hugh Dowding (1882–1970).

What: The *Luftwaffe* attempted to destroy the Royal Air Force and later to raze British cities.

Where: The skies above Britain and the English Channel.

When: 10 July 1940–10 May 1941

Why: Initially, the Germans needed control of the skies to cover Operation *Sea Lion*, the invasion of Great Britain. Later, the Blitz raids were primarily terror attacks.

Outcome: The *Luftwaffe* failed to subdue the RAF and break the will of the British people. Operation *Sea Lion* was cancelled.

FROM HIS ROOFTOP *vantage point, an air raid warden scans the skies above London for* Luftwaffe *bombers. The dome of St. Paul's Cathedral rises in the background.*

43

ABOVE: BRITISH PRIME MINISTER WINSTON CHURCHILL *visits coastal defences on the southern coast of England, August 1940.*

Operation *Sea Lion,* as the invasion was codenamed, would involve the marshalling of troops and matériel, as well as the rounding up of enough barges suitable for transporting the most formidable fighting machine in the world across the narrow expanse of the Channel. Still, all of the victories thus far, all of the planning and all of the *Führer's* bold rhetoric meant far less without mastery of the skies. Control of the air was a prerequisite to any successful invasion.

KANALKAMPF

Its opening phase was known as *Kanalkampf,* or the Channel Battle, to the Germans. For the rest of the world, the aerial conflict which began on 10 July 1940 and lasted fully 10 months was known collectively as the Battle of Britain. Less than three weeks after the Fall of France, *Reichsmarschall* Hermann Göring (1893–1946) and his *Luftwaffe* began the effort to take control of the skies above Britain. Hitler had initially set the date for the invasion as 15 August, and the German planes were to pound British harbours and shipping.

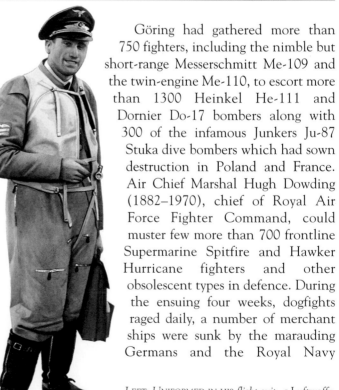

Göring had gathered more than 750 fighters, including the nimble but short-range Messerschmitt Me-109 and the twin-engine Me-110, to escort more than 1300 Heinkel He-111 and Dornier Do-17 bombers along with 300 of the infamous Junkers Ju-87 Stuka dive bombers which had sown destruction in Poland and France. Air Chief Marshal Hugh Dowding (1882–1970), chief of Royal Air Force Fighter Command, could muster few more than 700 frontline Supermarine Spitfire and Hawker Hurricane fighters and other obsolescent types in defence. During the ensuing four weeks, dogfights raged daily, a number of merchant ships were sunk by the marauding Germans and the Royal Navy

LEFT: *UNIFORMED IN HIS flight suit, a Luftwaffe bomber pilot proceeds to a pre-mission briefing.*

ABOVE: CONCEIVED AS A commercial airliner, the Heinkel He-111 was easily converted to a bomber.

relocated most of its ships and personnel to Portsmouth from Dover. The *Luftwaffe* failed, however, to sufficiently erode the strength of the Royal Air Force.

Early in the battle the British came fully to appreciate the value of accurate intelligence and a new early warning device called radar, both of which provided advance notice to them of incoming German air raids. It was also quickly determined that the lumbering Stukas were unfit for air-to-

BELOW: COURAGEOUS MEMBERS OF the London Fire Brigade wrestle a hose into position to combat a fire ignited by Luftwaffe incendiary bombs.

air combat, easy prey for RAF fighters. Although they had lost 300 planes, while half that number of British aircraft had fallen, the Germans considered their initial operations sufficiently effective to begin round two of the aerial preparations for invasion.

DER ADLERTAG

Still confident of victory, German airmen often sang a jaunty tune with the lyric, *'Wir fliegen gegen England'* ('We are flying against England'). Göring scheduled *Adlertag*, or

THE MESSERSCHMITT ME-109 *was the premiere* Luftwaffe *fighter aircraft of World War II. It was heavily armed and skilfully piloted, but its limited range allowed only 20 minutes of fighting time in hostile airspace over Britain.*

Eagle Day, for 13 August 1940. The second phase of the Battle of Britain was intended to bring the RAF to its knees, through the systematic bombing of its airfields in southern and central England; the destruction of the 93m (300ft) towers and installations which comprised the early warning radar stations strung along the English coastline; and, finally, the elimination of the planes and pilots of Fighter Command.

On Eagle Day, the Germans lost 46 planes, and the RAF 13. However, a week of nearly continuous daylight aerial combat followed. Citizens below could see the swirling vapour trails of the dogfighting planes. Occasionally they saw the puff of an exploding aircraft or the long, black trail of a burning machine as it hurtled towards the ground. At times, it actually seemed to be raining spent cartridges from British and German machine guns and cannon. Though its actual losses may have been fewer than those of the *Luftwaffe*, Fighter Command was being stretched to breaking point. Young pilots were often thrown into combat

with only a few hours of flying time, facilities had been bombed and strafed, and the rigours of combat had taken their toll on the remaining airworthy planes.

A CHANCE REPRIEVE

In concert with daylight raids, Göring also instructed his pilots to fly nocturnal bombing missions against military targets in Britain. Major cities, particularly London, had not been targeted due to the probability of retaliation by RAF bombers against German cities. However, on the night of 24 August 1940 a few *Luftwaffe* bombers strayed off course and dropped their ordnance on the city of London. The next night RAF bombers hit Berlin. Enraged, the *Führer* vowed to lay waste to British cities.

On 7 September 1940, Hitler authorized a change in strategy. The *Luftwaffe* was to bomb London into submission. A week later, however, he postponed Operation Sea Lion indefinitely. On the first night of the Blitz, more than 2000 Londoners were killed or wounded. The sacrifice of the civilian population proved to be the salvation of Fighter Command, which was given time to rest and refit. London was not the only city ravaged by German bombs in the months to come. On the night of 14 November 1940, Coventry was assailed by more than 400 *Luftwaffe* bombers, killing 568 civilians and injuring more than 1200 others. Birmingham, Liverpool and Manchester were hit. But the turning point had come with the change in German strategy and the refusal of the British people to buckle. The last *Luftwaffe* raids of the Blitz struck London on the night of 10 May 1941.

AN EASTWARD GAZE

Hitler's frustration with Göring's failure to destroy the RAF was tempered by his preoccupation with preparations for Operation *Barbarossa*, the invasion of the Soviet Union, which was scheduled for 22 June 1941. Some historians argue that the *Führer* had been reluctant to continue fighting the British, hoping that the fellow Anglo-Saxons might join in the war against the Soviet communists. At any rate, as early as the autumn of 1940, Hitler had concluded that the Battle of Britain could not be won. The opportunity for victory had been squandered and *Luftwaffe* losses continued to mount. British cities burned, but the RAF remained a potent force.

Prime Minister Winston Churchill (1874–1965) hailed the spirit of the British people and called the time of peril and suffering 'their finest hour'. On 20 August 1940, Churchill rose to address the House of Commons, praising the courage of the intrepid Royal Air Force pilots. 'Never in the field of human conflict,' he declared, 'has so much been owed by so many to so few.'

LONDONERS GAZE SKYWARDS *for any sign of approaching German aircraft as crews man anti-aircraft guns positioned in Hyde Park. Hitler and Luftwaffe chief Hermann Göring believed that the Blitz could bring Great Britain to its knees.*

SUPERMARINE SPITFIRE

Originally conceived in the 1930s by British aircraft designer Reginald Mitchell, the Supermarine Spitfire flew for the first time on 5 March 1936. Production began two years later. Powered by the Rolls-Royce Merlin engine and initially armed with a pair of 20mm (0.78in) cannon and four .303 Browning machine guns, the Spitfire represented the leading edge of technology deployed by the Royal Air Force during the Battle of Britain.

The superior performance of the Spitfire made it a worthy adversary of the German Messerschmitt Me-109. However, it was available in limited numbers compared to the older Hawker Hurricane. Therefore, the RAF instructed Spitfire squadrons to engage the German fighters, while the Hurricanes attacked the slower bomber formations. The aircraft depicted is a Spitfire Mk 1 of No. 66 Squadron.

BATTLE OF BRITAIN

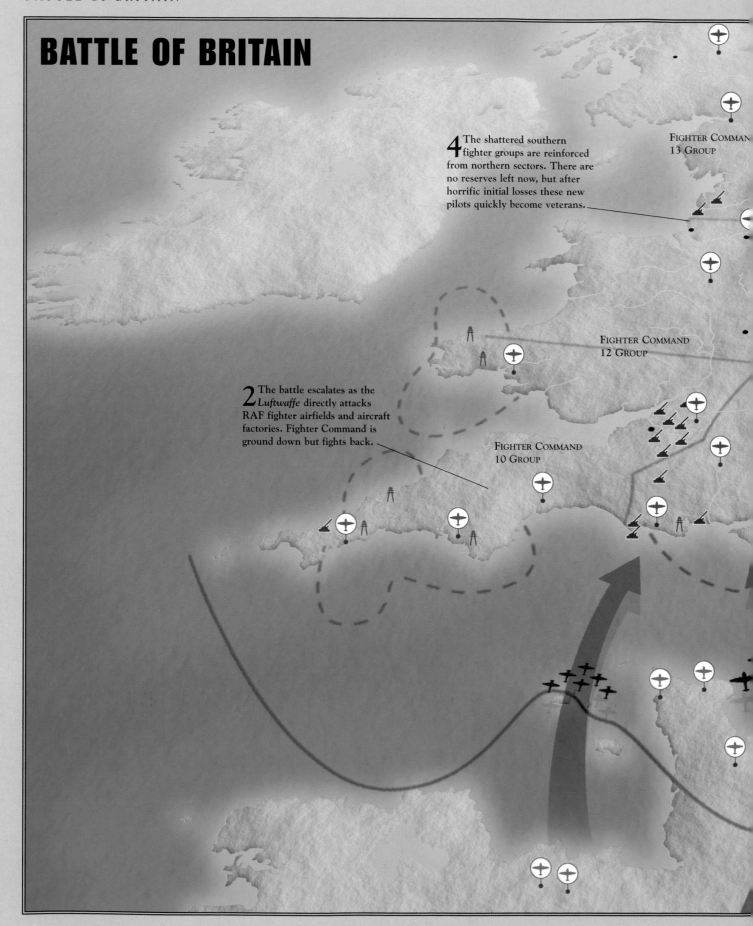

4 The shattered southern fighter groups are reinforced from northern sectors. There are no reserves left now, but after horrific initial losses these new pilots quickly become veterans.

FIGHTER COMMAN[D]
13 GROUP

FIGHTER COMMAND
12 GROUP

2 The battle escalates as the *Luftwaffe* directly attacks RAF fighter airfields and aircraft factories. Fighter Command is ground down but fights back.

FIGHTER COMMAND
10 GROUP

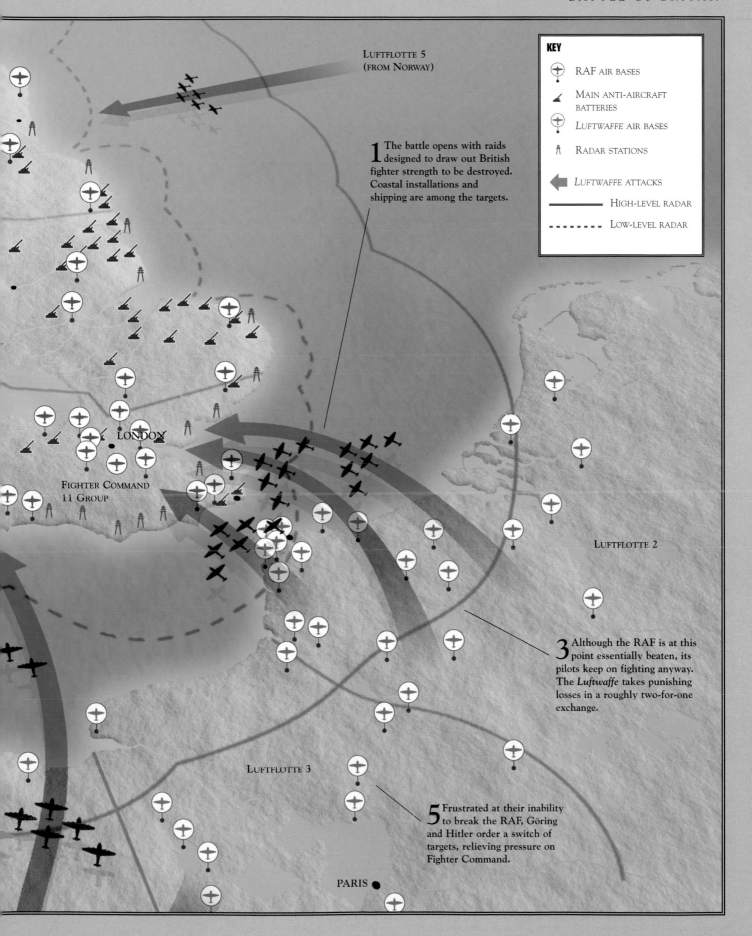

LUFTFLOTTE 5
(FROM NORWAY)

KEY

⊕ RAF AIR BASES

⟋ MAIN ANTI-AIRCRAFT
BATTERIES

⊕ *LUFTWAFFE* AIR BASES

𝚨 RADAR STATIONS

⬅ *LUFTWAFFE* ATTACKS

──────── HIGH-LEVEL RADAR

- - - - - - - - LOW-LEVEL RADAR

1 The battle opens with raids
designed to draw out British
fighter strength to be destroyed.
Coastal installations and
shipping are among the targets.

LONDON

FIGHTER COMMAND
11 GROUP

LUFTFLOTTE 2

3 Although the RAF is at this
point essentially beaten, its
pilots keep on fighting anyway.
The *Luftwaffe* takes punishing
losses in a roughly two-for-one
exchange.

LUFTFLOTTE 3

5 Frustrated at their inability
to break the RAF, Göring
and Hitler order a switch of
targets, relieving pressure on
Fighter Command.

PARIS ●

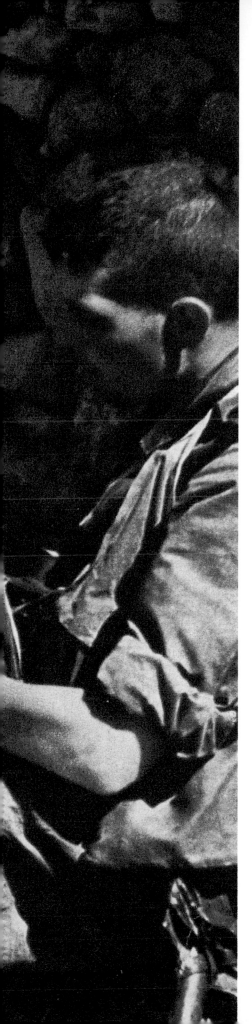

BATTLE FOR CRETE
1941

The German airborne assault of Crete, although successful in terms of conquest, came at a terrific cost in lives, and led to the sharp decline of the Luftwaffe's parachute arm as a surprise weapon. German airborne forces were never to launch an operation of this scale again.

Crete, a mountainous island 260km (160-mile) long, some 100km (60 miles) from mainland Greece and lying in the eastern Mediterranean, was from late April 1941 the sole piece of Greek territory left in Allied hands. One of the threats posed by Crete to the Germans was its key resource for the formidable presence of the Royal Navy at Suda Bay, to the east of the then capital, Khania. It was one of the Mediterranean's largest natural harbours and vital as a refuelling centre. British aircraft could also block naval convoys crossing the Mediterranean to supply Rommel's forces in North Africa. In addition, Hitler foresaw Crete as a

BATTLE FOR CRETE FACTS

Who: Overall commander of the 'Creforce' garrison, Major-General Bernard Freyberg VC (1889–1963) versus General Kurt Student (1890–1978), Commander of XI *Flieger* Corps, the *Luftwaffe's* elite airborne troops.

What: The Germans landed in Crete from the Greek mainland and in 10 days of fierce fighting drove out the bulk of Allied troops.

Where: Crete, the largest island in Greece and the second largest in the eastern Mediterranean.

When: The main German attack on Greece took place between 20 May and 2 June 1941.

Why: The Germans urgently sought a free gateway to the East and Crete posed a major threat to their operations, especially

the naval convoys crossing the Mediterranean to replenish Rommel's forces in North Africa.

Outcome: German forces occupied Crete until the end of 1944 when, along with Greece and Albania, the island was abandoned and Hitler ordered a major retreat from the Balkans.

GLIDER-BORNE TROOPS LANDED AS part of the airborne invasion of Crete, enjoy a rest and a meal of wurst.

potentially valuable fortress guarding the Balkan flank of his projected Operation *Barbarossa*, the invasion of the Soviet Union. Hitler ordered the invasion of Crete on 25 April to be designated Operation *Merkur* (Mercury). However, due to logistical problems, the date was postponed to 20 May.

PARATROOP WARFARE

General Kurt Student, begetter of the *Fallschirmjäger* ('Hunters from the sky'), was a strong advocate of aerial warfare and had pressed the case vigorously for an airborne assault on Crete. But Hitler had considered an air campaign too dangerous and had predicted an unacceptably heavy toll of casualties. However, following pressure from the *Luftwaffe* chief Hermann Göring (1893–1946) he had yielded.

In anticipation of invasion, Commonwealth forces in Crete were, in May 1941, organized in five widely separated defence areas along the north coast – around the three airfields at Heraklion, Rethymnon and Maleme, as well as at Suda Bay and the port of Khania. At dawn on 20 May, the island's defence garrison of Anzac (Australian, New

LEFT: ELITE GLIDER-BORNE FORCES *of German Gebirgsjäger (mountain troops) from the Greek mainland poised to land on Crete.*

BELOW: JU 52s CARRYING AIRBORNE *forces landed on key airports on the second day of the invasion, beginning with the capture of Maleme airport.*

GENERAL KURT STUDENT

General Kurt Student (1890–1978, pictured right) was a World War I fighter pilot, chosen by Göring in 1938 to form a parachute infantry force, which later expanded to around 4500 men. After the evacuation from Crete, Student's troops fought mainly as infantry. Student received no decoration for his services and his personal access to Hitler came to an end. Though he claimed little interest in Nazism, he was brought before an Allied military tribunal in 1947 on eight charges of war crimes in Crete, including sanctioning the execution of British prisoners of war. He was acquitted on certain counts but sentenced to five years in prison. The Greeks requested his extradition from Germany for war crimes but he was never handed over, and died at the age of 88.

EVERY SURVIVING MEMBER of Student's forces received an Iron Cross, but after such losses, he said, 'Crete was the grave of the German paratroops'.

Zealand), British and local troops was subjected to familiar heavy bombing and the scream of Stukas.

What followed a few hours later was a major invasion by elite airborne forces. The assault was in two waves: the first launched against Maleme and Khania to the west, the second against Rethymnon and Heraklion, further to the east. This consisted of transport and 100 gliders, launched from bases on the Greek mainland. These delivered 6000 paratroopers and airborne infantry on and around Maleme with bombers pounding New Zealand troop positions.

General Student divided his forces into three battle groups: West, Centre and East, concentrating particularly on Khania and the prominent hunk of the Akrotiri peninsula. He would thus be given both an airfield and harbour where the battle line could be reinforced, the main object being the capture of the capital.

With more than 40,000 defenders – ANZAC and British troops, Greek and Cretan irregulars – was the 'Creforce' Commander, Major-General Bernard Freyberg, a VC from World War I. He faced serious problems: tired and demoralized troops, battered tanks from North Africa, no air cover and paucity of communications. But Freyberg was receiving intelligence from deciphered German codes alerting him to Student's intentions. He also had the support of a fiercely loyal local population.

BRIDGEHEADS ESTABLISHED

Although many of the German paras presented easy targets as they drifted down over New Zealand positions, many survived to regroup and fight fiercely, on Maleme. A severe

A MEMBER OF 7TH FLIEGER DIVISION (7th Air Division) of the Fallschirmjäger *units, consisting of airborne light infantry which made a drop during the battle of Crete.*

blow on the first day was the loss of a small hill known to the military as Hill 107, commanding the Maleme airfield from the south. The area around the airfield and hill was made up of 5 square kilometres (2 square miles) of rough territory, much of it giving poor visibility. There was a significant build-up of German forces, notably paratrooper battalions and dive bombers forming up to the southeast of the airfield. Lieutenant-Colonel Les Andrew, the area's New Zealand commander, was determined to go on the offensive.

Receiving no extra support, he attacked the invaders on his own initiative but could not contend with the overwhelming superiority of the paratroopers holding the hill. His small force was soon beaten back and his tanks immobilized. A promise of reinforcements came to nothing and Andrew was given permission to withdraw. Hill 107 was taken unopposed and control of the airfield passed to the Germans.

Student, more determined than ever to consolidate the Maleme bridgehead, flew in over the next two days a total of 3200 mountain troops and paras. He encountered fierce local resistance. But the Germans beat it off and the Stukas went in. On 25 May, the New Zealanders under Colonel Howard Kippenberger had some success with a counterattack near Galatas, lying to the southwest of Khania. But this simply delayed the German advance and Kippenberger had no resources to recover.

FLIMSY CANVAS AND WOOD-BUILT German gliders were vulnerable targets. Many crashed into olive trees or were shattered on landing, their fleeing crews cut down by the defenders.

The remainder of the Maleme position had to be yielded in the face of the presence of 2000 additional German mountain troops. The defenders retreated to Khania, which fell on 27 May. Resistance to the overwhelming air and eventually land power of the Germans became impossible, not least through lack of ammunition which severely weakened the Allied divisions. All was now set for a general evacuation.

Withdrawal from Suda Bay was covered by flown-in British commandos, while between 28 May and 1 June Britain's Mediterranean Fleet took off around 17,000 men, from Sphakia on the island's south coast, mostly from open beaches during a few short hours of darkness. Nine ships were sunk by the *Luftwaffe*. Back on land, 5000 men had to be left behind after being separated from their units. The Germans lost 1990 killed in action, while British and Commonwealth forces lost 1742. For the Allies, the debacle of Crete was complete.

ABOVE: GERMAN PARATROOPERS *move forward past the bodies of Allied soldiers after their successful air invasion of Crete.*

AFTERMATH

Hitler, severely shaken by figures for casualties in Crete, informed Student that he considered the days of the parachutist over, since its arm was no longer a surprise weapon. During the battle for Crete, over 1700 ANZAC and British troops had died, a similar number were wounded and around 12,000 were taken prisoners. The full extent of German losses differ, one of the highest figures being 3986 killed and missing with about 2000 having perished in the parachute drop alone.

Subsequent airborne operations by the Germans were strictly limited. As it turned out, the occupation of Crete proved a mixed blessing. The Cretans put up unremitting guerrilla resistance, forcing the Germans to garrison more troops than they wished, thereby making them unavailable elsewhere.

LEFT: ALTHOUGH MANY BRITISH 'TOMMIES', *such as these on Suda Bay, were forced to surrender, others escaped in small craft or fled into the mountains to fight with partisans.*

BATTLE FOR CRETE

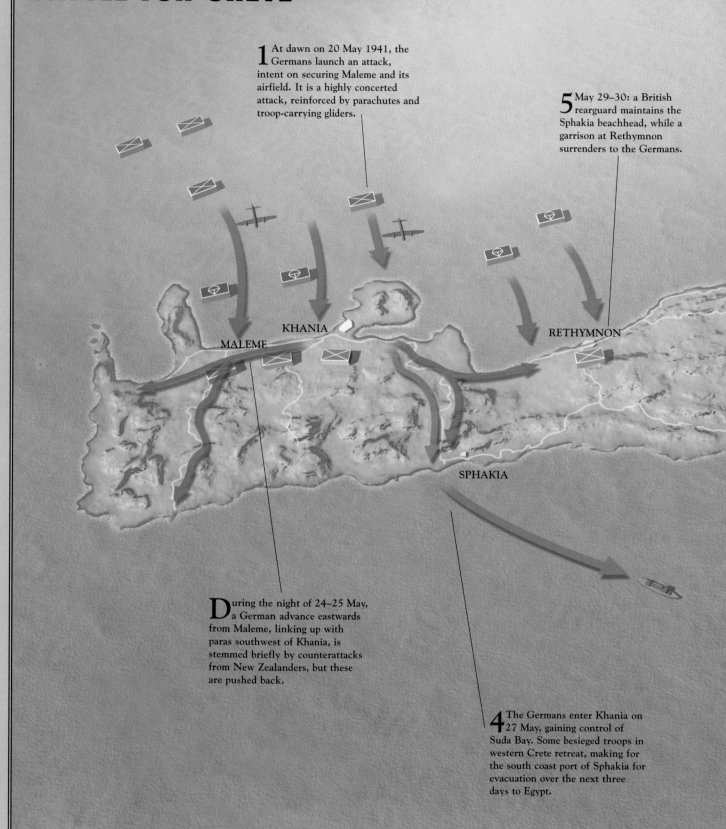

1 At dawn on 20 May 1941, the Germans launch an attack, intent on securing Maleme and its airfield. It is a highly concerted attack, reinforced by parachutes and troop-carrying gliders.

5 May 29–30: a British rearguard maintains the Sphakia beachhead, while a garrison at Rethymnon surrenders to the Germans.

MALEME

KHANIA

RETHYMNON

SPHAKIA

During the night of 24–25 May, a German advance eastwards from Maleme, linking up with paras southwest of Khania, is stemmed briefly by counterattacks from New Zealanders, but these are pushed back.

4 The Germans enter Khania on 27 May, gaining control of Suda Bay. Some besieged troops in western Crete retreat, making for the south coast port of Sphakia for evacuation over the next three days to Egypt.

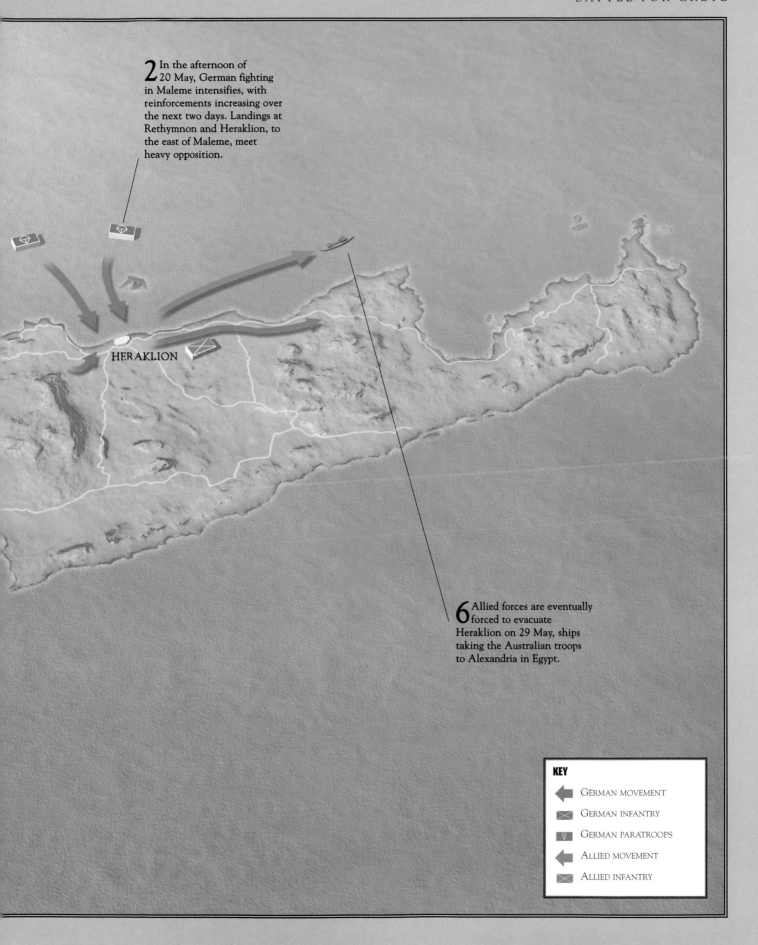

2 In the afternoon of 20 May, German fighting in Maleme intensifies, with reinforcements increasing over the next two days. Landings at Rethymnon and Heraklion, to the east of Maleme, meet heavy opposition.

HERAKLION

6 Allied forces are eventually forced to evacuate Heraklion on 29 May, ships taking the Australian troops to Alexandria in Egypt.

KEY

←	GERMAN MOVEMENT
✉	GERMAN INFANTRY
▽	GERMAN PARATROOPS
←	ALLIED MOVEMENT
✉	ALLIED INFANTRY

HUNT FOR THE BISMARCK

1941

By the summer of 1941, the Battle of the Atlantic had become a struggle for the survival of Great Britain. Not only were Nazi U-boats ravaging convoys and sinking merchant vessels laden with precious cargoes, but surface raiders of the Kriegsmarine (German Navy) also posed a significant threat.

From January to April, more than 610,000 tonnes (672,410 tons) of Allied shipping were lost. Then in May the worst fears of the British Admiralty were realized. The massive 42,800-tonne (47,200-ton) battleship *Bismarck* had weighed anchor and Operation *Rheinübung* (Rhine Exercise) was under way. In company with the heavy cruiser *Prinz Eugen*, the great battleship might wreak havoc on Allied merchant shipping with its eight 380mm (15in) guns.

HUNT FOR THE BISMARCK FACTS

Who: Elements of the British Royal Navy under Admiral John Tovey (1885–1971) versus the German battleship Bismarck and cruiser *Prinz Eugen*, under Admiral Günther Lütjens (1889–1941).

What: The *Bismarck* and *Prinz Eugen* tried to attack Allied shipping but were confronted by the Royal Navy.

Where: The North Atlantic near Allied convoy routes.

When: 18–27 May 1941

Why: The Germans hoped to inflict substantial losses on Allied merchant shipping, thereby strangling the supply line to Great Britain.

Outcome: During an epic chase, the Royal Navy sank the *Bismarck*. The *Kriegsmarine* mounted no more serious surface threats to Allied shipping in the Atlantic.

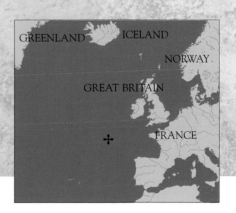

FAIREY SWORDFISH TORPEDO PLANES, *the flying anachronisms that slowed the German battleship* Bismarck, *are lashed to the flight deck of the aircraft carrier HMS Victorious amid an angry sea.*

Recognizing the imminent danger, Admiral John Tovey (1885–1971), commander of the British Home Fleet at Scapa Flow, began to marshal his scattered surface assets to find and sink the Bismarck. Meanwhile Admiral Günther Lütjens (1889–1941), at sea aboard the German behemoth, knew that his movements during daylight hours had been observed by the Swedish cruiser *Gotland* and patrol planes from the neutral country. On 21 May, the battleship was photographed by a British reconnaissance aircraft.

BREAKOUT AND PURSUIT

Lütjens was determined to break out into the open sea and chose the Denmark Strait, one of three options, as his avenue of approach. Shadowed by a pair of British cruisers (*Suffolk* and *Norfolk*), the Bismarck and Prinz Eugen were engaged in the pre-dawn darkness of 24 May by the brand new battleship HMS *Prince of Wales* and the venerable battlecruiser HMS *Hood*. Launched in 1918, the *Hood* was equal in firepower to the *Bismarck* but it was vulnerable to the enemy's heavy guns, its designers having sacrificed armour protection for speed more than 20 years earlier.

Seconds into the fight, a German shell penetrated the *Hood's* thin armour and detonated an ammunition magazine. A gigantic explosion enveloped the warship and the pride of the Royal Navy was gone. Only three of the battle-cruiser's 1421 sailors survived. The *Prince of Wales* was seriously damaged, one German shell wrecking her bridge. Although the *Bismarck* sustained only three hits, one of these gashed her forecastle and tonnes of seawater poured in. Another ruptured a fuel tank and precious oil leaked in a telltale slick. Urged by the *Bismarck's* captain, Ernst Lindemann, to head back to Germany, Lütjens instead dispatched the *Prinz Eugen* to continue prowling for merchantmen and turned his wounded battleship towards the French port of Brest. En route, he hoped that U-boats might offer protection and air cover from planes based in France might soon appear.

ADMIRAL GÜNTHER LÜTJENS, commander of the Kriegsmarine *task force which included the battleship* Bismarck *and the heavy cruiser* Prinz Eugen, *wearing his Knight's Cross.*

THE BISMARCK

Named in honour of the Iron Chancellor of a unified Germany, the battleship *Bismarck* undertook Operation Rhine Exercise on 18 May 1941. Displacing nearly 43,000 tons, the warship posed a major threat to Allied shipping in the Atlantic. The *Bismarck's* main armament consisted of eight 380mm (15in) guns.

Capable of achieving speed in excess of 30 knots, the *Bismarck* was relentlessly pursued by heavy units of the Royal Navy. It was disabled by Swordfish torpedo planes and was eventually sunk on 27 May. However, the battleship and her consort, the heavy cruiser *Prinz Eugen*, had previously achieved a great success: the sinking of the battlecruiser HMS *Hood*, the pride of the Royal Navy.

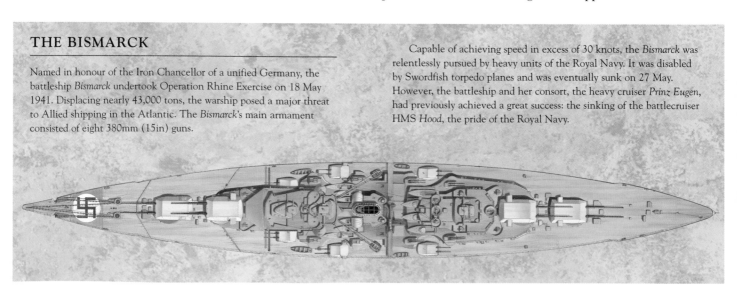

SAILORS OF THE German Navy, or Kriegsmarine, stand at attention during an inspection by officers prior to their departure from an anchorage on the Baltic Sea.

PERSEVERANCE AND LUCK

Devastated by the loss of the *Hood*, the British nevertheless continued their pursuit of the *Bismarck*. The Germans gave the shadowing cruisers the slip on the night of the 24 May after beating back an attack by Fairey Swordfish torpedo lauched planes from the aircraft carrier *Victorious*. Lütjens then inexplicably began to broadcast a lengthy radio message to Berlin, unaware that he had temporarily shaken the British off his trail. The British picked up the signal, corrected a navigational error which had sent them steaming in the wrong direction and locked on to their quarry once again.

On the morning of 26 May, a Consolidated PBY Catalina flying boat spotted the *Bismarck* less than 1300km (800 miles) from the French coast and nearing the range of a protective *Luftwaffe* air umbrella. Several of the Royal Navy warships initially engaged in the chase were obliged to turn for home as fuel ran low. The battleship HMS *King George V*, with Tovey aboard, ploughed ahead. Detached from convoy duty, the battleship HMS *Rodney* joined the pursuit, as did Gibraltar-based Force H, under Admiral James Somerville (1882–1949). The British had lost critical time and distance, though. The *Bismarck* might still escape.

SWORDFISH AT SUNSET

Tovey had one more card to play. The Fairey Swordfish was a flying anachronism, a biplane constructed primarily of wood, canvas and wire. Fifteen of these planes,

SAILING IN LINE ASTERN, the Bismarck *as seen from the rear of the* Prinz Eugen *as they head out into the North Atlantic.*

torpedoes slung beneath their bellies, took off from the pitching deck of the Force H aircraft carrier HMS *Ark Royal* on the afternoon of the 26 May. Several mistakenly attacked the cruiser HMS *Sheffield* and luckily did not score a hit.

In the gathering twilight, the remaining 'Stringbags' pressed home their attacks through a curtain of withering anti-aircraft fire. Two torpedoes struck home. One of these hits was inconsequential. The other was catastrophic for the Germans. Flying only 15.5m (50ft) above the water and in gale force winds, Sub-Lieutenant John Moffat released his plane's weapon, which slammed into the *Bismarck's* stern and jammed her rudders 15° to port. As a result, the great ship was able to steer only one course, northwest towards the assembling might of the vengeful Royal Navy.

TORRENT OF SHELLS

Every sailor aboard the *Bismarck* now knew that the fate of their ship was sealed. Lindemann ordered the storage areas open and allowed the men to take what provisions they could. A cable from Hitler – 'The whole of Germany is with you' – seemed a forlorn hope. The Royal Navy would come with morning light and the death struggle would follow.

At 8.47 a.m. on 27 May, the 406mm (16in) guns of the *Rodney* barked from a range of 19km (12 miles). The *King George V* joined in. The crew of the *Bismarck* fought valiantly, but repeated hits seriously damaged her fire control system and disabled her main armament. The British battleships closed to less than 3.2km (2 miles) and bodies of dead and wounded sailors littered the *Bismarck's* decks. By 11 a.m., the ship was still afloat but blazing from bow to stern and unable to fight back. Shortly afterwards, the battleship rolled to port and sank stern first.

LINGERING CONTROVERSY

Three torpedo hits from the cruiser HMS *Dorsetshire* have long been credited with administering the *coup de grâce*. However, survivors of the *Bismarck* have insisted that they opened the vessel's seacocks and scuttled the ship. Exploration of the wreckage tends to support their claim but remains inconclusive. Only 110 of the *Bismarck's* complement of more than 2000 sailors were pulled from the chilly waters of the Atlantic. More might have been rescued, but a U-boat alarm sounded and the British were forced to abandon many sailors to the sea.

ABOVE: FAIREY SWORDFISH BIPLANES, torpedoes slung beneath their fuselages, in flight. Constructed primarily of wood and canvas, the Swordfish proved effective against the Bismarck.

The epic *Bismarck* chase resonates through history as a classic tale of naval warfare. In a practical sense, the loss of the great warship effectively ended the threat of the *Kriegsmarine* surface fleet to Allied merchant shipping in the Atlantic. Hitler simply became unwilling to risk his few capital ships in such an endeavour. Far to the north, German warships, including another giant, the battleship *Tirpitz*, menaced Allied convoys to the ports of Murmansk and Archangel in the Soviet Union. However, the Atlantic was to be the domain of the U-boats until they too were defeated.

BELOW: DAMAGED AND DOWN by the bow, the Bismarck ploughs through the waters of the Atlantic prior to its deadly rendezvous with the Royal Navy, principally the battleships King George V and Rodney.

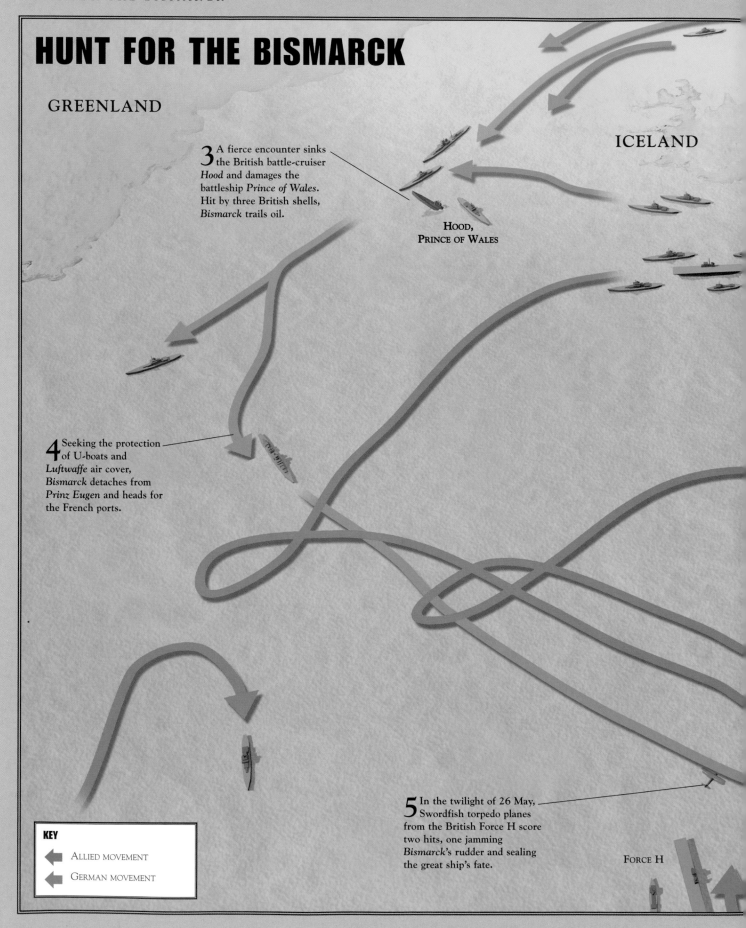

HUNT FOR THE BISMARCK

GREENLAND

ICELAND

3 A fierce encounter sinks the British battle-cruiser *Hood* and damages the battleship *Prince of Wales*. Hit by three British shells, *Bismarck* trails oil.

HOOD,
PRINCE OF WALES

4 Seeking the protection of U-boats and *Luftwaffe* air cover, *Bismarck* detaches from *Prinz Eugen* and heads for the French ports.

5 In the twilight of 26 May, Swordfish torpedo planes from the British Force H score two hits, one jamming *Bismarck*'s rudder and sealing the great ship's fate.

FORCE H

KEY

← ALLIED MOVEMENT

← GERMAN MOVEMENT

64

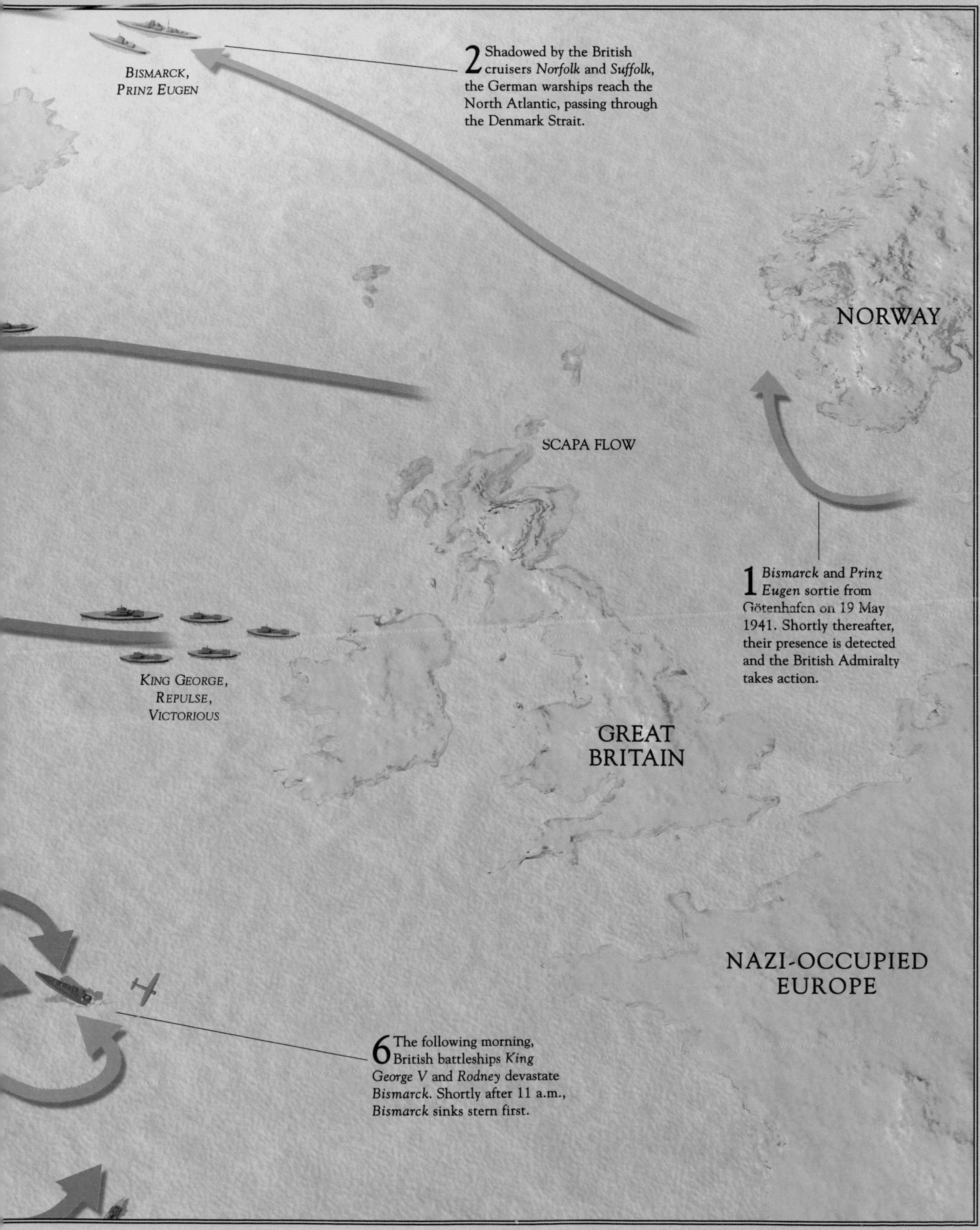

2 Shadowed by the British cruisers *Norfolk* and *Suffolk*, the German warships reach the North Atlantic, passing through the Denmark Strait.

BISMARCK, PRINZ EUGEN

NORWAY

SCAPA FLOW

1 *Bismarck* and *Prinz Eugen* sortie from Götenhafen on 19 May 1941. Shortly thereafter, their presence is detected and the British Admiralty takes action.

KING GEORGE, REPULSE, VICTORIOUS

GREAT BRITAIN

NAZI-OCCUPIED EUROPE

6 The following morning, British battleships *King George V* and *Rodney* devastate *Bismarck*. Shortly after 11 a.m., *Bismarck* sinks stern first.

OPERATION BARBAROSSA 1941

A massive German army of 3.3 million men supported by over 3000 tanks and almost as many aircraft invaded the Soviet Union on 22 June 1941. The huge invasion force was to capture Moscow, the Ukraine and Leningrad in short order.

The largest military operation of all time, codenamed *Barbarossa* ('Red Beard'), was under way. It would see the German *Wehrmacht* achieve its most spectacular victories. It did not lead to ultimate victory, however, and the Red Army would storm Berlin four years later.

Hitler had placed the greatest emphasis in his plans for the capture of Leningrad – the USSR's second city and primary naval base – and the clearing of the Baltic States. Yet he had allocated the least number of troops, some 26 divisions to Army Group North under Marshal von Leeb (1876–1956). As a consequence,

OPERATION BARBAROSSA FACTS

Who: Three German Army Groups (North, Centre and South) led respectively by Marshals Ritter von Leeb (1876–1956), Fedor von Bock (1880–1945) and Gerd von Rundstedt (1875–1953) were charged by Hitler to destroy the Red Army in two months.

What: Barbarossa was the decisive turning point of the war. If the Soviet Union survived the German onslaught, Hitler's Reich would face a two-front war.

Where: By July 1941, when Finland had joined the German onslaught in the north, the Eastern Front would eventually stretch from the Black Sea to the Arctic North and the Germans would almost reach the gates of Moscow.

When: 22 June–5 December 1941

Why: Undaunted by his failure to subdue Britain during the summer of 1940, Hitler gambled that his *Wehrmacht* would be able to knock out the Soviet Union before the United States eventually intervened in the war on the side of Britain.

Outcome: Ultimately the outcome of *Barbarossa* would decide the outcome of World War II.

A CZECH-BUILT 35(T) TANK PASSES *a burning manor house in White Russia in early June 1941 as the* blitzkrieg *rips through Soviet territory.*

Leeb's advance was slow and it was not until September that his exhausted troops managed to cut off Leningrad from the rest of the USSR. And instead of a swift capture of the great city, a long and ultimately fatal siege ensued.

UKRAINIAN VICTORIES, ROSTOV SETBACK

Marshal Gerd von Rundstedt's (1875–1953) Army Group South – 41 divisions, including five panzer and 14 Romanian divisions – were entrusted with the vital task of taking the Ukraine. With its abundant grain fields and the industrial might of the Donbass region, it was a prize that was much needed.

Unfortunately for Rundstedt, however, the Southwestern Front, the strongest of the Soviet army groups, offered fierce

HISTORY TENDS TO SEE THE GERMAN ARMY as a fast-moving, motorized force. However, the reality was that a great deal of equipment was moved by horse power – 750,000 horses were used in the invasion of the Soviet Union.

resistance, led ably by its commander General Mikhail Kirponos (1892–1941). As a result, Army Group South was able to advance only slowly and deliberately. Nevertheless, the panzer forces of Army Group Centre intervened, converging on 10 September with those of Rundstedt's panzers east of Kiev.

Three massive Soviet armies (Fifth, Twenty-Sixth and Thirty-Seventh) were now trapped in and around Kiev. Kirponos died trying to escape the German trap and a staggering 665,000 of his men were captured.

THE 'LIBERATOR' SOON turned to savage oppressor: a German landser (infantryman) with a burning Russian cottage in the background.

On 30 September, the 1st Panzer Group attacked and had, by 6 October, trapped much of the Soviet Southern Front in a large pocket in southeast Ukraine. Two armies (the Ninth and Eighteenth) were destroyed, yielding 100,000 prisoners.

The German advance continued towards Rostov on the Don river, which was captured on 20 November. However, the Soviet High Command (*Stavka*) launched a vigorous counterattack with three armies against the by now over-extended German lines. By 29 November, this strategically located city was back in Soviet hands and the Germans had narrowly escaped an early version of Stalingrad.

ADVANCE OF ARMY GROUP CENTRE

When Napoleon had invaded Russia in 1812, he ultimately reached Moscow but still did not achieve victory. Hitler's generals – especially Fedor von Bock (1880–1945), the commander of Army Group Centre – believed that the Soviet Union would collapse if Moscow was captured. Here, as in the south, the Germans scored some major successes. A string of armies were trapped inside the Bialystok salient and in a vast pocket west of Minsk, yielding 300,000 prisoners. Stalin had the Western Front's commander, General Dimitri Pavlov (1897–1941), fired and shot upon his return to Moscow for his failures. His place was taken by Marshal Simeon Timoshenko (1883–1973), an experienced and hard-headed commander.

The Red Army continued to suffer catastrophic reverses, however. Smolensk, the gateway to Moscow, fell on 16 July. Stalin was now determined to block the German advance, and a series of counterattacks were launched by the Western Front armies, costing them yet another 300,000 men and 3000 tanks. Among the Germans, the feeling spread that

GENERAL HEINZ GUDERIAN

Heinz Guderian (1888–1954) was Hitler's most successful tank commander, who combined brilliant brains with outstanding abilities as a practical and hard-headed field commander. He was made head of the 2nd Panzer Division in 1935, took part in the Polish campaign (September 1939) and broke through at Sedan on 14 May 1940. During the *Barbarossa* campaign, Guderian was in command of the 2nd Panzer Group, renamed simply 'Guderian'. He was set to march on Moscow, having taken Smolensk in July when his panzer forces were diverted south. Guderian was called '*Schneller Heinz*' (Hurrying Heinz) by his hard-pressed but admiring troops. During Operation *Typhoon*, Guderian held command of the Second Panzer Army but was fired on 25 December and remained without a command until 1943.

with each success they were no closer to victory and that the Red Army's reserves were inexhaustible.

Hitler, who did not share his generals' views, diverted most of Army Group Centre's panzer divisions to take part in the battle for Kiev. For more than a month, the Central Front of 800km (496 miles) remained unchanged, giving the Red Army invaluable time to prepare its defences. General Andrei Yeremenko (1892–1970) had three armies (30 divisions) at Bryansk, and Timoshenko had six armies with 55 divisions at Vyazma. Incredibly, all these forces had been either wiped out or captured by October.

BELOW: A GERMAN PAK-36 team knocks out a light Soviet tank during the fighting of the summer of 1941.

LEFT: AS RUSSIA FACES yet another savage invasion, these Ukrainians dig antitank ditches during the late summer of 1941.

The march on Moscow, codenamed Operation *Typhoon*, was unleashed early in the morning of 2 October in brilliant sunshine. Army Group Centre numbered a million men in 77 divisions with 1700 tanks and almost a thousand planes.

Five days later, General Höppner's Fourth Panzer Group co-operating with General Hermann Hoth's (1885–1971) Third Panzer Group had trapped Timoshenko's six armies in a massive pocket in and around Vyazma.

THE BATTLE FOR MOSCOW

On 9 October, Hoth and Hoeppner linked up with Guderian's panzer forces, trapping the Third, Thirteenth and Fiftieth Soviet armies north and south of Bryansk. Leaving only a minimum of troops to seal up the pockets at Vyazma and Bryansk, the Army Group's panzer groups aimed for Mozhaiska and Tula. These pockets were eliminated by 14 and 20 October respectively, leaving eight armies destroyed. The yield was as massive as at Kiev – some 673,000 prisoners, more than 1000 tanks and 5000 guns.

Despite torrential rains that turned the roads into quagmires, the Germans had covered two-thirds of the distance to Moscow by the middle of the month. Finally, Soviet morale snapped. On 16 October, law and order collapsed in the capital, a million of its citizens fleeing for their lives in the 'Great Flight'. Only a policy of shooting to kill by the NKVD (Soviet Secret Police) stemmed the panic and prevented further looting and chaos.

In early November, the weather turned colder, enabling the Germans to advance again across frozen and hard roads. But it was soon too cold with temperatures of -21°C (-6°F),

RIGHT: OCTOBER 1941 – Soviet propaganda trying to show a united nation rallying to the defence of the capital. In reality, there was oppression, corruption and defeatism before the onset of winter.

and a new commander had appeared on the Soviet side, General Georgi Zhukov (1896–1974), who had already saved Leningrad and was now planning a counterattack against the exhausted Germans. By 18 November, Zhukov had 21 rested, fully equipped and battle-hardened Siberian divisions ready to be unleashed against Bock's army.

The German plan was for a frontal assault with 36 divisions while the three panzer groups encircled the Soviet defenders around Moscow. On 27 November, 2nd Panzer Division was just 22km (14 miles) from the capital and could see the spires of the Kremlin palaces through the haze.

Bock's Army Group now held a front almost 1000km (600 miles) long with a mere 60 divisions. The crawling offensive came to a halt on 5 December when temperatures plunged to a bone-chilling -35°C (-31°F). That same day Zhukov ordered General Ivan Konev's (1897–1973) Kalinin Front to attack, and the following day his own Western Front went on to the offensive.

The attack took the Germans completely by surprise, and over the next two months the Red Army held the initiative on the Central Front. Hitler gave orders that there was to be no retreat and this probably saved Army Group Centre from a complete collapse.

The failure of *Typhoon* spelled the defeat of *Barbarossa*. In the long run, the Soviet counterattack sounded the death-knell to the German Nazi Reich as well. Two days after Zhukov began his offensive, the United States entered the war, and Hitler's defeat was now only a question of time.

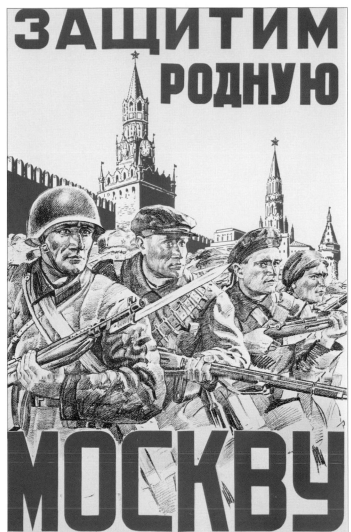

ЗАЩИТИМ РОДНУЮ МОСКВУ

BELOW: THE PANZER MK III (this model belonging to the 2nd Panzer Division) was the sturdy workhorse of the German Panzer forces but was no match for the Soviet T-34.

OPERATION BARBAROSSA

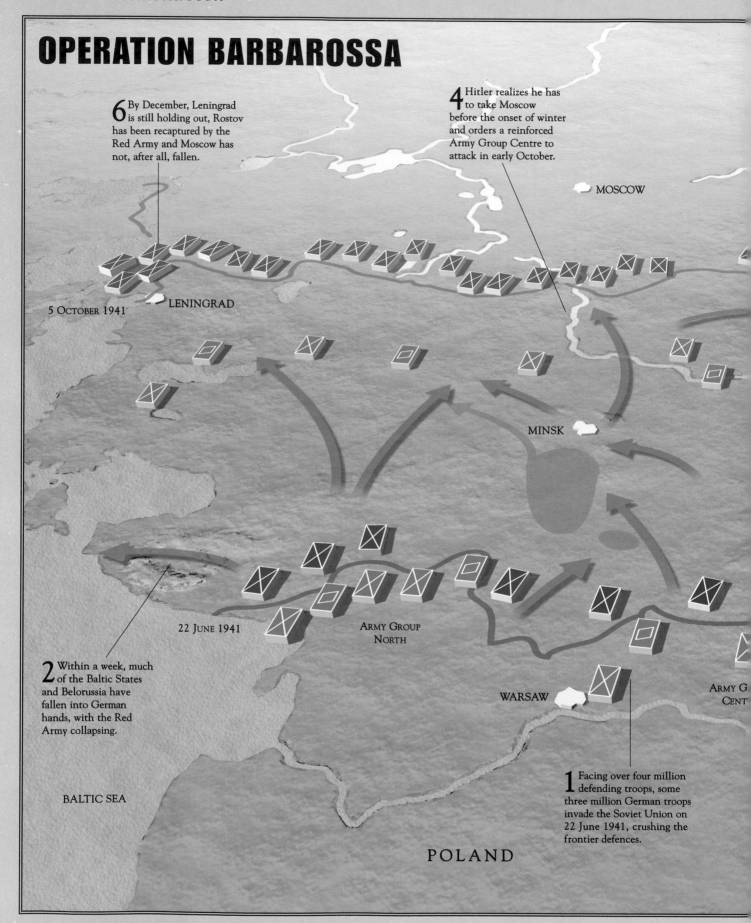

6 By December, Leningrad is still holding out, Rostov has been recaptured by the Red Army and Moscow has not, after all, fallen.

4 Hitler realizes he has to take Moscow before the onset of winter and orders a reinforced Army Group Centre to attack in early October.

MOSCOW

5 OCTOBER 1941

LENINGRAD

MINSK

22 JUNE 1941

ARMY GROUP NORTH

2 Within a week, much of the Baltic States and Belorussia have fallen into German hands, with the Red Army collapsing.

WARSAW

ARMY G
CENT

1 Facing over four million defending troops, some three million German troops invade the Soviet Union on 22 June 1941, crushing the frontier defences.

BALTIC SEA

POLAND

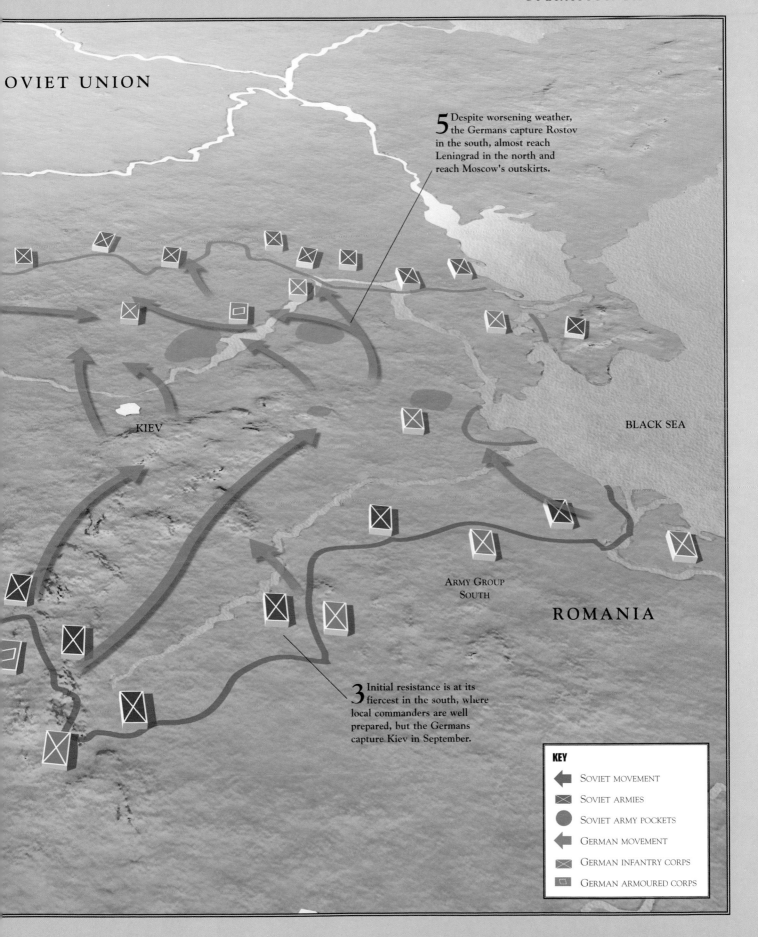

SOVIET UNION

5 Despite worsening weather, the Germans capture Rostov in the south, almost reach Leningrad in the north and reach Moscow's outskirts.

KIEV

BLACK SEA

ARMY GROUP SOUTH

ROMANIA

3 Initial resistance is at its fiercest in the south, where local commanders are well prepared, but the Germans capture Kiev in September.

KEY

⬅	SOVIET MOVEMENT
⊠	SOVIET ARMIES
●	SOVIET ARMY POCKETS
⬅	GERMAN MOVEMENT
⊠	GERMAN INFANTRY CORPS
▱	GERMAN ARMOURED CORPS

SIEGE OF LENINGRAD 1941–44

The siege of Leningrad was a ghastly epic of endurance that cost the lives of up to 1.5 million people, both soldiers and civilians. In total, it ran for nearly 900 days.

On 22 June 1941, German forces surged across the Soviet border in Operation *Barbarossa*. The *Wehrmacht* was split into three major formations – Army Groups North, Centre and South – each with its own objectives. Army Group North under the command of Field-Marshal Wilhelm von Leeb (1876–1956), had Leningrad as its goal, a large urban zone of a million souls located on the Gulf of Finland. Von Leeb's forces, as with the other elements of *Barbarossa,* made vigorous progress, pushing on through the Baltic states and breaking across the Luga river just 120km (75 miles) south of Leningrad on 9 August.

SIEGE OF LENINGRAD FACTS

Who: The German Army Group North under several commanders versus the Soviet Volkhov and Leningrad Fronts, commanded by General Kirill Meretskov (1897–1968) and Marshal Leonid Govorov (1897–1955) respectively.

What: A partial blockade of Leningrad by Army Group North reduced Leningrad to starvation conditions, the blockade being broken only by a succession of Soviet offensives over nearly three years.

Where: Leningrad (now renamed St Petersburg), a city in the far north of Russia, nestling on the Gulf of Finland.

When: The siege effectively ran from September 1941 to January 1944.

Why: Leningrad was an early target of Hitler's Operation *Barbarossa,* but by the end of 1943 the German operations there had little military function besides maintaining the overall German frontline.

Outcome: A million civilians died from starvation, bombing and shelling, but the ultimate defeat of the Germans was a key ingredient in the German Army's defeat on the Eastern Front.

A RED ARMY UNIT makes a characteristic attack in the Leningrad sector, winter 1943 – a simple charge backed by heavy machine-gun support.

ABOVE: JU-87 STUKA DIVE-BOMBERS were used intensively as 'flying artillery' to intercept Soviet supply runs into Leningrad from across Lake Ladoga.

SAVED FOR A SIEGE

The fate of the city seemed assured, not least because German-allied Finnish forces were fighting down from the north between Lake Ladoga and the sea. Important road and rail links into Leningrad fell to the Germans one by one – Novgorod on 16 August, Chudovo on the 20th – and by 1 September the German artillery shells were dropping into the city itself. The inhabitants of Leningrad prepared themselves for a battle for survival. From 9 September, the esteemed Soviet General Georgi Zhukov (1896–1974) was in the city, transforming it from a beautiful northern city into a massive fortress ringed by defensive positions, pillboxes and trenches. Yet the direct German assault on Leningrad did not come. On 6 September, Hitler switched the priority of *Barbarossa* to objectives further south and drew off much of von Leeb's panzer strength to support the offensive. Therefore Leningrad would have to be defeated by siege and bombardment.

Throughout September and October, the strategic situation for Leningrad worsened considerably. The major railway stations at Schlisselburg and Mga to the east fell into German hands, and in October von Leeb began an offensive towards the vital railway centre at Tikhvin, which fell on 8 November. A ring of steel was closing around Leningrad, but the fighting was far from easy for the Germans. The offensive had grossly overstretched an already weakened Army Group North and it faced pressing resistance from the armies of the Volkhov Front commanded by General Kirill Meretskov (1897–1968).

By 10 December 1941, Tikhvin was back in Soviet hands following a huge but crudely handled Red Army offensive and by early January the Germans were forced to re-establish their frontlines further west. Only

LEFT: A WELL-EQUIPPED Red Army infantryman, seen here in the autumn of 1941, armed with the Tokarev SVT-40, an early Soviet semi-automatic rifle.

ABOVE: THE LIFELINE – A TRUCK CONVOY moves across a frozen Lake Ladoga. Under such conditions, up to 400 trucks a day were able to make the journey.

the narrowest of supply corridors, however, remained for Leningrad's already desperate people.

STARVATION AND RESISTANCE

As the German and Soviet armies outside Leningrad battled for dominance, a horrifying battle against starvation was under way within the city itself. In an especially bitter winter, the citizens of Leningrad were beginning to starve in their thousands, their predicament worsened by a collapse in fuel supplies for warmth.

By the end of November, people were trying to survive on a daily ration of less than 250g (9oz) of bread. Bodies littered

RIGHT: GERMAN INFANTRY BATTLE the Russian winter, late 1941. As elsewhere, the harsh Russian climate hampered German mobility on the Leningrad Front.

every street – people would literally die on their feet or curled up in doorways. On one day alone, 13,500 deaths occurred. Film footage of the period shows old people scraping out refuse bins with spoons and putting what they found into their mouths. Cannibalism became one way of surviving, and disturbing-looking meat appeared on sale by some street vendors. Every animal, wild or domestic, was killed for food, and other items, such as linseed oil and tallow candles, found their way on to the menu. Against this horrifying backdrop was the constant German air and artillery bombardment.

The main lifeline to the city was Lake Ladoga, though it was hardly adequate. Supplies were moved by land to Tikhvin, then to disembarkation points, such as Novaya Ladoga and Lednevo. Small boats of every military and civilian variety sailed the waters in the non-winter months, frequently under heavy German air assault, to dock in Osinovets, northeast of Leningrad. When Lake Ladoga froze over, up to 400 trucks a day shuttled supplies straight across the ice and took back refugees on the return

ABOVE: LENINGRAD CIVILIANS GATHER in a small group to distribute what meagre supplies are available, transporting them across icy streets on sledges.

BELOW: THE T34/76 TANK WAS the primary Soviet armoured fighting vehicle of the Leningrad Front, and its numbers were critical in breaking the German siege in 1944.

journey. Conditions for the supply convoys were grim: many truck crews, ship crews and refugees found their graves at the bottom of Ladoga. However, in the spring of 1942 fuel and electricity pipelines were laid across the river, bringing power for cooking and heating. Yet although conditions had improved by the end of 1942, blockade conditions existed for nearly 900 days, during which time about one million people died out of a population of 2.5 million. Some sources put the death toll as high as 1.5 million.

BREAKING THE SIEGE

In 1942, the Soviets looked to make further gains. In January, a large offensive by the Volkhov Front between Novgorod (just north of Lake Ilmen) and Spasskaya Polist made a 60km (37-mile) salient in the German frontline, but the offensive had stalled by March, leaving the Germans to nip out of the salient and completely destroy the Soviet Second Shock Army. Nevertheless, the Soviet attack had alarmed Hitler enough for him to replace von Leeb as commander of the Army Group North (von Leeb had requested a tactical withdrawal in the face of the offensive) with Field-Marshal Georg von Küchler (1881–1968). Küchler himself would go in August 1942 after he resisted Hitler's idea for a general offensive to crush Leningrad, codenamed *Northern Lights*. Manstein then took what was proving to be a poisoned chalice for German commanders.

Between 27 August and 25 September 1942, there was considerable movement around Leningrad. An offensive by Meretskov against the bottleneck was eventually stopped by Manstein, but his counteroffensive also ground to a halt against the Soviet defence. The critical change in fortunes, however, came in January 1943. The Soviet Leningrad Front under Marshal Leonid Govorov (1897–1955), four armies strong, launched a combined offensive with the Volkhov Front against the German forces in the bottleneck. The sheer weight of men and armour was irresistible and Schlisselburg was back in Soviet hands by 19 January. By early February, the Soviets were running direct rail journeys into Leningrad, albeit ones under constant German bombardment – the corridor secured by the Red Army was only 10km (6.2 miles) wide.

SIEGE OVER

The worst of the siege was over but the partial blockade ran until January 1944. The Germans held their lines even as they were weakened by Hitler's redeployment of forces for his 1943 offensives in the Ukraine. On 14 January 1944, an overwhelming Soviet offensive by both Red Army fronts flooded over the German defences and put the *Wehrmacht* troops on the retreat. On 27 January, with the recapture of the Leningrad–Moscow rail line, Stalin officially declared the siege of Leningrad over.

THE BETRAYAL OF LENINGRAD

The siege of Leningrad became iconic in the years following its liberation, with artists, writers, musicians and historians enshrining the resistance in their work. This publicity soon fuelled Stalin's paranoia – he had long suspected that Leningrad (as Russia's second city) could produce a rival power base to his own. In 1946, he acted against the figures behind Leningrad's resistance, arresting them on false charges. The Leningrad Party Organization was purged and some 2000 people were executed, imprisoned or exiled between 1946 and 1950, including Pyotr Popkov, Aleksei Kuznetsov and Nikolai Voznesensky, important players in Leningrad's survival and attempted post-war renaissance.

LOCAL PEOPLE MARK the fiftieth anniversary of the end of the siege of Leningrad at the St. Petersburg Cemetery, 1994.

SIEGE OF LENINGRAD

FINLAND

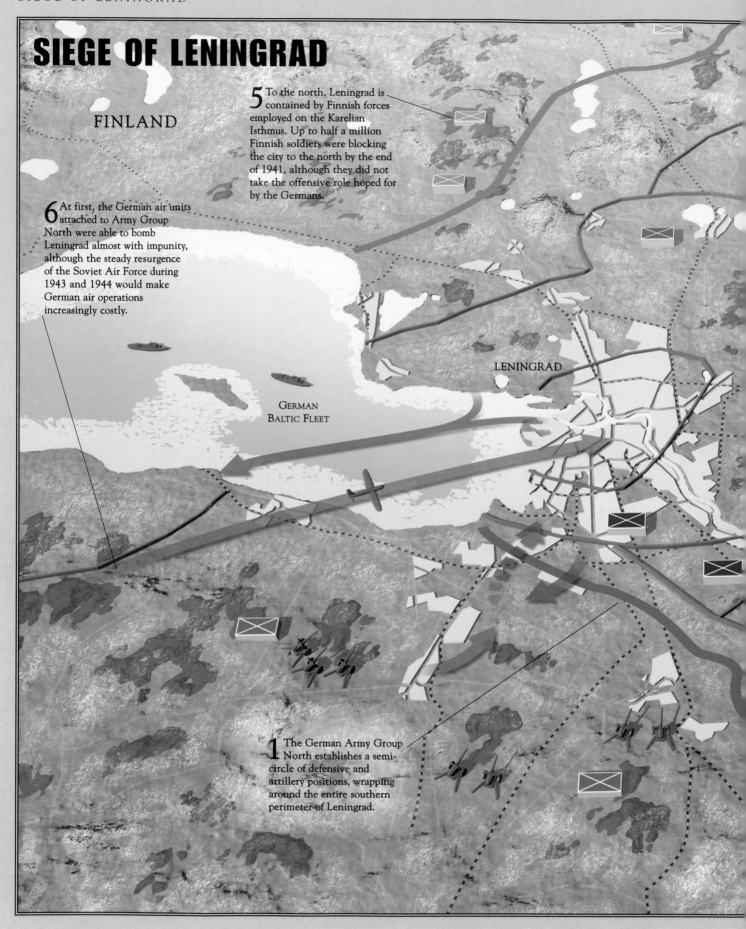

5 To the north, Leningrad is contained by Finnish forces employed on the Karelian Isthmus. Up to half a million Finnish soldiers were blocking the city to the north by the end of 1941, although they did not take the offensive role hoped for by the Germans.

6 At first, the German air units attached to Army Group North were able to bomb Leningrad almost with impunity, although the steady resurgence of the Soviet Air Force during 1943 and 1944 would make German air operations increasingly costly.

GERMAN
BALTIC FLEET

LENINGRAD

1 The German Army Group North establishes a semi-circle of defensive and artillery positions, wrapping around the entire southern perimeter of Leningrad.

3 Ladoga provides the primary supply route for Leningrad during 1941/42. Ships carry supplies during the summer months, and truck convoys move across the frozen ice during the winter.

LADOGA FLOTILLA

4 The limit of the German frontline is established by the forces of the Soviet Volkhov Front. The Front made numerous localized offensives, although it was not until 1944 that a massive three-Front attack put the Germans into general retreat.

WSEWOLOSHKI

2 Schlisselburg is captured in September 1941, cutting off the city from an overland supply route. In January 1943, the Soviets subsequently open a narrow supply channel across the top of the German 'bottleneck'.

KEY

⬅ SOVIET MOVEMENT

⬛ SOVIET FORCES

⬅ GERMAN MOVEMENT

⬛ GERMAN FORCES

⬜ FINNISH FORCES

IN THE BALANCE

With the entry of the United States into the war in December 1941, Winston Churchill famously 'slept the sleep of the saved and the thankful' because 'there was no more doubt about the end.' Yet Germany remained ascendent and Japan was rampaging through the Far East. American power would take time to deploy decisively and the war was by no means won.

It took desperate and bloody battles at El Alamein in the Western Desert and on a far greater scale at Stalingrad and Kursk on the Eastern Front to turn the tide against the Germans, and at Midway, Guadalcanal and Imphal to do the same against the Japanese in the Pacific theatre.

US MARINES TAKE COVER *amidst landing operations in the Solomon Islands, 30 June 1943. The crucial battles at Midway and Guadalcanal proved to be the turning point in the war in the Pacific.*

PEARL HARBOR 1941

When Japanese warplanes swept in to attack the US naval base at Pearl Harbor and other installations on the Hawaiian island of Oahu on 7 December 1941, the act was the culmination of years of growing tension between the two countries. Japan, seeking preeminence in Asia and the Pacific, required land and other natural resources to sustain its growing population and fuel its formidable military machine.

In 1931, Japan's army had invaded Manchuria, and a decade of fighting in China followed. By 1941, Japan had occupied all of Indochina. Recognizing the US and the traditional European powers as the chief impediments to the establishment of its 'Greater East Asia Co-Prosperity Sphere', Japan prepared for a war that its militaristic leaders considered inevitable.

In response to the growing threat, President Franklin D. Roosevelt (1882–1945) utilized political and economic pressure to curb Japanese ambitions. In May 1940, he ordered the US Pacific Fleet, already in Hawaiian waters for

PEARL HARBOR FACTS

Who: The Japanese Combined Fleet under strategic command of Admiral Isoroku Yamamoto (1884–1943) and tactical command of Vice-Admiral Chuichi Nagumo (1887–1944) versus the US Pacific Fleet under Admiral Husband Kimmel (1882–1968) and US Army forces under General Walter Short (1880–1949).

What: The Japanese Combined Fleet assembled six fleet carriers to launch an audacious attack on the US Pacific Fleet base of Pearl Harbor 5472km (3400 miles) away.

Where: Pearl Harbor and US military facilities on the Hawaiian island of Oahu.

When: 7 December 1941

Why: In the face of US and British sanctions, Japan needed to neutralize US naval power in the Pacific, at least temporarily, in order to seize British and Dutch resources in the region, especially oil.

Outcome: Tactically Japan caused considerable damage at little cost to itself, but, in the words of Vice-Admiral Nagumo, it managed only 'to awaken a sleeping giant and fill her with a terrible resolve'.

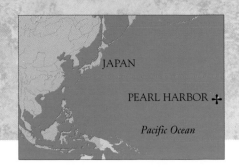

JAPAN

PEARL HARBOR ✛

Pacific Ocean

STRUCK BY SEVERAL JAPANESE *torpedoes, the battleship USS* West Virginia *burns and settles to the shallow bottom of Pearl Harbor. In the foreground, sailors pull a survivor from the water.*

LEFT: JAPANESE PREMIER HIDEKI TOJO led his nation to war with the United States. After the war, Tojo survived a suicide attempt. He was later tried, convicted, and executed for war crimes.

exercises, to remain on station at Pearl Harbor rather than return to its home port of San Pedro, California. In the summer of 1940, he prohibited the export of strategic minerals, chemicals and scrap iron to Japan. On 26 July 1941, in retaliation for Japan's occupation of Indochina, he imposed an embargo on oil, nationalized the Filipino Army and froze Japanese assets in the United States.

WAR WARNINGS

Admiral Isoroku Yamamoto (1884–1943), Commander-in-Chief of the Combined Fleet, was reluctant to go to war with the United States. Nevertheless he became the architect of what was conceived as a crippling blow to American military power in the Pacific, a pre-emptive strike by carrier-based aircraft against the US Pacific Fleet anchored at Pearl Harbor. For months, the Japanese pilots trained in secret. Then, on 26 November 1941, the powerful

BELOW: THE ENGINES OF JAPANESE Mitsubishi Zero fighters roar to life aboard the aircraft carrier Shokaku. The Zeroes provided air cover for the attackers at Pearl Harbor.

armada sailed from Hittokapu Bay in the Kurile islands. Two battleships, three cruisers, nine destroyers and three submarines escorted the heart of the strike force, six aircraft carriers, *Akagi, Kaga, Soryu, Hiryu, Shokaku* and *Zuikaku*.

American military leaders and diplomats acknowledged that war with Japan was imminent. However, they were convinced that the first blow would fall in the Philippines or Southeast Asia. The day after the Japanese fleet sailed, US commanders across the Pacific received a war warning. But the commander of the US Pacific Fleet, Admiral Husband Kimmel (1882–1968), and his Army counterpart, General Walter Short (1880–1949), were preoccupied with safeguarding installations and equipment from sabotage. They also fell victim to a series of communication failures.

EARLY WARNINGS IGNORED

In the pre-dawn hours of 7 December, the Japanese strike force had reached its appointed station 370km (230 miles) north of the island of Oahu. At 3.30 a.m. Pacific time, US cryptanalysts in Washington DC intercepted the last of a 14-part message from Tokyo to its emissaries there. The message seemed to indicate the opening of hostilities by Japan within a matter of hours.

At 3.45 a.m., the minesweeper USS *Condor*, on routine patrol, sighted what appeared to be a submarine periscope in

A JAPANESE PILOT wearing leather headcover, goggles and flight suit, strides towards his waiting aircraft. At the time of Pearl Harbor, many Japanese fliers had combat experience, gained in China.

a restricted area near the entrance to Pearl Harbor. The sighting was probably one of five Japanese midget submarines which were tasked with entering the harbour and firing torpedoes at American warships. Although the submarines failed in their assigned task, their two-man crews were lionized as heroes in Japan – with one notable exception. After his disabled midget submarine was beached, Ensign Kazuo Sakamaki was captured and became the first Japanese prisoner of war in World War II.

As streaks of daylight brightened the eastern sky, 183 Japanese planes of the first attack wave were being launched from the decks of the carriers. At 6.40 a.m., the destroyer USS *Ward*, patrolling the entrance to Pearl Harbor sighted and attacked one of the

THE VERSATILE 'VAL'

Designed in 1935 as the Dive Bomber Type 99 Model 11, the Aichi D3A1 was the primary dive bomber of the Imperial Japanese Navy until 1942. Designated the 'Val' by the Allies, this aircraft was utilized in large numbers during the attack on Pearl Harbor, 7 December, 1941.

In the hands of a skilled pilot, the Val proved a highly accurate platform for the delivery of ordnance, achieving a success rate of greater than 80 per cent at its peak. However, following severe losses of veteran airmen, particularly at the battles of the Coral Sea and Midway and during the prolonged actions in the vicinity of the Solomons, the combat efficiency of the Val suffered.

midget submarines. The destroyer's second 75mm (3in) shell struck the conning tower of the craft, which sank immediately. The *Ward*'s message concerning hostile contact was dismissed as another phantom sighting. Just 20 minutes later, the US Army's Opana radar station at Point Kahuku on Oahu picked up and reported an unidentified formation of aircraft. This warning was also discounted. By 7.30 a.m., the 170 planes of the Japanese second wave were airborne.

TORA, TORA, TORA!

Unmolested by US fighters or antiaircraft defences, the bombers of Lieutenant-Commander Mitsuo Fuchida (1902–1976) cleared the mountains west of Pearl Harbor. When it was apparent that the attackers had achieved complete surprise, Fuchida transmitted the message, '*Tora, Tora, Tora!*' to the Japanese fleet. The first bombs fell on Ford Island at 7.55 a.m.; Kaneohe Naval Air Station, Wheeler Field, Bellows Field, Hickam Field and Ewa Marine Corps Air Station came under attack from bombers and strafing fighters, destroying most American aircraft on the ground.

Moored along Battleship Row southeast of Ford Island, the pride of the US Pacific Fleet lay at anchor. Seven battleships – *Nevada*, *Arizona*, *West Virginia*, *Tennessee*, *Oklahoma*, *Maryland* and *California* – represented easy targets for screeching dive bombers and torpedo planes, which skimmed the harbour at barely 15.5m (50ft) to launch their deadly weapons. The flagship of the fleet, the battleship USS *Pennsylvania*, lay in a nearby drydock.

ABOVE: EDGY AMERICAN SOLDIERS, *one with a pair of binoculars, scan the skies above Pearl Harbor following the Japanese attack. Their weapons are Browning 7.5mm (0.3in) machine guns.*

BELOW: WITH THE SMOKE *from the effects of the Japanese attack blackening the sky, the USS Shaw explodes with spectacular consequences during the Japanese raid on Pearl Harbor.*

Within minutes, Pearl Harbor was ablaze. Four battleships were sunk. The *West Virginia* was hit by seven torpedoes and two bombs. The *California* took two torpedoes and a bomb. The *Oklahoma* was hit by at least five torpedoes and capsized, trapping many sailors below decks. A bomb fashioned from a modified 355mm (14in) shell originally intended for a naval cannon penetrated the deck of the *Arizona* and ignited a catastrophic explosion that shattered the ship and took the lives of 1177 men. The *Pennsylvania*, *Maryland*, *Nevada* and *Tennessee* were heavily damaged. The cruisers *Helena*, *Raleigh* and *Honolulu*; the destroyers *Cassin*, *Downes* and *Shaw*; the seaplane tender *Curtiss* and the repair ship *Vestal* were damaged, and the target ship *Utah* and minelayer *Oglala* were sunk.

THE WAKES OF JAPANESE torpedoes reach out towards Battleship Row at Pearl Harbor on 7 December 1941, while the shock waves of prior hits and oil haemorrhaging into the harbour are also visible.

STUNNING BLOW

In little more than two hours, Japan had altered the balance of power in the Pacific. The bold attack had taken the lives of 2403 Americans. Eighteen of 96 vessels at Pearl Harbor were sunk or damaged heavily. A total of 165 US aircraft were destroyed and 128 others damaged. In exchange, the Japanese lost 29 aircraft, five midget submarines, one fleet submarine and 185 dead.

Although they had achieved a great victory, the Japanese failed to achieve two major goals. The US aircraft carriers, their primary objective, were at sea and thus spared the attack. The marauding planes had also neglected nearly 23 million litres (5 million gallons) of fuel oil stored in tanks around Pearl Harbor and barely touched repair facilities, which would prove essential to future operations. The day after the attack, President Roosevelt asked a joint session of Congress for a declaration of war and called 7 December 1941 'a date which will live in infamy'.

PEARL HARBOR

3 At 7.55 a.m., 'Kate' torpedo bombers target ships to the northwest of Ford Island. This was where the missing carriers were normally berthed.

6 The USS Nevada attempted to make for the safety of open water, but was attacked by wave after wave of torpedo and dive bombers.

MIDDLE LOCH

FORD ISLAND NAVAL AIR STATION

USS CALIFORNIA

US NAVY YARD

5 Attacked by both the first and second waves, Hickam Field suffers the heaviest damage of Oahu's airbases.

SOUTHEAST LOCH

2 At 7.53 a.m., 'Val' dive bombers approach from the northwest. Their targets are the aircraft parked on Hickam Field and Pearl Harbor NAS on Ford Island.

OKLAHOMA

USS ARIZONA

USS WEST VIRGINIA

USS NEVADA

1 The first wave of 'Kate' torpedo bombers attack Battleship Row from the southeast at 7.50 a.m. They are followed by waves of Japanese bombers attacking from a high level.

4 The second wave arrive at 8.49 a.m. and attack Battleship Row again, as well as the ships in harbour, and make further raids on the airfields.

OIL TANKS

KEY

⬅ US NAVY MOVEMENT

✈✈ JAPANESE AIRCRAFT

BATTLE OF MIDWAY

DVD TRACK 5

1942

Reluctant to go to war in the first place, Admiral Isoroku Yamamoto (1884–1943), Commander-in-Chief of the Japanese Combined Fleet, had warned prior to the attack on Pearl Harbor, 'For six months, I will run wild in the Pacific. After that, I make no guarantees.'

Yamamoto was familiar with the United States, having attended Harvard University and served as a naval attaché in Washington DC. He recognized the huge industrial might of the United States and was convinced that a series of rapid victories and the destruction of the US Pacific Fleet were Japan's only hope of winning the war.

Although the Pearl Harbor attack had been a success, the American aircraft carriers had been at sea and were not destroyed. Yamamoto realized that he had

BATTLE OF MIDWAY FACTS

Who: Japanese naval forces under Admiral Isoroku Yamamoto (1884–1943) and Admiral Chuichi Nagumo (1887–1944) versus the US Pacific Fleet under Admirals Chester Nimitz (1885–1966), Frank Jack Fletcher (1885–1973) and Raymond Spruance (1886–1969).

What: A Japanese armada of four aircraft carriers carrying 256 aircraft, 11 battleships and numerous smaller vessels opposed an American force that included three aircraft carriers, 234 carrier- and land-based planes, and a variety of smaller craft.

Where: The central Pacific west of Hawaii and the northern Pacific near the Aleutians.

When: 4–7 June 1942

Why: The Japanese attempted to capture Midway atoll and occupied the islands of Attu and Kiska in the Aleutians.

Outcome: A turning point in the Pacific War, the battle was a devastating defeat for Japan. Four aircraft carriers were sunk and the invasion of Midway was cancelled.

CREWMEN ABOARD THE aircraft carrier USS Yorktown *tend planes on the ship's flight deck. Damaged at Coral Sea, the* Yorktown *was repaired within 72 hours of returning to Pearl Harbor.*

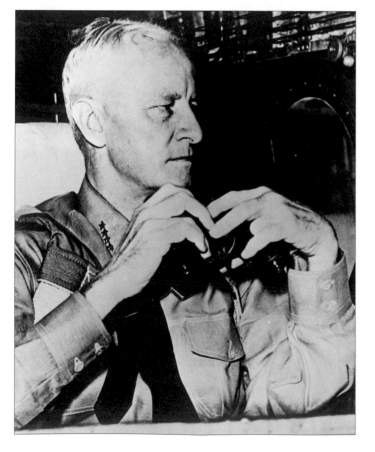

ABOVE: THE CREWMEN OF *the American search plane that located the Japanese invasion force headed for Midway atoll pose beside their Consolidated PBY Catalina flying boat.*

unfinished business. It was still necessary to engage the bulk of the US warships in a decisive battle. Despite the setback at Coral Sea in May, he forged ahead in the first week of June 1942 with plans for the capture of Midway, a tiny atoll less than 1930km (1200 miles) west of Hawaii and composed of two small islands, Sand and Eastern. With Midway in Japanese hands, the defensive perimeter of the Empire would be extended considerably. Hawaii itself might be open to invasion. In the process, Yamamoto would annihilate what remained of the US Pacific Fleet.

READING ENEMY MAIL

Yamamoto was unaware, however, that US Navy cryptanalysts based at Pearl Harbor had cracked the Japanese naval code, JN 25, and that Admiral Chester Nimitz (1885–1966), Commander-in-Chief of the US Pacific Fleet, was planning to counter the Midway operation. Nimitz ordered the aircraft carriers USS *Enterprise* and USS *Hornet* and their escorts to join the

LEFT: ADMIRAL CHESTER W. NIMITZ *became the Commander of the Pacific Fleet after Pearl Harbor. Aggressive and willing to take risks, he played decisive roles in the American victories at the battles of Coral Sea and Midway.*

ABOVE: THE GRUMMAN TBF AVENGER *torpedo bomber was also capable in level bombing and anti-submarine roles. A number of these large, multipurpose aircraft were present at Midway.*

USS *Yorktown* – seriously damaged at Coral Sea but returned to service following a Herculean 72-hour repair effort at Pearl Harbor – northeast of Midway, to lie in wait for the Japanese. Admiral Frank Jack Fletcher (1885–1973), aboard the *Yorktown*, was to assume overall command of the American naval force, while Admiral Raymond Spruance (1886–1969) operated with a great deal of autonomy in command of the *Enterprise* and *Hornet*.

Yamamoto, meanwhile, stuck to his penchant for complex operations and formulated a plan that would initially involve a feint against the islands of Attu and Kiska in the Aleutian Islands far to the north. He further divided his forces into a powerful surface fleet formed around the super battleship *Yamato*, an invasion force transporting 500 soldiers to capture Midway and a carrier force consisting of four aircraft carriers, *Akagi*, *Kaga*, *Soryu* and *Hiryu*, which together transported 234 combat aircraft. Yamamoto himself sailed aboard the *Yamato*, while Admiral Chuichi Nagumo (1887–1944) commanded the carrier force.

BELOW: THE DOUGLAS SBD DAUNTLESS *dive bomber was responsible for inflicting the lethal damage against four aircraft carriers of the Imperial Japanese Navy during the Battle of Midway.*

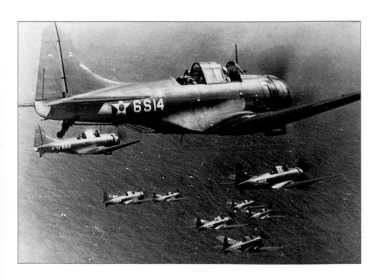

BATTLE JOINED

On the morning of 3 June, a US search plane spotted the Japanese invasion force, but subsequent attacks by aircraft based at Midway failed to achieve any success. The next day, the Japanese carrier force emerged from dense fog and rain as Nagumo launched more than 100 planes to strike Midway

BELOW: THE LAST SURVIVOR *of the Japanese battle fleet at Midway, Hiryu was struck by SBD Dauntless dive bombers late on 4 June 1942. Burning fiercely, the carrier was abandoned and scuttled some 12 hours later.*

in an effort to render its airstrip unusable and soften up the atoll's defences.

The attack was only partially effective and Nagumo faced a dilemma. A portion of his aircraft had been retained and armed with torpedoes to hit the American carriers if and when they were sighted. A second attack on Midway would require that these planes have their torpedoes exchanged for bombs, a hazardous and time-consuming process. The need for a second attack on Midway was confirmed by the appearance of American land-based bombers overhead. Although they scored no hits, Nagumo ordered planes not returning from the first Midway raid to be rearmed with bombs.

Moments later, however, Nagumo's resolve was again tested when a Japanese reconnaissance aircraft reported

10 US ships, including a carrier, steaming just over 320km (200 miles) to the northeast. Nagumo considered ordering the planes already rearmed with bombs to take off against Midway while those still carrying torpedoes attacked the American ships.

To complicate matters, the planes returning from the first Midway attack and the Zero fighters flying protective combat air patrol above his ships were low on fuel and needed to land. Finally, Nagumo decided to recover planes that were airborne and to equip with torpedoes the bombers which had been withheld. In their haste to land and refuel

BELOW: BADLY DAMAGED IN A collision with its sister ship, Mogami, and by repeated US air attacks, the Japanese heavy cruiser Mikuma drifts prior to sinking on 6 June 1942.

BELOW: DISPLACING 19,800 TONS and carrying 71 aircraft, the Japanese carrier Soryu (Green Dragon) was a veteran of Pearl Harbor. Hit by three American bombs at Midway, Soryu was turned into a blazing inferno and sunk.

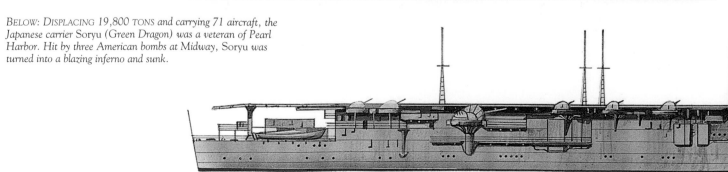

aircraft while rearming others, Japanese crewmen stretched fuel lines across the carrier decks and stacked bombs below without properly securing them. For a dangerously long time, the Japanese aircraft carriers were as vulnerable as they could possibly be. Fletcher and Spruance swung into action when a search plane located the enemy carrier force at about 5.30 a.m. on 4 June. Near the limits of their range, more than 150 dive bombers, torpedo bombers and fighters took off from the *Hornet*, *Enterprise* and *Yorktown*.

FATAL MISCALCULATION

Some of the formations drifted off course and the opportunity for a coordinated attack was lost. In a twist of fate, however, this worked to the advantage of the Americans. The slow, obsolete torpedo bombers found the Japanese first but were decimated by anti-aircraft fire and the covering Zeros.

Nearly every one was lost without scoring a single hit. Shortly after 10 a.m., the Japanese carriers began the launch of their own planes. As the first aircraft roared down the flight decks, lookouts shouted the warning. Unmolested by the fighters, which were off chasing the last of the torpedo planes, 50 American dive bombers pressed home their attacks. In a flash, the course of the Pacific War was changed. Bombs exploded among aircraft waiting to take off and amid the ordnance stacked below decks. *Akagi*, *Kaga* and *Soryu*, engulfed in flames, were doomed.

The lone surviving Japanese carrier, the *Hiryu*, had been steaming in a rain squall some distance away and managed to launch a strike against *Yorktown*, seriously damaging the veteran of the Coral Sea fight. Although damage control parties worked to save the ship, *Yorktown* was spotted by a Japanese submarine and sunk along with the destroyer USS *Hammann* on 7 June. The *Hiryu*, however, did not outlive her sisters for long. US dive bombers scored four hits on the afternoon of 4 June, turning the last Japanese carrier into a blazing hulk.

AN EMPIRE SHATTERED

The action in the waters around Midway on 4 June 1942 turned the tide of World War II in the Pacific. The loss of four aircraft carriers, a cruiser, 332 aircraft and more than

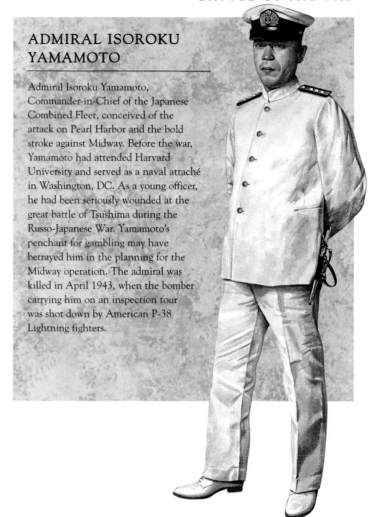

ADMIRAL ISOROKU YAMAMOTO

Admiral Isoroku Yamamoto, Commander-in-Chief of the Japanese Combined Fleet, conceived of the attack on Pearl Harbor and the bold stroke against Midway. Before the war, Yamamoto had attended Harvard University and served as a naval attaché in Washington, DC. As a young officer, he had been seriously wounded at the great battle of Tsushima during the Russo-Japanese War. Yamamoto's penchant for gambling may have betrayed him in the planning for the Midway operation. The admiral was killed in April 1943, when the bomber carrying him on an inspection tour was shot down by American P-38 Lightning fighters.

2000 men was a crippling blow from which the Japanese never recovered. In contrast, the US lost one carrier, a destroyer, 137 planes and 307 men.

Yamamoto briefly entertained the prospect of bringing his overwhelming superiority in battleships and cruisers to bear in a surface engagement against the Americans. Spruance would have none of it. He had recognized a great victory, remembered the admonition of Nimitz to employ the 'principle of calculated risk' and retired out of harm's way. The invasion of Midway was cancelled. The defeated Japanese retreated and for the remainder of the war were obliged to fight defensively.

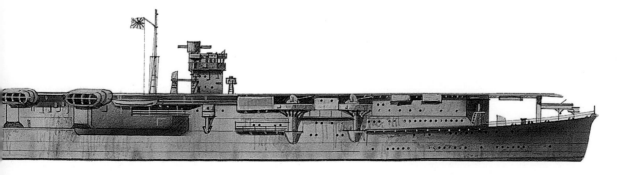

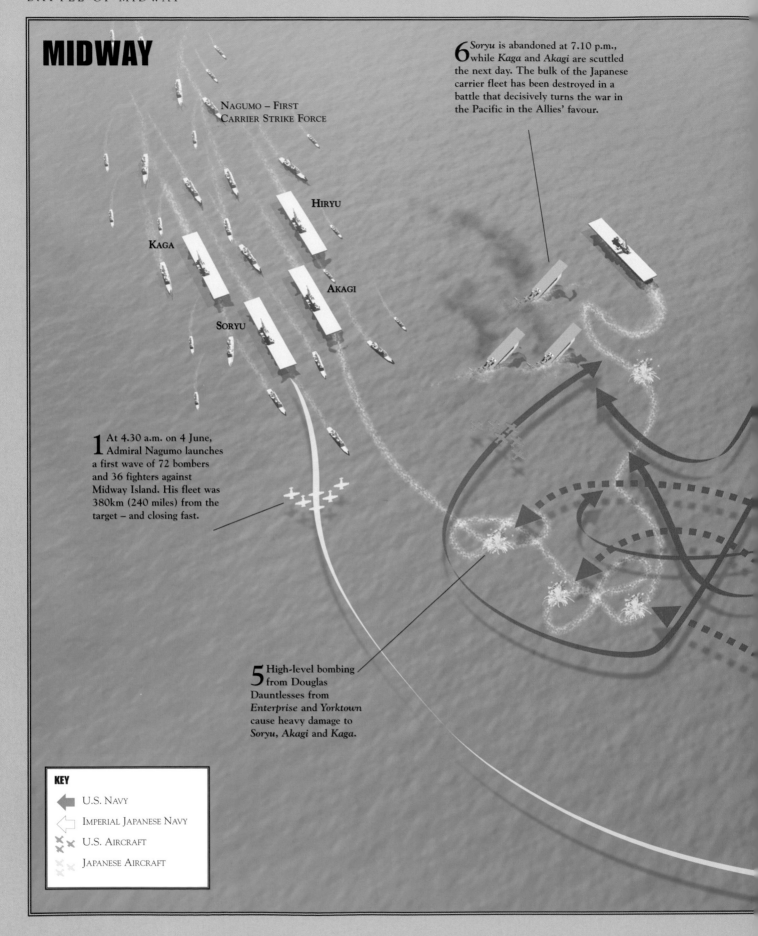

MIDWAY

NAGUMO – FIRST
CARRIER STRIKE FORCE

6 *Soryu* is abandoned at 7.10 p.m.,
while *Kaga* and *Akagi* are scuttled
the next day. The bulk of the Japanese
carrier fleet has been destroyed in a
battle that decisively turns the war in
the Pacific in the Allies' favour.

HIRYU

KAGA

AKAGI

SORYU

1 At 4.30 a.m. on 4 June,
Admiral Nagumo launches
a first wave of 72 bombers
and 36 fighters against
Midway Island. His fleet was
380km (240 miles) from the
target – and closing fast.

5 High-level bombing
from Douglas
Dauntlesses from
Enterprise and *Yorktown*
cause heavy damage to
Soryu, Akagi and *Kaga*.

KEY

◄ U.S. NAVY

◁ IMPERIAL JAPANESE NAVY

✕✕✕ U.S. AIRCRAFT

✕✕✕ JAPANESE AIRCRAFT

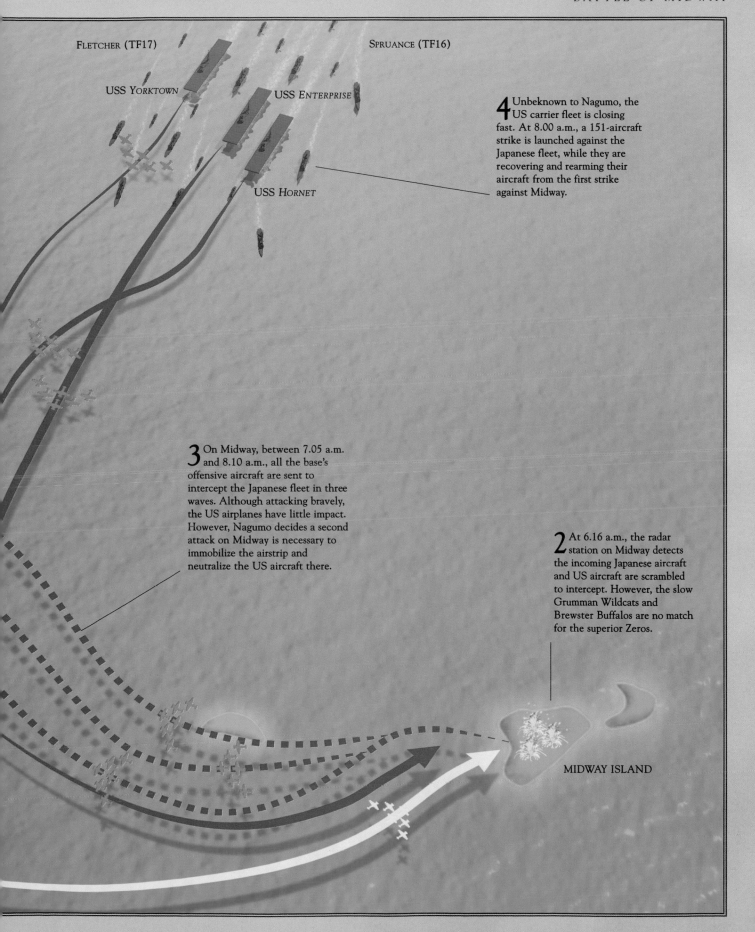

FLETCHER (TF17)

SPRUANCE (TF16)

USS YORKTOWN

USS ENTERPRISE

USS HORNET

4 Unbeknown to Nagumo, the US carrier fleet is closing fast. At 8.00 a.m., a 151-aircraft strike is launched against the Japanese fleet, while they are recovering and rearming their aircraft from the first strike against Midway.

3 On Midway, between 7.05 a.m. and 8.10 a.m., all the base's offensive aircraft are sent to intercept the Japanese fleet in three waves. Although attacking bravely, the US airplanes have little impact. However, Nagumo decides a second attack on Midway is necessary to immobilize the airstrip and neutralize the US aircraft there.

2 At 6.16 a.m., the radar station on Midway detects the incoming Japanese aircraft and US aircraft are scrambled to intercept. However, the slow Grumman Wildcats and Brewster Buffalos are no match for the superior Zeros.

MIDWAY ISLAND

CONVOY PQ-17 1942

Convoy PQ-17 was in some ways a triumph for the heavy surface raiders, even though they played no part in the actual attacks. The threat that a battleship was at large was enough to force the convoy to scatter, at which point its fate was sealed.

At the outbreak of World War II, the *Kriegsmarine* possessed a handful of powerful heavy cruisers and capital ships. These were not enough to threaten the Royal Navy but they did affect the course of the war.

The strategy of a 'fleet in being' meant that rather than coming out to fight a battle that they would certainly lose, the German major units tied down, merely through their existence, large segments of the Allied fleet that could be used elsewhere such as in the Mediterranean or the Pacific.

Traditionally, weaker naval powers have resorted to 'cruiser warfare' – ie, raiding the sea traffic of their enemies. While this is normally the province of cruisers and submarines, a capital ship could swiftly slaughter a convoy and its escorts.

CONVOY PQ-17 FACTS

Who: An Allied convoy of 33 ships with an escort of four cruisers, three destroyers and two Royal Navy submarines sailing to the Soviet Union, versus 10 submarines, aircraft based on the Norwegian mainland and the threat of surface attack.

What: A gradual massacre of the merchant ships and their escorts.

Where: North of Norway in the Arctic Sea, close to the island of Spitzbergen.

When: June–July 1942

Why: The convoy scattered in response to a supposed surface threat.

Outcome: Massive casualties among the Allied merchant ships, with only 11 ships arriving at their destination. Shortly afterwards, the Allies suspended Arctic convoys because of the heavy losses.

DEPTH CHARGES EXPLODE *in the Arctic twilight. Whether or not the submarine was destroyed, aggressive depth-charging could prevent it from making a successful attack while the convoy moved on. The submarines of the period were too slow to catch up with most convoys once they were past.*

THE TYPE IX U-BOAT *was capable of long-range operations, though it had to travel mostly on the surface. These boats could strike anywhere on a convoy route and remain at sea for long periods waiting for a suitable target.*

The big surface raiders of the German Navy were thus a serious threat to Allied supply lines. Although raiding cruises by the heavy ships had not achieved as much as might have been hoped, an attack on a concentrated high-value target, such as a major convoy, could achieve results of strategic importance.

Much effort was expended on keeping the major units of the *Kriegsmarine* bottled up, especially when a critical convoy was under way. Some convoys were protected by old battleships or given distant heavy covering forces that could counter a sortie by the major raiders. However, some areas were simply too hazardous for capital ships. One such was the Arctic passage to Murmansk.

The German attack on Russia in 1941 brought the Soviet Union into the war on the side of the Allies and ultimately doomed the Axis to defeat. However, there was a time when the situation in Russia was desperate and the new allies needed to send support. The only practicable way was to ship vast quantities of tanks, vehicles, artillery, aircraft and other war matériel into Russian ports, and the only available route was through the Arctic Ocean, around the north of Norway and into the Kola Inlet on the White Sea.

ARCTIC CONVOYS

Arctic convoys were difficult enough without enemy interference. Ice was a constant hazard – not just in the water but forming on ships. It jammed turrets and winches and, more dangerously, increased topweight so that ships rolled more and could become unstable. Ice clearance was a constant task. The Arctic Ocean largely freezes in the

winter; pack ice advances far south. This requires ships making the passage to travel relatively close to the northern coastline of Norway, which was at the time occupied by German forces. Aircraft and submarines based there not only had less far to travel to find the convoy but also a smaller area to search in.

However, winter convoys were at least covered by darkness – that far north, there were months of night in which the sun barely rose above the horizon. In the summer, convoys could take a more northerly route, putting some

U-BOATS WERE VULNERABLE to aircraft and surface vessels, so maintaining a good lookout was essential. This was a miserable job in rough weather, as the top of the conning tower was constantly lashed with icy spray.

distance between the ships and their enemies, but the constant daylight offset this defensive advantage.

Convoys were given a code name and number that indicated, to those who knew the system, their route and sometimes composition or speed. 'Fast' convoys received a different designation to those that could make a relatively low average speed. Each route had its own pair of code

TYPE VIIC U-BOAT

Coming into service in 1941, just as the 'happy time' for U-boats was ending, the Type VIIC was smaller than the Type IX and had a shorter range as well as a smaller torpedo load. It was the mainstay of the German U-boat service for the remainder of the war and several hundred were built.

Although the tide was slowly turning against the U-boats, the Type VIIC was highly successful in combat. Many received *Schnorkels* from 1944 onwards, increasing their underwater endurance. Others were modified into flak boats to counter air attacks near the U-boat bases in the Bay of Biscay.

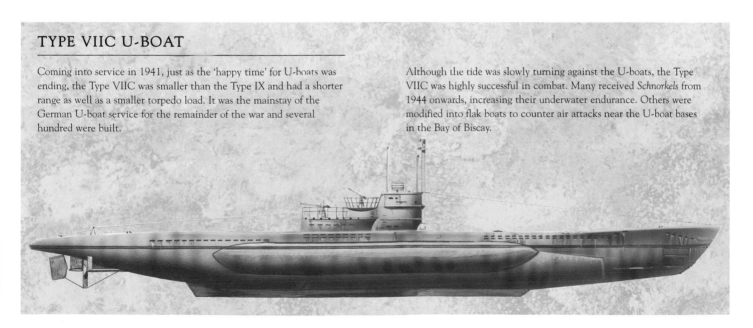

letters. Arctic convoys to Russia were designated PQ, with returning convoys labelled QP.

PQ convoys began with PQ-1, which assembled in Iceland and set sail on 29 September 1941. Only one ship was lost among the 103 that set out before the spring of 1941, but the sinking of a destroyer by a U-boat on January 1942 warned of things to come. Losses mounted, with increasing pressure from air and submarine units. PQ-16 lost five of its 30 merchant ships, four others arriving damaged.

CONVOY PQ-17

It was with the expectation of a tough passage that PQ-17 formed up. It was the largest convoy thus far, with 36 merchant ships. The close escort consisted of four destroyers, 10 lighter craft (mostly armed trawlers) and two anti-aircraft ships. Distant cover was provided by four cruisers and four destroyers. A heavy force containing two battleships, two cruisers and an aircraft carrier was available for the first part of the route but could not be risked past the North Cape.

German high command considered breaking the Arctic convoy route to be of great importance and had made plans for heavy air and submarine attacks plus a possible sortie by heavy

POOR VISIBILITY WAS a mixed blessing for the Arctic convoys. It helped them to avoid submarine and air attack but also concealed the U-boats that did find the convoy as they closed in to make their attack.

surface units. The Allies were aware that this was a prospect, though they could not know whether an attack was planned.

The convoy sailed on 27 June 1942. It took a very northerly route, passing close to the Svalbard archipelago, to keep as much distance between it and the enemy's northern bases as possible. This meant struggling through sea ice at times and some ships were damaged. One had to be sent back to join another that had turned back just after leaving Iceland.

Despite this and being spotted first by U-boats and later by aircraft, the convoy suffered no losses until 4 July. Two ships were sunk after three days of intermittent air attack. However, something much more serious happened that day. The Allies received word that the battleship *Tirpitz* was out.

Tirpitz was the most powerful ship in the German fleet. Modern and well-designed, she was quite probably capable of defeating a single Allied battleship if she met one; the convoy escorts and cruisers would stand no chance. *Tirpitz* was fast enough to destroy the escorting cruisers and then chase down the slow merchant ships; if she got into range of the convoy, it would be a massacre. Worse, she was reported as sailing in company with two heavy cruisers and several destroyers. The only chance to save any of the convoy was to scatter it and to hope that the heavy raiders found only some of the ships.

The British intelligence service was subsequently able to establish that this was not a sortie against PQ-17 but merely a redeployment. The damage had been done, though. The order to scatter was sent and the covering force was pulled back. Many of the warship crews were sickened by what they heard on the radio. Unable to help, they heard the scattered merchant ships struggling on under submarine and air attack – vessels calling for help and then going off the air.

Many of the escort crews met a hostile reception in the bars of their home ports. Challenged by other sailors for 'abandoning' PQ-17, they gave vent to their own bitter emotions. There were many fights, and several men were killed. The 'stigma' of PQ-17 took a long time to erase, even though none of what happened was the sailors' fault: the Admiralty ordered the convoy to scatter and the ship captains were bound to obey.

On 5 July, the convoy came under heavy attack from aircraft and lost six ships, while submarines accounted for six more. The remaining close escorts did what they could for nearby vessels, but without an organized convoy the merchants were desperately vulnerable, especially to submarines. With no destroyer force to counter them, U-boats could make their attacks at leisure and consequently were very effective.

Similarly, the *Luftwaffe* was able to press home its attacks with great precision, since there was little anti-aircraft fire. This, too, increased the effectiveness of the sorties. As a consequence, nine more ships were sunk over the following five days. The survivors began to arrive in Russia on 10 July. Eleven ships straggled in over the next week. More than half the convoy had been destroyed by aircraft and submarines. Some of the ships would have been sunk whether or not the full escort had been available. However, the circumstances leading to the destruction of PQ-17 were brought about just by the threat of attack. The very existence of the 'fleet in being' brought ruin upon the Arctic convoy route.

AFTERMATH

The effect of the 'abandonment' on the psyche of the escort crews is summed up by a statement made by one of the captains involved. During Operation *Pedestal*, a convoy to Malta facing heavy opposition, this officer said: 'I don't care what signals I get from whom, so long as there's a merchant afloat I'm putting my ship alongside her and we're going to Malta.' His was one of three destroyers that rescued the crippled tanker *Ohio* and somehow got her into Grand Harbour, quite probably changing the course of the war.

ABOVE: A ROYAL NAVY OFFICER *dressed for Arctic convoy service. The cold was a deadly enemy; men keeping watch or venturing above decks risked hypothermia, and falling overboard was a death sentence.*

LEFT: CAPTAIN HEINZ BEILFELD *of U-703 is congratulated by a superior officer after the successful raid against convoy PQ-17.*

CONVOY PQ-17

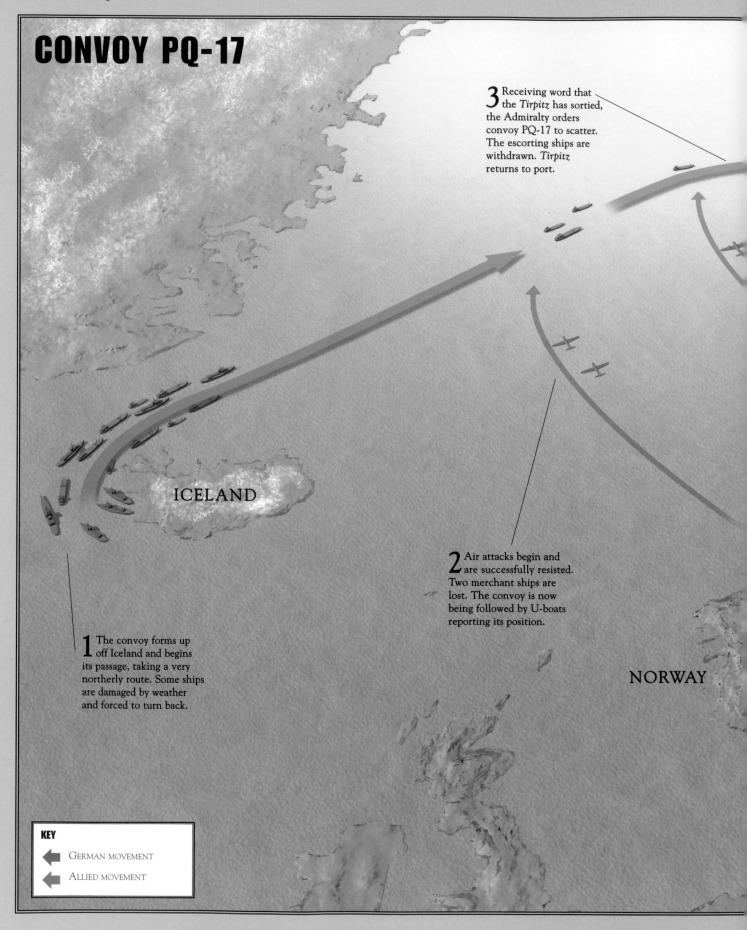

3 Receiving word that the *Tirpitz* has sortied, the Admiralty orders convoy PQ-17 to scatter. The escorting ships are withdrawn. *Tirpitz* returns to port.

2 Air attacks begin and are successfully resisted. Two merchant ships are lost. The convoy is now being followed by U-boats reporting its position.

1 The convoy forms up off Iceland and begins its passage, taking a very northerly route. Some ships are damaged by weather and forced to turn back.

ICELAND

NORWAY

KEY

GERMAN MOVEMENT

ALLIED MOVEMENT

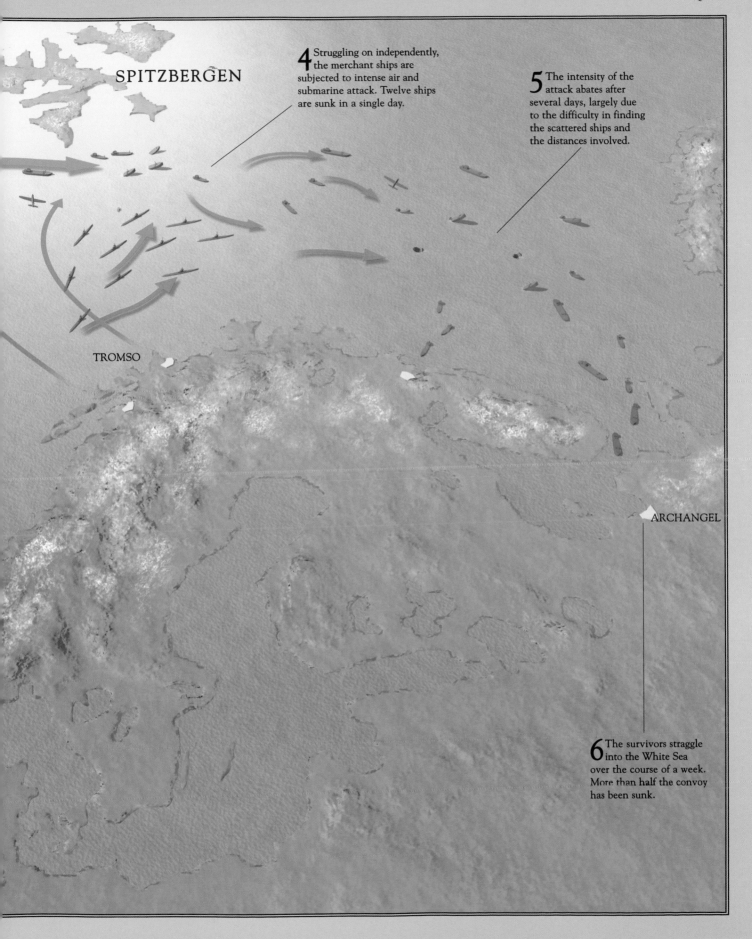

SPITZBERGEN

4 Struggling on independently, the merchant ships are subjected to intense air and submarine attack. Twelve ships are sunk in a single day.

5 The intensity of the attack abates after several days, largely due to the difficulty in finding the scattered ships and the distances involved.

TROMSO

ARCHANGEL

6 The survivors straggle into the White Sea over the course of a week. More than half the convoy has been sunk.

EL ALAMEIN

1942

The Battle of El Alamein, 23 October–4 November 1942, taking its name from an Egyptian railway halt west of Alexandria, marked a turning point in the war in North Africa. The British Prime Minister Winston Churchill (1874–1965) claimed that, 'Before Alamein we never had a victory. After Alamein we never had a defeat.'

Although Churchill's pronouncement was something of an exaggeration, the German–Italian army was forced into full-scale retreat and its position worsened considerably after the Allied landings in French North Africa on 8 November. However, for the Commonwealth army the battle also had the psychological effect of finally breaking the myth of German invincibility.

The war in the Western Desert had swung back and forth over the course of nearly two years. Field-Marshal Erwin Rommel's (1891–1944) German–Italian Panzer Army Africa had driven the British back past the Egyptian border, where it

EL ALAMEIN FACTS

Who: The Commonwealth Eighth Army (British, Australian, New Zealand, Indian and South African troops) led by Lieutenant-General Bernard Montgomery (1887–1976) faced Field Marshal Erwin Rommel's (1891–1944) Panzer Army Africa, renamed the German–Italian Panzer Army on 25 October 1942.

What: Operation Lightfoot was a carefully planned and prepared set-piece offensive launched by Montgomery on the Axis forces, who had shifted to the defensive after being defeated at Alam Halfa in September.

Where: El Alamein, a small Egyptian railway halt, 95 kilometres (60 miles) west of Alexandria.

When: 23 October to 4 November 1942

Why: Growing British material strength allowed Montgomery to shift decisively to the offensive against Rommel's over-extended forces and finally ensure the safety of the Suez Canal and the Middle Eastern oil fields.

Outcome: Although Rommel was able to escape with a large proportion of his army, El Alamein marked a clear turning point in the Western Desert Campaign with the initiative shifting decisively to the Allies.

A PROBABLY STAGED photograph of troops of the 51st Highland Division running past a knocked-out German Panzer Mark III at El Alamein.

ABOVE: FIELD MARSHAL ERWIN ROMMEL, *the charismatic, energetic commander of German and Italian forces in the Western Desert.*

BELOW: BRITISH ARTILLERY BOMBARDS *German positions during the buildup to the offensive at El Alamein, Operation* Lightfoot.

was stopped by General Claude Auchinleck's (1884–1981) Eighth Army between 1 and 4 July 1942, at the first battle of El Alamein. By the time Rommel was ready to try again, Auchinleck had been replaced as Army Commander by Lieutenant General Bernard Law Montgomery (1887–1976). Montgomery was a meticulous planner and superb trainer of men, and set about rebuilding the Eighth Army, both in terms of matériel and confidence.

When Rommel attacked in September at Alam Halfa, the British were well prepared and he was soundly defeated. At the end of a long logistical chain, plagued by shortages of fuel and facing an increasingly strong Commonwealth Army, Rommel, debilitated by ill health, shifted to the defensive. The Germans and Italians set about establishing a system of strong points set among deep minefields. Rommel's mobile troops were held back behind his infantry to counter any breakthrough, but the desperate lack of fuel meant they were held closer to the front than normal. In the north, he placed 15th Panzer, 90th Light and the Italian *Littorio* armoured divisions; and in the south, 21st Panzer and *Ariete*.

SET-PIECE BATTLE

Montgomery refused to be pushed by Churchill into attacking before he believed he was ready. He would launch his offensive only when he was sure his men were trained to the peak of perfection and completely in his grip, ready to do exactly what he wanted of them. Unlike so many previous desert battles, Alamein would be a set-piece affair, with both

RIGHT: A PRIVATE FROM THE 9TH Australian Division with his Short Magazine Lee-Enfield Rifle. He is well wrapped-up to withstand the rigours of the desert at night.

flanks soundly anchored by the Mediterranean to the north and the impassable Qattara Depression to the south. Montgomery could muster 195,000 men to Rommel's 105,000, of whom 53,000 were German. He fielded 1000 tanks to the enemy's 500 and roughly double the amount of aircraft.

The Commonwealth forces, broadly speaking, held a two-to-one advantage in most weapon systems. Montgomery's plan was that four infantry divisions of Lieutenant-General Oliver Leese's (1884–1978) XXX Corps would clear a path through the German positions in the north to allow the two armoured divisions of Lieutenant-General Herbert Lumsden's (1897–1945) X Corps to push through and take defensive positions in the west. Then the infantry would break up the German line to the north and south – 'crumbling' as Montgomery called it. Brian Horrocks's (1895–1985) XIII Corps would make strong representations to the south.

THE OFFENSIVE OPENS

Operation *Lightfoot*, a codename in somewhat poor taste given the 445,000 German mines, opened with a massive barrage on the evening of 23 October. It took the Germans by surprise and seriously disrupted Axis communications. General George Stumme (1886–1942), commanding in Rommel's absence on sick leave, died of a heart attack going forward to find out what was happening. The battle started well but resistance began to stiffen quickly, particularly in the 51st Highland Division's sector. The northernmost 9th Australian Division took all its objectives, but the armour

RIGHT: A HEAVILY DECORATED GERMAN tank man swigs from his water, standing atop his Panzer Mark III.

was to advance through the Highlanders and the 2nd New Zealand Division, where more difficulties had been encountered and heavy casualties suffered. The Commonwealth forces had failed to reach their first day objectives. Bitter fighting continued over the next couple of days and, although progress was slow, a couple of serious German counterattacks were repulsed. Rommel returned on 26 October and concentrated what armour he could muster after the attritional fighting of the previous few days to counterattack a salient created by British 1st Armoured Division on the slight rise of Kidney Ridge. Both 21st Panzer and 90th Light Divisions were stopped dead by well-served antitank guns, artillery and air power. Meanwhile, Montgomery's forces slowly reduced the Axis positions, although progress was much slower than expected.

SUPERCHARGE LAUNCHED

The failure to make much headway forced Montgomery to come up with another plan. Operation *Supercharge* shifted the weight of the offensive away from the north to the Kidney Ridge area on the night of 1 November. Led by Lieutenant-General Bernard Freyberg's (1889–1963) New Zealanders, bolstered by three British brigades, *Supercharge*

THE US-BUILT M3 Medium Tank (known to the British as the Lee or Grant) first saw service in the Western Desert in early 1942. Although it had a number of flaws, the British appreciated the fire power provided by its hull-mounted 75mm (2.95in) gun.

penetrated deep into the Axis position and convinced Rommel that the battle was lost.

On 3 November, he began to pull back his armoured forces and ordered the rest of his men to disengage. The New Zealanders and 1st Armoured Division, then 7th Armoured Division threatened to cut off the escape, which was in itself hampered by Hitler ordering Rommel to stand fast. Rommel managed to extricate large numbers of his forces, although 30,000 – about a third of them German – were taken prisoner. The Battle of El Alamein was over and had cost the Allies 13,560 casualties, Major-General Douglas Wimberley's (1896–1983) inexperienced

51st Highland Division taking the brunt, with the other infantry divisions also suffering heavily.

PURSUIT AND DEFENCE

Montgomery was hesitant in the pursuit and Rommel was able to retreat westwards about 1000km (620 miles) before turning to make a serious stand in January 1943. By then, the strategic situation had worsened even further for the Axis, as on 8 November US and British forces landed in French North Africa seriously threatening Rommel's rear. The remorseless logic of a two-front campaign doomed the Axis presence in Africa.

GENERAL BERNARD MONTGOMERY

Bernard Montgomery combined undeniable charisma and flair for showmanship with a single-minded dedication to the profession of arms. He proved to be a superb trainer of men and meticulous planner, who did much to banish the myth of German invincibility. He was seriously wounded in World War I, but by the outbreak of World War II he commanded 3rd Division, which he led with distinction through the French campaign of 1940.

Corps and Area commands in Britain followed. Then, in August 1942, the death of Lieutenant-General William Gott, Churchill's first choice as commander for the Eighth Army, gave Montgomery his opportunity.

ABOVE: A GERMAN TANK MAN *surrenders to Commonwealth infantry in another probably staged photo from the period.*

El Alamein was the climax of the campaign in the Western Desert and the turning point in the war in North Africa. Montgomery had approached the battle with determination and a hard-headed will to succeed. He had also proved flexible enough – although he would never admit it – to change his plan midway through the battle. More importantly, he had proved himself to be a general capable of defeating the Germans. This was vital for the morale of the Eighth Army, vital for Churchill, who was under political pressure at home, and vital for the British nation as a whole.

LEFT: THE MARK II MATILDA *had been a mainstay of British tanks forces in the early part of the desert war, but by El Alamein it was obsolescent.*

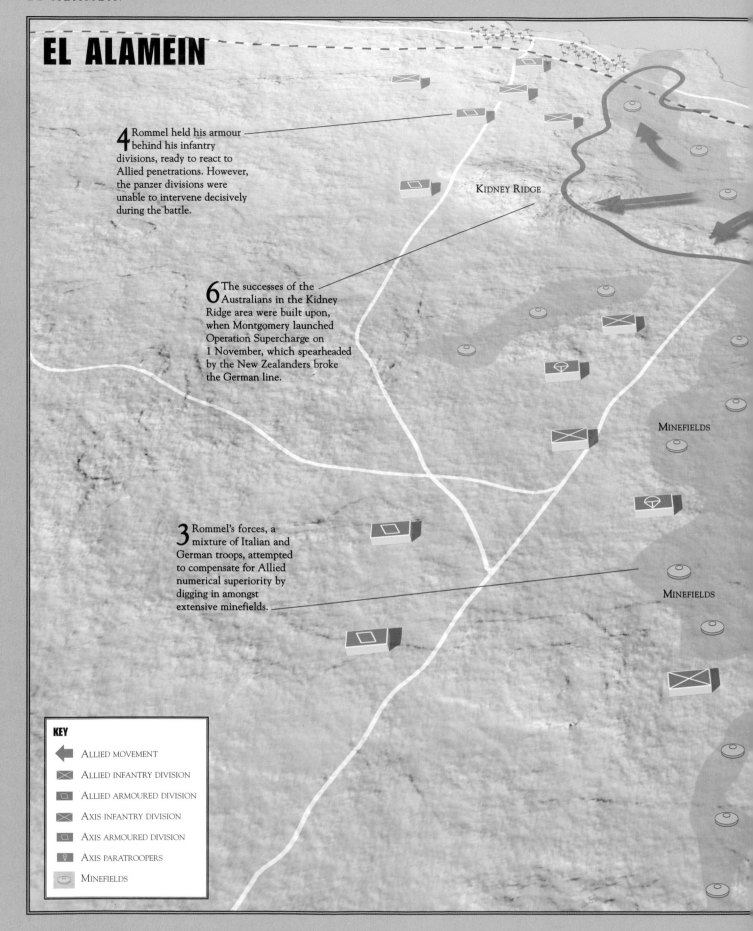

EL ALAMEIN

4 Rommel held his armour behind his infantry divisions, ready to react to Allied penetrations. However, the panzer divisions were unable to intervene decisively during the battle.

KIDNEY RIDGE

6 The successes of the Australians in the Kidney Ridge area were built upon, when Montgomery launched Operation Supercharge on 1 November, which spearheaded by the New Zealanders broke the German line.

MINEFIELDS

3 Rommel's forces, a mixture of Italian and German troops, attempted to compensate for Allied numerical superiority by digging in amongst extensive minefields.

MINEFIELDS

KEY

◄ ALLIED MOVEMENT

⊠ ALLIED INFANTRY DIVISION

▭ ALLIED ARMOURED DIVISION

⊠ AXIS INFANTRY DIVISION

▱ AXIS ARMOURED DIVISION

▽ AXIS PARATROOPERS

◉ MINEFIELDS

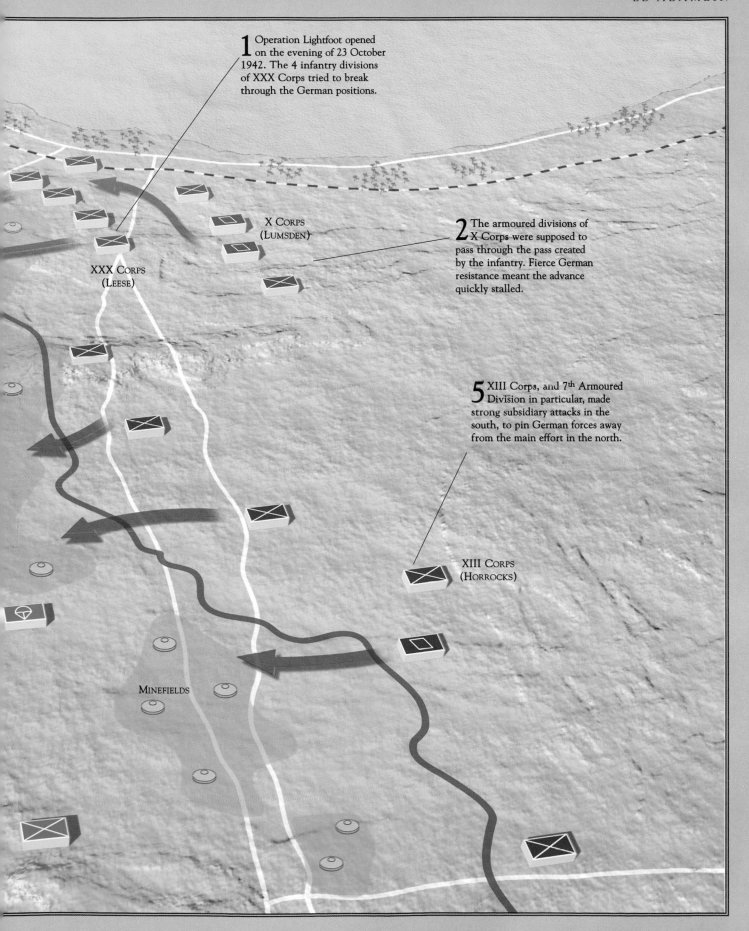

1 Operation Lightfoot opened on the evening of 23 October 1942. The 4 infantry divisions of XXX Corps tried to break through the German positions.

2 The armoured divisions of X Corps were supposed to pass through the pass created by the infantry. Fierce German resistance meant the advance quickly stalled.

5 XIII Corps, and 7th Armoured Division in particular, made strong subsidiary attacks in the south, to pin German forces away from the main effort in the north.

X CORPS
(LUMSDEN)

XXX CORPS
(LEESE)

XIII CORPS
(HORROCKS)

MINEFIELDS

BATTLE OF GUADALCANAL 1942–43

After defeating the Imperial Japanese Navy at the Battle of Midway in June 1942, the Allies set about clearing Japanese bases from the Solomon Islands. This required amphibious operations against several islands – including Tulagi, where a seaplane base needed removing, and Guadalcanal, where a major airbase was being constructed.

The Allies assembled an invasion force at Fiji under US Vice-Admiral Frank Fletcher (1885–1973), with ground forces led by Major-General Alexander Vandegrift (1887–1973), commander of the US 1st Marine Division, which provided most of the ground forces.

BATTLE OF GUADALCANAL FACTS

Who: Allied forces from the United States, Australia and New Zealand versus Japanese ground, air and naval forces.

What: The Battle of Guadalcanal was a drawn-out fight lasting several months and involving land, naval and air forces. Allied forces captured the island and held it against determined attack.

Where: Guadalcanal in the Solomon Islands, in the South Pacific.

When: August 1942–February 1943

Why: The island was important to both sides as a base for future operations.

Outcome: With its eventual success, the Allies won their first major ground victory against the Japanese. Despite heavy losses on both sides, the island was held by the Allies and used as a forward base.

US MARINES GO ASHORE *in August 1942. There was little opposition to the initial landings on Guadalcanal, though later the island was bitterly contested until the Japanese finally gave up.*

LEFT: A US DESTROYER off the coast of Guadalcanal. Although the fate of the island was decided on land, naval power greatly influenced the battle by limiting Japanese reinforcements and supply runs.

This was met by carrier-based fighters, with casualties on both sides. Some attacks got through and caused damage to transport ships not yet unloaded. Soon afterwards, the carrier force had to withdraw for lack of fuel.

An attack by a powerful Japanese cruiser force under Vice-Admiral Gunichi Mikawa (1888–1981) resulted in heavy losses to Allied cruisers off Savo island, and the decision was taken to withdraw the surviving naval vessels from the area. This meant it became necessary to pull the half-unloaded transports out as well – they were too vulnerable to air attack without carrier cover and surface ships without cruisers to protect them.

The forces ashore on Guadalcanal at this point comprised some 11,000 marines, but much of their heavy equipment was still aboard the transports steaming away towards safety. Nevertheless they proceeded with the plan and finished building the airfield the Japanese had started, naming it Henderson Field.

SECURING THE ISLAND

Some Japanese forces had dispersed around the island after the Allied landings, and these were reinforced by a small number landed by destroyer. Patrols and expeditions were launched to locate and remove these holdouts, and though success was mixed the enemy was largely kept away from the airfield, which received its first aircraft – a mix of fighters and dive bombers.

The island was harassed by air attacks more or less constantly, but the Japanese commanders were not satisfied: they wanted the Allies driven off Guadalcanal and the rest of the Solomons, and so planned an

Approaching under cover of bad weather, the assault force went ashore on 7 August 1942. The main objective was the capture of Guadalcanal itself and the airbase there. Other forces were tasked with capturing Tulagi and other smaller islands in the group.

On Guadalcanal itself, things went very well. The terrain, which was mostly jungle, proved more of a problem than enemy resistance for the first day, and by the end of the second the airfield was in Allied hands, along with stores, supplies and construction equipment abandoned there.

Although heavily outnumbered, the Japanese troops on the other islands put up a stiff fight and had to be eliminated almost to a man. This sort of fanatical resistance became familiar as the war went on and resulted in heavy casualties for the Allies, even when dealing with quite small outposts.

Meanwhile, the Allies came under attack from aircraft out of Rabaul on the island of New Britain in New Guinea.

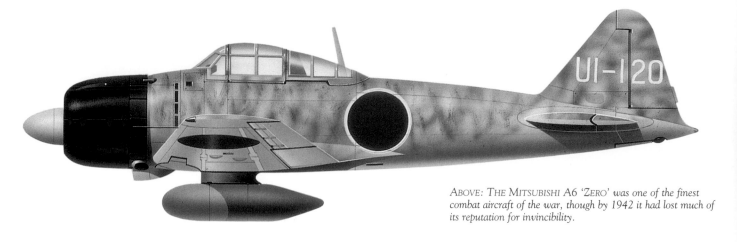

ABOVE: THE MITSUBISHI A6 'ZERO' was one of the finest combat aircraft of the war, though by 1942 it had lost much of its reputation for invincibility.

ABOVE: US MARINE GENERAL VANDERGRIFT and US Navy Admiral Kelly were in command of the land and naval components of the operation respectively. Amphibious operations of this kind required close cooperation between services.

amphibious attack of their own. The task fell to Seventeenth Army, which was already heavily committed to the battles for New Guinea.

Some elements of Seventeenth Army were available for an operation against Guadalcanal but they arrived in piecemeal fashion. The first assault force was a contingent of about 1000 men of the 28th Infantry Regiment under Colonel Kiyonao Ichiki (1892–1942). This inadequate force was landed from destroyers and immediately moved west to engage the defenders.

Although it was outnumbered more than ten to one Ichiki's force attacked towards Henderson Field under cover of darkness. Japanese casualties were extremely high and the attack achieved nothing. A subsequent marine counterattack scattered the survivors after Ichiki himself was killed.

A second force, about 2000 strong, was also on its way and its approach was covered by Japanese naval forces, including three carriers. This resulted in the Battle of the Eastern Solomons as the Allied carrier forces engaged the Japanese fleet. Amid this action, aircraft out of Henderson field attacked the Japanese troop transports and caused heavy casualties. The survivors were eventually landed from destroyers.

During this period, the Allied forces on Guadalcanal were reinforced with additional aircraft, steadily increasing the strength of the island's air group despite losses in combat. Guadalcanal became a big threat to Japanese intentions in the area and both sides knew that a major operation to eliminate Henderson Field and its air group was going to be launched.

General Vandergrift set his marines, now reinforced, to improving their positions. Units were redeployed to create a better overall defence while minor operations were undertaken against the increasing Japanese forces on the island. Dysentery was a serious problem for the garrison, with as much as 20 per cent of the force down at any given time, and the island's terrain also made offensive operations difficult.

THE TOKYO EXPRESS

After losing many transports to air attack, Japanese commanders decided that a traditional amphibious operation was not feasible and instead implemented what became known as the Tokyo Express, whereby destroyers and light cruisers dashed in under cover of night to land relatively small forces and re-supply them.

The Tokyo Express was a clever solution to the problem of getting troops on to Guadalcanal, but it had its limitations. Small warships could not carry heavy equipment or artillery and ships engaged in these operations were not available for war-fighting missions elsewhere. Nevertheless the Tokyo Express ran several thousand Japanese troops into Guadalcanal over the next few weeks until sufficient forces had been built up for an attack.

RIGHT: THE JAPANESE DEPLOYED large numbers of naval infantry personnel to defend the Pacific islands. Marines by any other name, these troops put up a determined fight on Guadalcanal and elsewhere.

THE M3 STUART was too light for anything but reconnaissance duty in the European theatre, but in the Pacific island terrain the light tank really came into its own.

On 31 August, General Kawaguchi arrived to take command of all Japanese forces on Guadalcanal, and on 7 September he gave the order for an assault on Henderson Field. A raid by US Marines hit the supply base of one of these groups the next day, giving an indication that a large force was on the island and an attack was imminent.

JAPANESE ATTACKS

The Japanese plan was to attack at night, in three groups from the east, west and south. However, the Allies were forewarned and had posted troops on a rise to the south of Henderson Field. This later became known as Edson's Ridge after Lieutenant-Colonel Merritt Edson (1897–1955), who led the defence. They were right in the path of the main Japanese force when the attack went in on 12 September.

Fighting on the ridge was heavy and the defenders, who were outnumbered more than three to one, were eventually pushed on to a central high point. There they resisted several assaults, but were unable to prevent other Japanese troops bypassing them. Those who got past Edson's Ridge ran into other defenders, who were able to hold and eventually repel them. Attacks in other sectors were likewise halted. Finally, after two days of intense fighting, the Japanese pulled back to regroup.

Both sides rebuilt their forces and defences as best they could. More Allied troops were brought in, although the sea routes were hotly contested. The US carrier *Wasp* was sunk during this operation. General Vandergrift reorganized his forces and promoted some men, including Edson.

After a period of bad weather, the air battle resumed on 27 September, with even greater intensity as both sides had been reinforced. On the ground, more Japanese troops arrived while US forces tried to drive the scattered survivors of previous attacks away from their defences and prevent the new arrivals from establishing themselves close to the airfield. The result was several clashes in late September and early October which disrupted Japanese offensive preparations.

However, the island's defenders were under pressure from the air and the Japanese buildup was causing concern. Reinforcements were requested and in due course set sail.

The timing was fortuitous. US naval units covering the reinforcement convoy ran into a major Japanese force shipment that included vessels tasked to bombard Henderson Field. In the resulting Battle of Cape Esperance, the US vessels inflicted a heavy defeat on the Japanese navy, though the associated Tokyo Express convoy got through and unloaded on Guadalcanal.

Another bombardment was ordered for 13 October while yet more troops were brought in. This time, the attack included two battleships and did major damage to the airfield, which nevertheless was restored to minimal function in time to launch strikes against the Japanese troop transports.

By the middle of October, the Japanese had brought several thousand troops on to Guadalcanal and had repeatedly shelled the airfield. Ground forces began to move into position for the assault. Some 20,000 Japanese troops were available, the main attack coming in from the south with additional flanking operations. The attack was dislocated by delays in preparation, and communication problems meant that some forces attacked on 23 October and some the day after. The assault was sustained, and in

DESPITE GREAT DETERMINATION, many of the Japanese attacks on US positions were ill-advised given the tactical situation. Heavy casualties were inevitable.

some places the Japanese got through the outer defences despite heavy casualties. A handful of tanks were used but were easily disabled by the defenders.

Although under pressure, the defenders held out on the ground while the air forces fought off air and naval attacks. Repeated frontal charges were cut up by infantry weapons and artillery firing over open sights. Finally, on 26 October, the assault was called off, and the Japanese retreated.

ENDGAME

Land warfare in the Pacific was heavily influenced by the situation at sea. Whichever side had sea control could bring in supplies and reinforcements, tipping the balance of the land engagement. Thus the naval actions off Guadalcanal were vital to the land campaign. Several battles were fought at sea in the vicinity of Guadalcanal, including the Battles of Savo Island and Cape Esperance. On 13 November 1942, a Japanese force attempting to bring reinforcements to the islands and to bombard Henderson Field clashed with US ships in a close-range brawl that cost both sides dearly and left the US Navy very short of ships to defend Guadalcanal when the Japanese Navy came back to try again.

Further Japanese attempts to reinforce their presence on the island were unsuccessful and US forces began taking the offensive, pushing the enemy away from the airfield. Cut off from re-supply and being ground down, the remaining Japanese forces were evacuated in early February, ending the campaign. Guadalcanal was the first clear-cut land victory

over the Japanese and did much to restore Allied confidence. It also deprived the Japanese of an important forward base. The battle had a wider significance too.

After the failure of the first big attack, Japanese commanders realized that the struggle for Guadalcanal was a battle of real strategic significance and gave it great prominence. One consequence of this was that forces advancing on Port Moresby in New Guinea were pulled back and denied reinforcements. Thus the fighting on Guadalcanal indirectly assisted the Allied cause elsewhere.

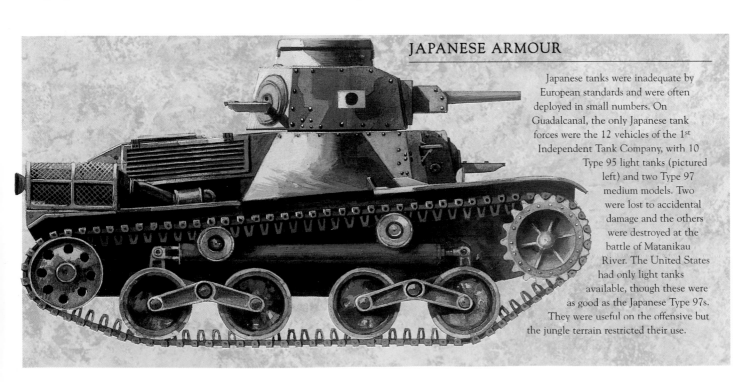

JAPANESE ARMOUR

Japanese tanks were inadequate by European standards and were often deployed in small numbers. On Guadalcanal, the only Japanese tank forces were the 12 vehicles of the 1st Independent Tank Company, with 10 Type 95 light tanks (pictured left) and two Type 97 medium models. Two were lost to accidental damage and the others were destroyed at the battle of Matanikau River. The United States had only light tanks available, though these were as good as the Japanese Type 97s. They were useful on the offensive but the jungle terrain restricted their use.

GUADALCANAL

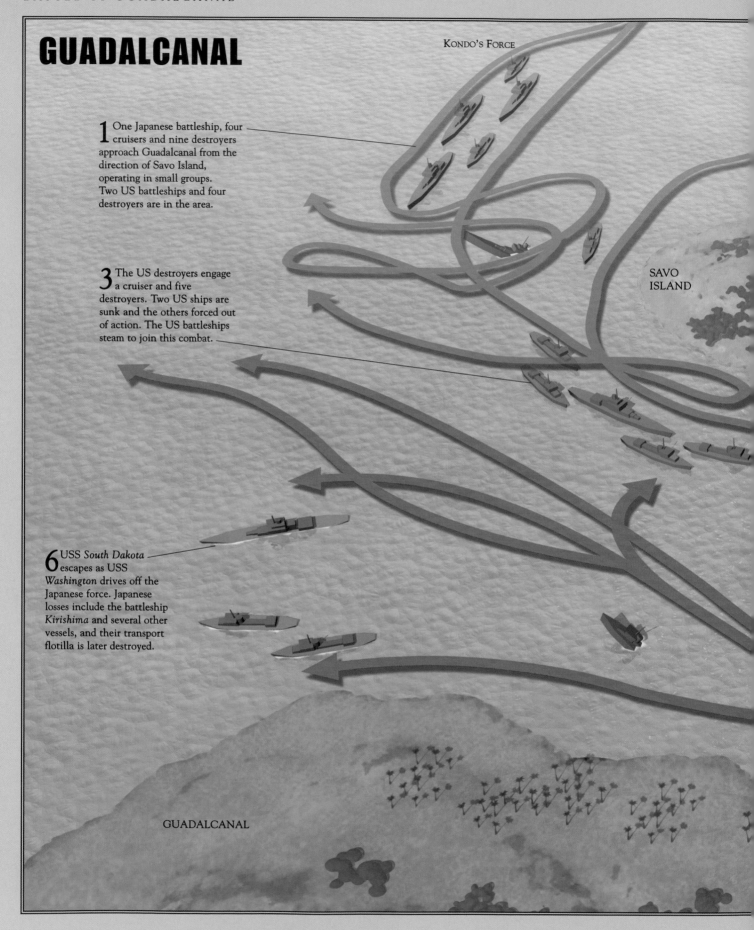

KONDO'S FORCE

1 One Japanese battleship, four cruisers and nine destroyers approach Guadalcanal from the direction of Savo Island, operating in small groups. Two US battleships and four destroyers are in the area.

3 The US destroyers engage a cruiser and five destroyers. Two US ships are sunk and the others forced out of action. The US battleships steam to join this combat.

6 USS *South Dakota* escapes as USS *Washington* drives off the Japanese force. Japanese losses include the battleship *Kirishima* and several other vessels, and their transport flotilla is later destroyed.

SAVO
ISLAND

GUADALCANAL

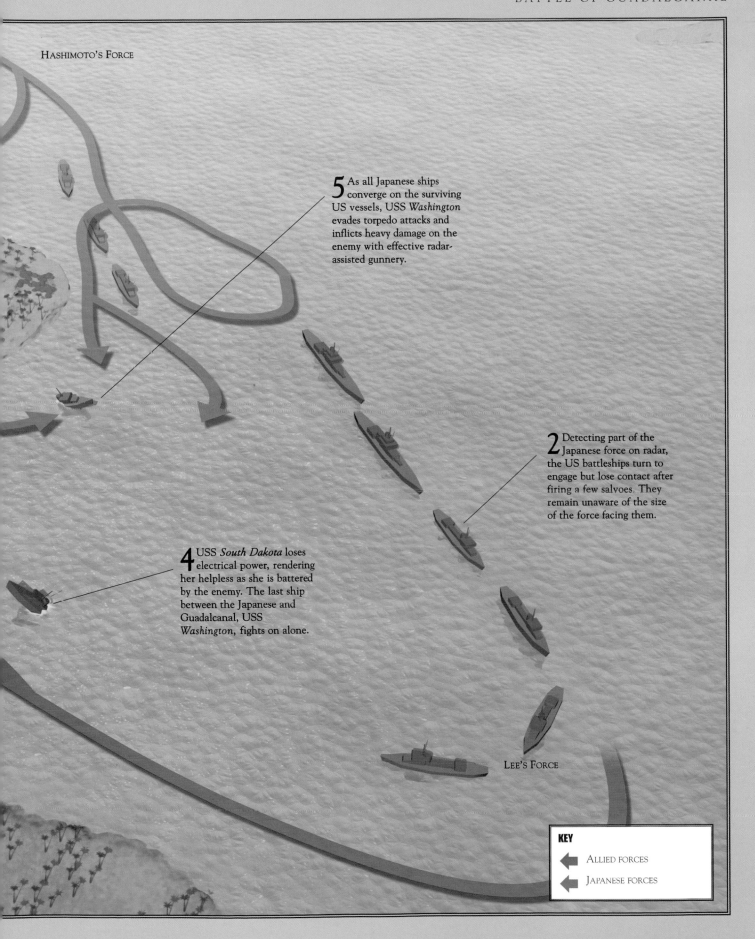

HASHIMOTO'S FORCE

5 As all Japanese ships converge on the surviving US vessels, USS *Washington* evades torpedo attacks and inflicts heavy damage on the enemy with effective radar-assisted gunnery.

2 Detecting part of the Japanese force on radar, the US battleships turn to engage but lose contact after firing a few salvoes. They remain unaware of the size of the force facing them.

4 USS *South Dakota* loses electrical power, rendering her helpless as she is battered by the enemy. The last ship between the Japanese and Guadalcanal, USS *Washington*, fights on alone.

LEE'S FORCE

KEY

← ALLIED FORCES

← JAPANESE FORCES

STALINGRAD 1942–43

Stalingrad changed the face of World War II. In a cataclysmic struggle, the Wehrmacht *experienced its first major army-sized defeat and the strategic advantage on the Eastern Front began to shift to the Red Army.*

As the crushing Russian winter of 1941–42 ran its course, Adolf Hitler was faced with a critical strategic decision. His *Barbarossa* campaign to smash the Soviet Union, which began in June 1941, had stalled before Moscow and was even put into temporary retreat by a Soviet counteroffensive on 5–6 December. Only the late spring would return the *Wehrmacht* to mobility and Hitler decided to apply this mobility in a new direction. Instead of renewing the Moscow offensive, much as the Soviets expected, Hitler ordered Operation *Blue* – a massive offensive by his Army Group South through the Ukraine and into the Crimea towards the Caucasus. The ultimate objective was to capture the Soviet oilfields of the Caucasus, oilfields upon which Germany relied to power its war machine.

STALINGRAD FACTS

Who: The German Sixth Army under General Friedrich Paulus (1890–1957), along with elements of the Fourth Panzer Army under General Hermann Hoth (1885–1971), versus the Red Army's Stalingrad Front, principally the Sixty-Second Army under Major-General Vasily Chuikov (1900–1982).

What: German forces nearly succeeded in conquering Stalingrad, but with massive losses. A Soviet counteroffensive trapped 250,000 Germans within the city. About 100,000 of these men were killed and 110,000 went to almost certain death in Soviet captivity.

Where: The city of Stalingrad, set on the Volga river.

When: 14 September 1942 to 2 February 1943

Why: The Stalingrad battle was part of a German campaign to occupy the Soviet Union's southern oilfields in the Caucasus. Stalingrad needed securing to protect the German left flank.

Outcome: Stalingrad marked the beginning of the German defeat on the Eastern Front, with the Red Army maintaining an offensive drive for the rest of the war.

AMIDST THE DEVASTATION OF STALINGRAD, *a heavily armed German platoon prepares to make yet another assault on Soviet positions.*

A *TWO-MAN GERMAN* MG34 *machine-gun team occupies a shell-hole in the ruined Stalingrad suburbs, September 1942.*

Operation *Blue* began on 28 June, consisting of 1.3 million men (including 300,000 German allies, principally Romanians and Italians) and 1500 aircraft. Army Group South was divided into Army Groups A and B, and the plan was for both groups to converge on the city of Stalingrad on the banks of the Volga, at which point Army Group B would remain on the Don and Volga rivers to provide flank protection for Army Group A's assault into the Caucasus. As with the *Wehrmacht* operations of the previous spring/summer, the Germans made good headway, and by mid-July the Sixth Army under General Friedrich Paulus (1890–1957) – the main component of Army Group B – was closing in on Stalingrad.

On 23 July, Hitler gave the order to take the city itself. General Hermann Hoth's (1885–1971) Fourth Panzer Army was deployed south of Stalingrad to assist in the assault. On the same day, Stalin issued his own directive stating that Stalingrad

would be defended to the last. Soviet forces in the newly designated Stalingrad Front consisted of the Sixty-Second, Sixty-Third and Sixty-Fourth Armies. Although Stalingrad was an important industrial centre, the fact that it bore Stalin's name gave the Soviet leader a definite psychological imperative to see that it did not fall.

STREET BATTLE

The prelude to fighting within the city was a heavy air bombardment by *Luftlotte* 4, which reduced much of the city to rubble and killed more than 30,000 people. By 12 September, German troops were already pushing into the city's suburbs, where they faced a defence of almost psychotic vigour from the troops of Chuikov's Sixty-Second Army within the city. Chuikov, a rough-edged commander in contrast to the urbane Paulus, had a numerical disadvantage within the city compared to the Germans (roughly 54,000 Soviets to 100,000 Germans).

Yet the battle for Stalingrad was to be pure street fighting, a form of warfare depriving the Germans of the mobility that was their accustomed route to success in battle. Moreover, Chuikov deliberately pushed his troops into extreme close-quarters battle, ordering them to 'hug' the German troops and thus limit enemy use of air bombardment and heavy artillery fire, both of which would

risk the danger of 'friendly fire' casualties. The effect was that every building, and every room in every building, became a battleground, the Germans paying for each yard with blood.

By the end of September, Paulus and Hoth had taken around two-thirds of Stalingrad. An offensive launched on 14 September by LI Corps penetrated deep inside the city, taking the Mamayev Kurgan heights (a salient feature of the

Below: All available Soviet personnel were used in the defence of Stalingrad – this group includes sailors and civilians.

ABOVE: TROOPS AND ARMOUR of the Soviet Twenty-First Army advance during Operation Uranus, the two-pronged offensive designed to trap German forces in Stalingrad.

city) and driving through towards the No 1 Railway station. The aim was to reach the Volga and destroy the Soviet landing stages, which were receiving resupply and reinforcements boated across the river (a harrowing experience for boat crews and passengers, who were bombed remorselessly by German attack aircraft). However, last-

BELOW: THE ITALIAN EIGHTH ARMY begins its long retreat from positions on the left flank of the German Sixth Army, December 1942.

minute reinforcements from Major-General Aleksandr Rodimtsev's (1905–1977) 13th Guards Division meant that the station changed hands 15 times before it finally fell to the Germans. Hoth's Fourth Panzers coming up from the south had a similar harrowing experience but made better progress, reaching the river by 13 October.

Between mid-October and mid-November, the Germans slowly squeezed the Soviets back, battling through the factory district at appalling cost (major battlegrounds were the Barrikady, Krasny Oktyabr and Tractor factories). Stalingrad was by now utterly destroyed, but the rubble created by German firepower actually made a convoluted landscape that was easier to defend and harder to attack. By 18 November, the Soviets held only a thin broken strip of territory on the Volga, little more than 10 per cent of the city. Winter was beginning, however, and the Germans were shattered and depleted from the last weeks of fighting.

THE SOVIET OFFENSIVE

On 19 November, Soviet forces around Stalingrad played their masterstroke, a counteroffensive planned by General Georgy Zhukov (1896–1974). North of Stalingrad, the Soviet Southwest Front and Don Front launched a six-army push southwards across the Don, smashing weak Romanian resistance. The next day, the Stalingrad Front attacked north from positions south of Stalingrad, once again overcoming weak German flank protection. On 23 November, the two

A YAK 1B of the 37th Guards IAP. The Soviets had a total of about 1400 aircraft at Stalingrad, flying about 500 sorties a day.

'pincers' met behind Stalingrad, trapping the Sixth Army and much of the Fourth Army – more than 250,000 men – within the city. A German disaster was unfolding.

In the early days of the offensive, a German breakout was possible but it was refused by Hitler. Instead, he opted for one of Hermann Göring's wildly optimistic aerial resupply plans, which was never realistic, and then for a relief offensive by Manstein's Eleventh Army. This offensive – Operation *Winter Storm* – was launched on 12 December and made some progress but was eventually battered to a standstill 48km (30 miles) from Stalingrad. Two weeks later, Manstein's forces were in retreat from fresh Soviet offensives, leaving the German soldiers in Stalingrad to a ghastly fate.

Horrific fighting continued in Stalingrad for over a month as the Soviets steadily crushed the German occupiers. Although 34,000 Germans were evacuated by air before the final airfield fell on 25 January, more than 100,000 *Wehrmacht* troops were killed in this period. Finally, between 31 January and 2 February, Paulus and some 110,000 German survivors surrendered, destined for Soviet labour camps from which only 5000 men would emerge alive.

THE BEGINNING OF THE END

The German defeat at Stalingrad tilted the balance of the war both strategically and psychologically. Strategically, it put paid to Operation *Blue* and began, in effect, the German retreat that would end in Berlin in 1945. Psychologically it gave the Soviets an enormous boost of confidence and showed that they could compete with the Germans on both tactical and strategic levels. For the Germans, it was an undeniable sign that they could be defeated – the glory days of 1939–40 were now forgotten.

FIELD-MARSHAL FRIEDRICH PAULUS

Friedrich Paulus (1890–1957) cut his military teeth as an army captain during World War I and showed the ability and ambition that enabled him to rise to the rank of general by 1939. He subsequently served as deputy to General Franz Halder, the German Chief of Staff, before taking his most infamous command, that of the Sixth Army, in 1941. Paulus was an urbane 'old school' officer whose loyalty to the military led him, initially, to obey Hitler's ludicrous 'to the last man' defence orders at Stalingrad. On 31 January 1942, Hitler made Paulus a field-marshal, knowing that no field-marshal in German history had ever surrendered or been captured alive. (Hitler was in effect requesting his suicide.) At this point, however, Paulus chose to ignore the precedent and surrendered, going on to be a vocal critic of the Nazi regime while in captivity. His last career posting was as an adviser to the East German Army in the mid-1950s.

FIELD-MARSHAL PAULUS (left) and his chief-of-staff Arthur Schmidt (right) seen after their surrender in early 1943.

STALINGRAD

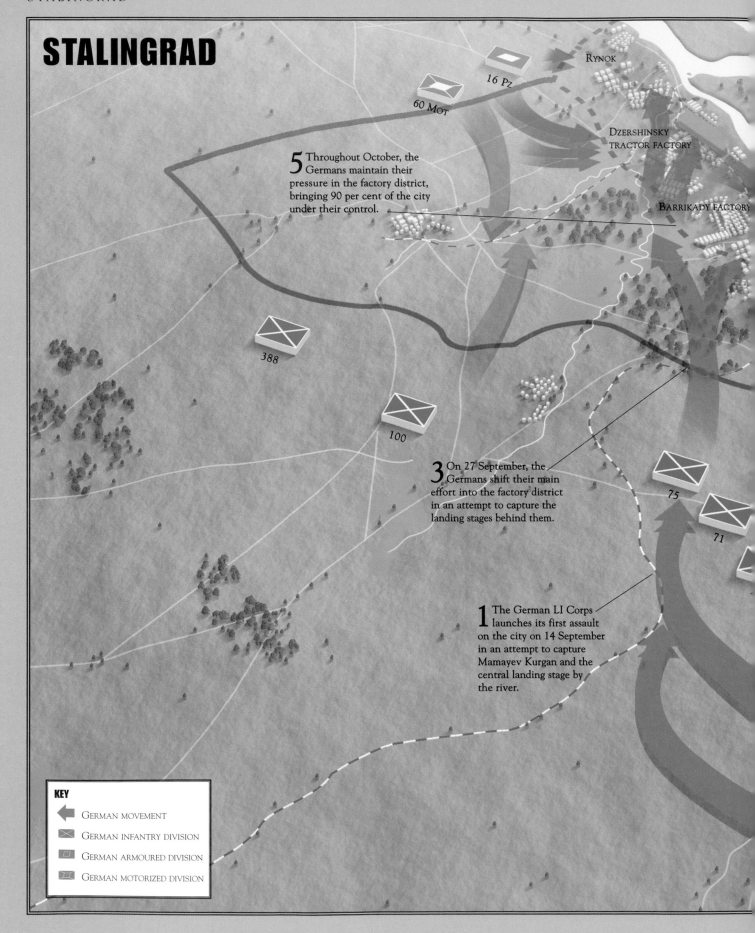

RYNOK

16 Pz

60 Mot

DZERSHINSKY
TRACTOR FACTORY

BARRIKADY FACTORY

5 Throughout October, the
Germans maintain their
pressure in the factory district,
bringing 90 per cent of the city
under their control.

388

100

3 On 27 September, the
Germans shift their main
effort into the factory district
in an attempt to capture the
landing stages behind them.

75

71

1 The German LI Corps
launches its first assault
on the city on 14 September
in an attempt to capture
Mamayev Kurgan and the
central landing stage by
the river.

KEY

⬅ GERMAN MOVEMENT

✉ GERMAN INFANTRY DIVISION

▭ GERMAN ARMOURED DIVISION

▭ GERMAN MOTORIZED DIVISION

6 The last major German attack begins on 11 November. Eight days later, the Soviets launch Operation Uranus, cutting off the Sixth Army in the city.

4 The Soviets managed to maintain their supply lines across the Volga, providing the Sixty-Second Army with just enough men and matériel to hang on to their foothold in the city.

RED OCTOBER FACTORY

MAMAYEV KURGAN

KRASNAYA SLOBODA

GRAIN SILO

RIVER VOLGA

94

14 Pz

24 Pz

29 Mot

2 The Fourth Panzer Army attacks in support in the south of the city, but is held up by fanatical resistance around the grain silo.

THIRD BATTLE OF KHARKOV 1943

The Third Battle of Kharkov is generally considered to be the last German victory on the Eastern Front. It stands as a classic example of armoured manoeuvre tactics executed under difficult conditions against a well-prepared and numerically superior enemy.

When Hitler ordered the invasion of the Soviet Union in 1941, he did not envisage a long war. There was a time when a knockout blow might have been achieved, but the Soviets averted defeat long enough for the weather to close in. This granted some time to prepare and allowed renewed German offensives to be halted.

The German army tried again in 1942 and then 1943, but decisive victory proved elusive and all the time Soviet strength was increasing. The odds became

THIRD BATTLE OF KHARKOV FACTS

Who: 160,000 German troops led by Field Marshal Erich von Manstein (1887–1973) versus approximately 300,000 Soviet troops of the Bryansk, Volkhov and South Western Fronts led by generals Golikov and Vatutin (1901–1944).

What: Committed to the operation by the Red Army were the Bryansk, Voronezh and the South Western Fronts. These included the Fortieth, Sixty-Ninth and Third Tank armies. The Germans' counteroffensive was led by the Fourth Panzer Army and included the II SS Panzer Corps, comprising the *Leibstandarte Adolf Hitler* and *Das Reich* divisions.

Where: The city of Kharkov in the Ukraine.

When: February–March 1943

Why: The city was important politically and as a transport nexus.

Outcome: The city was captured by the Germans but was lost again in August to a Soviet offensive.

PANZERGRENADIERS OF THE SS DIVISION *Das Reich ride into Kharkov on the engine deck of a Panzer III. Early 1943 was the last period in which the war on the Eastern Front was winnable for Germany.*

T-34 TANKS IN Dzerzhinsky Square, Kharkov. After the fall of Stalingrad, it seemed that the Germans could be swiftly pushed out of Soviet Russia, but their recapture of Kharkov challenged that assumption.

slimmer each year, but there was no choice: Germany had to attack and defeat the enemy its leader had chosen.

By the beginning of 1943, the tide was turning against Germany. Defeats in North Africa had dealt a serious blow to German prestige. Her allies were reconsidering their position and there seemed little prospect of persuading others – such as Turkey – to join the fight. Meanwhile at home there were economic problems and social unrest.

SOVIET SUCCESSES

The fall of Stalingrad after months of bitter fighting was a serious blow to German morale and prestige while their opponents were riding a wave of success. The Red Army began advancing, urged on by a jubilant Stalin, who believed that he could sweep the invaders out of Russia with a headlong offensive. Leningrad was relieved and the threat to Moscow greatly diminished. In the south, Soviet troops were making gains against the tired and depleted Germans.

There was a danger that the German Army Group South might be cut off and forced to surrender and matters were not helped by a catastrophic defeat in Stalingrad. However, the German commander Field-Marshal Von Manstein (1887–1973) ignored his orders to die in place and organized a fighting retreat that not only got his army out

of the trap in condition to fight on but also bought time for reinforcements to arrive.

The Soviets were running ahead of their logistics capability and beginning to falter, but were forced to push on by Stalin's urgings. The Soviet high command did not believe that the battered German army could do anything but retreat westwards, putting up local resistance. A counterattack was obviously out of the question.

REINFORCEMENTS ARRIVE

In fact, the German army did possess the capability to counterattack. Reinforcements had begun to arrive. In some cases, these were damaged units pushed back into the line after receiving some replacement personnel and equipment and were in little better shape than the line formations. However, some very powerful units were placed at Manstein's disposal.

Most significantly Manstein was given control of I SS Panzer Corps. This comprised the SS *Totenkopf*, *Liebstandarte* and *Das Reich* divisions, all of which had been

THESE WAFFEN-SS SOLDIERS show the benefits of their period of rest and refitting. Their good morale and better supply situation enabled them to defeat a larger number of Soviet troops in the battle for Kharkov.

refitting and were well rested. More importantly perhaps, they were equipped with the new Panzer VI Tiger tank armed with a formidable 88mm (3.46in) gun. Much of the divisions' tank strength was made up of lesser vehicles but the Tigers made a potent spearhead.

The first arrivals were formed into a battle group and pushed into the line to halt the Soviet advance. Remnants of German and Italian units retreated past them, but despite heavy Soviet attacks the battle group was able more or less to hold its positions. A period of repositioning then followed as the German army tried to establish defences that would prevent the strategic city of Kharkov being encircled.

Although the Soviets were suffering severe ammunition shortages and were becoming disorganized, they pushed forward faster than expected. It became obvious that an attack on Kharkov could not be prevented by defensive measures. The SS troops were ordered to attack.

The Soviet advance on Kharkov took the form of a pincer movement, in which the southern arm was much more powerful. The advancing Soviets were hit from the flank with armoured units and dive-bombers savaging their rear echelon support units before falling on the disorganized combat formations.

The attack was a success and halted the advance for a time. However, the Soviets were still able to drive forwards and despite inflicting heavy casualties the SS troops were pushed back. Again the German force was threatened with encirclement. The SS commander Paul Hausser (1880–1972) asked for permission to retreat.

Although Hitler himself refused permission to retreat and commanded the SS troops to hold at all costs, Hausser decided to ignore this order. He launched a local counter-

T-34/76: THE GREATEST TANK OF WORLD WAR II?

The T-34 was among the most important weapons systems in the Red Army in World War II. At the time it was first fielded in 1940, it was easily the finest tank design in the world. Individually, T-34s were workmanlike rather than excellent combat vehicles. They were well protected, mobile, and possessed a good gun that could knock out enemy tanks at a respectable range. However, they were also prone to mechanical problems, especially with the transmission.

One for one, German tanks were generally better, but the phrase 'all things being equal' never applies in warfare. Tanks did not fight one on one but as part of a military/technical/industrial partnership in which the fighting capabilities of the vehicle were only one aspect. The ability to repair or replace breakdowns and get tanks back into the fight was also critical, as was the capacity to manufacture them in large enough numbers to make a difference. It was in this context that the T-34 was a world-beater.

attack with tanks to blunt the Soviet offensive and pulled his force back on 15 February. Disregarding renewed orders to stand his ground, Hausser was able to bring his force out in reasonably good order despite large Soviet forces entering the city.

Hitler was enraged and ordered Manstein to use Hausser's command as the spearhead of an attack to retake the city of Kharkov. This suited Manstein. A deep salient had appeared in the battle front where the Soviets had pushed forwards. This created an ideal opportunity for a double envelopment against the shoulders of the salient, pincering off and encircling the advancing Soviets for destruction.

Plans were made while the SS troops reorganized themselves, amalgamating their depleted tanks and other assets into scratch battalions. This method of creating effective battle groups from the remains of heavily damaged units was a hallmark of the German forces during World War II and allowed the shrinking formations to go on fighting long after the individual units they were created from had ceased to be useful.

ABOVE: GENERAL PAUL HAUSSER *defied Hitler's orders to fight to the last and instead pulled his troops out of a bad position, creating the opportunity for a successful counterattack.*

ABOVE: A MACHINE-GUN TEAM *of the SS Division* Liebstandarte. *In close-quarters urban fighting, the observer's sub-machinegun and grenade might prove more useful than the support weapon.*

MANSTEIN'S COUNTERATTACK

Manstein's counterattack went in on 19 February 1943. The SS formations spearheaded the northern half of the pincer attack while regular Panzer units led the southern arm. Despite minefields and foul weather that included both snow and fog, the SS troops advanced to contact and hit the enemy flank. Early successes included cutting the main road link to the river Dnieper, hampering Soviet movements.

Renewing the advance, the SS force fought several small but sharp encounter battles with Soviet units moving up to the front, capturing the town of Pavlograd on 24 February. Elsewhere, the flanking movements had thrown the Soviets into confusion and their advance to the Dnieper was brought to a halt, then pushed back. The way to Kharkov was now open and the *Das Reich* division led the way towards the city. The Soviet high command issued 'hold at all costs' orders. Reinforcements were rushed into Kharkov and attacks made elsewhere to try to divert German resources. This measure failed. The strategic rail junctions at Lasovaya were taken by the *Das Reich* and *Totenkopf* divisions.

Still Soviet reinforcements continued to arrive. The Third Tank Army (equivalent to a Panzer corps) managed to get between the *Das Reich* and *Liebstandarte* divisions. This was a perilous situation – or a great opportunity to smash it from both sides, depending on your viewpoint.

Hausser took the latter view and launched an attack that became a three-day slogging match. Despite appalling weather, the landscape rapidly turning into a sea of mud and critical supply shortages, the SS troops gradually came out on top. By the time it was over, three Soviet tank brigades, three infantry divisions and an entire corps of cavalry were shattered or captured.

Under this punishing onslaught, the Soviet forces pulled back in some areas, and on 11 March a battle group of SS troops established itself within the city limits. On 12 March, the battle for the city began. Despite extremely stubborn resistance, notably around the railway station and the industrial district, the Soviets were gradually pushed out of the city.

By now, the Soviets were in a state of confusion and thoroughly demoralized. Driving ever eastwards, the SS divisions, though heavily depleted, smashed up two Guards Tank Corps and four infantry divisions. The last organized resistance was around a tractor factory outside the city. Once this was taken, Kharkov was firmly in German hands.

Subsequent operations cleared Soviet forces out of the immediate area and stabilized the front before the spring

BELOW: COSSACK CAVALRY WERE more often used for scouting operations, but if they achieved surprise and got in among enemy infantry, their sabres and pistols were highly effective.

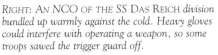
RIGHT: AN NCO OF THE SS DAS REICH division bundled up warmly against the cold. Heavy gloves could interfere with operating a weapon, so some troops sawed the trigger guard off.

thaw turned everything to mud and brought a halt to offensive operations on both sides.

AFTERMATH

Hitler remained angry at Hausser for ignoring his orders and refused to decorate him even though his troops had performed brilliantly in the battle for the city. His command did receive considerable replacements and much of its artillery was upgraded to self-propelled guns. The formation was re-designated II SS Panzer Corps.

In the wake of the victory at Kharkov, plans were formulated to launch a new offensive in the summer. Codenamed Operation *Citadel*, it would smash the Soviet forces facing Army Group South and tip the balance of the war back in the direction of Germany – if it succeeded. The stage was thus set for the Battle of Kursk; the greatest armoured clash of all time.

THIRD BATTLE OF KHARKOV

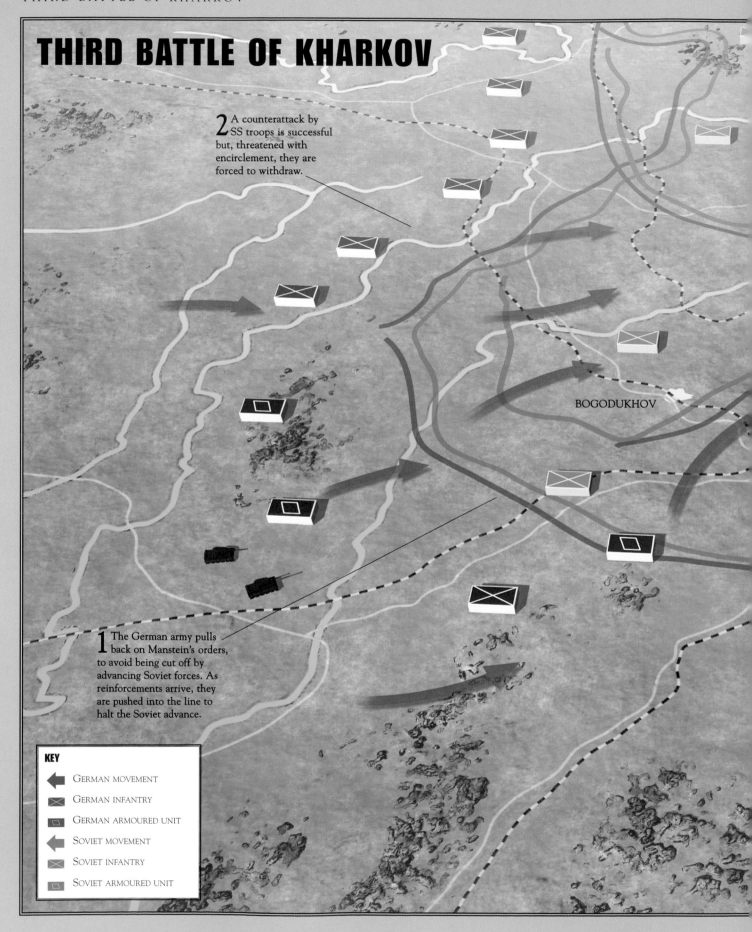

2 A counterattack by SS troops is successful but, threatened with encirclement, they are forced to withdraw.

BOGODUKHOV

1 The German army pulls back on Manstein's orders, to avoid being cut off by advancing Soviet forces. As reinforcements arrive, they are pushed into the line to halt the Soviet advance.

KEY

◄ GERMAN MOVEMENT

⊠ GERMAN INFANTRY

▭ GERMAN ARMOURED UNIT

◄ SOVIET MOVEMENT

⊠ SOVIET INFANTRY

▭ SOVIET ARMOURED UNIT

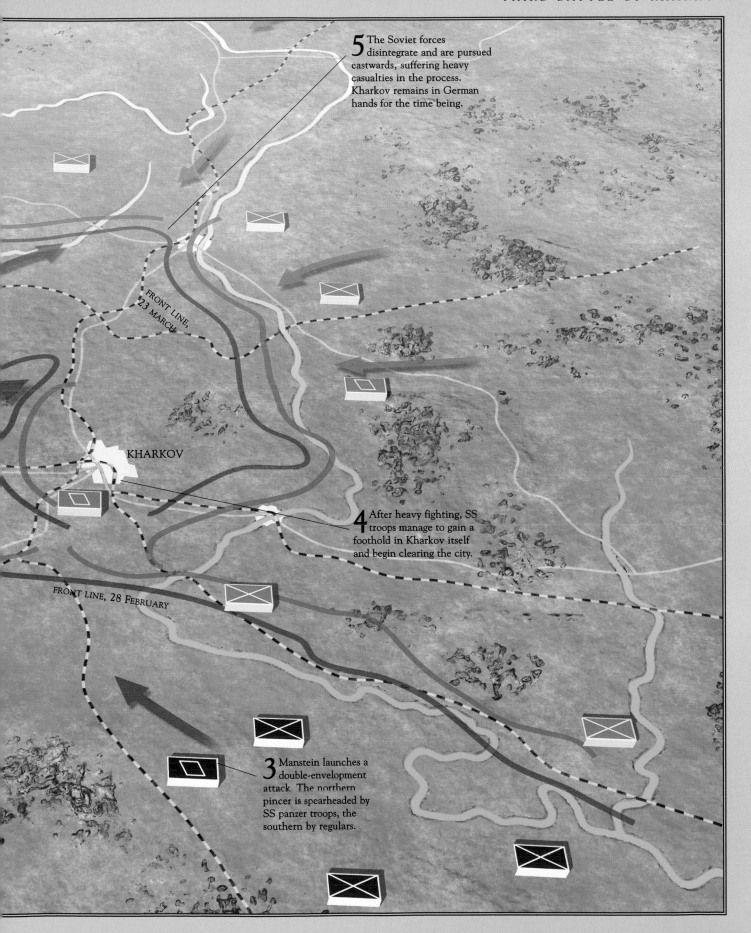

5 The Soviet forces disintegrate and are pursued eastwards, suffering heavy casualties in the process. Kharkov remains in German hands for the time being.

FRONT LINE, 23 MARCH

KHARKOV

4 After heavy fighting, SS troops manage to gain a foothold in Kharkov itself and begin clearing the city.

FRONT LINE, 28 FEBRUARY

3 Manstein launches a double-envelopment attack. The northern pincer is spearheaded by SS panzer troops, the southern by regulars.

KURSK 1943

The July 1943 Battle of Kursk was the greatest clash of armoured forces yet seen in warfare. The origins of this German offensive – Operation Citadel – lay in the disastrous start to 1943, when Soviet counterattacks not only destroyed the Sixth Army in Stalingrad but also imperilled Field-Marshal Erich von Manstein's Army Group Don.

However, between 18 February and 18 March von Manstein's effective counteroffensive destroyed the Soviet spearheads and subsequently a pause descended over the Eastern Front as the exhausted combatants rebuilt their shattered forces for the looming summer campaign. These battles left a large Soviet-held salient jutting west into the German lines around Kursk. Hitler ordered his forces to launch a double-pincer attack across the base of this salient to surround and destroy the sizable Soviet force trapped within. Such an offensive would accomplish this encirclement within a restricted geographical area, a sensible plan that reflected the *Wehrmacht*'s dwindling operational mobility. For

KURSK FACTS

Who: Elements of Field Marshal Günther von Kluge's (1882–1944) Army Group Centre and Field Marshal Erich von Manstein's (1887–1973) Army Group South faced Marshal Konstantin Rokossovsky's (1896–1968) Central Front and Marshal Nikolai Vatutin's (1901–1944) Voronezh Front under the direction of Supreme Commander-in-Chief Marshal Georgi Zhukov (1896–1974).

What: The German strategic offensive of 1943, aimed at eliminating the Soviet salient centred around Kursk.

Where: The area around Kursk in the Ukraine, an important rail junction 800km (497 miles) south of Moscow.

When: 4 to 13 July 1943

Why: Only having resources for a limited offensive in the east and needing a victory to reassure wavering allies, the Kursk salient provided the Germans with an apparently manageable strategic objective.

Outcome: The German offensive failed and the Soviet counterattack provided a launching point for further Soviet operations in 1943. The strategic balance in the East had shifted in favour of the Soviets for good.

A RARE PHOTOGRAPH of a Churchill tank from Fifth Guards Army, a unit equipped with a number of Lend-Lease vehicles from the Western Allies. It is passing a knocked-out German Sd Kfz 232.

ABOVE: A HEAVY PANZER BATTALION, equipped with Tiger Mark Is, deploys prior to the Battle of Kursk. Much hope was placed by the Germans on their new generation of armour.

Citadel, therefore, the Germans achieved a massive concentration of force by assembling 17 panzer/panzergrenadier divisions across a total attack frontage of just 164km (102 miles).

BELOW: FIELD MARSHAL MODEL (centre, with goggles on cap) addresses some of his soldiers in the build-up to the battle of Kursk.

DELAYS AND POSTPONEMENTS

The Germans set *Citadel* to begin in early May, but Hitler repeatedly postponed the offensive so that small numbers of Germany's latest weapons could reach the front. Hitler believed that with these 340 new 'war-winning' weapons – 250 Panther medium and 90 Tiger heavy tanks – the massive German forces committed to *Citadel* could smash any resistance the Soviets offered, however powerful. Yet the Germans proved unable to exploit their concentration of

PANZER V 'PANTHER' TANK

The Panther was built as a direct response to encountering the Soviet T-34 during 1941. The T-34 outclassed the current generation of German tanks and thus a counter was required. The MAN-produced Panther owed its sloping armour to the Soviet design, but maintained the German tradition of superbly designed, expensive and complex engineering. Its high velocity 75mm (3in) gun had excellent armour-piercing capabilities and proved very well protected.

A prototype was ready by September 1942 and the first production models by December. It was deployed for the first time at Kursk, although these early models were plagued with automotive problems.

force. The obvious German preparations for *Citadel* cast aside any element of surprise while Hitler's repeated postponements gave the Soviets sufficient time to construct the most powerful defensive system yet seen in the war. The Germans remained partially ignorant of the strength of these Soviet defences, thanks to the latter's skill at concealment and deception. Either that or they dismissed this strength; all it would mean was a bigger 'prize' when the German offensive successfully encircled the salient. Indeed, when *Citadel* commenced on 4–5 July the Germans were outnumbered by the Soviets – astonishing given that the offensive was of the Germans' choosing in timing, location and method.

PINCER MOVEMENT

The Germans deployed two main groupings for *Citadel*: in the north, elements of Field Marshal Günther von Kluge's (1882–1944) Army Group Centre; and in the south, forces from von Manstein's Army Group South. In the north,

SOVIET INFANTRYMEN deploy their 14.5mm (0.57in) Simov PTRS Rifle. By 1943, the antitank rifle was obsolescent and would struggle to pierce German armour from most angles, but it remained in service due to lack of anything else.

Above: Marshal Konstantin Rokossovsky was one of the new breed of successful Soviet commanders coming to the fore after the disasters of 1941–42. He commanded the Central Front at Kursk.

General Walter Model's (1891–1945) Ninth Army had at its disposal six panzer/panzergrenadier and 14 infantry divisions. In the south, Colonel-General Hermann Hoth's (1885–1971) Fourth Panzer Army and General Franz Kempf's (1886–1964) Army Detachment put into the field 11 panzer/panzergrenadier and 10 infantry divisions. The offensive commenced on 4 July, when von Manstein's forces initiated preliminary attacks from the salient's southern shoulder. At dawn the next day, 10 of Model's divisions assaulted the first Soviet defence line. By evening Model's forces had only managed painfully slow advances – at most, 10km (six miles) along a front some 40km (25 miles) long.

Meanwhile that same day, Hoth and Kempf's forces initiated their main assaults along the southern shoulder. By dusk, Hoth's forces had advanced only 10km (six miles) south to penetrate the first Soviet defensive line. Further east, Kempf's forces failed even to smash through the first Soviet defensive line. During the next day, Model's forces in the north attacked the Soviet second defence line, aiming to capture the Olkhovtka Ridge, from where they could surge through the open plain to the south. Though the repeated German attacks made some progress, intense Soviet counterattacks prevented the capture of Ponyri.

Between 7 and 9 July, both sides threw in their reserves as Model repeatedly attempted to capture this village in the face of fanatical resistance that included powerful counterattacks. Finally, between 10 and 11 July, these Soviet counterattacks halted Model's advance. The northern German thrust had proven a dismal failure: despite a week of intense and costly attacks, it had managed to advance just 15km (9 miles).

In the south, on 6 July, Hoth's XXXXVIII Panzer Corps pushed north towards the second Soviet defence line near Oboyan despite counterattacks by fresh Soviet armoured reserves. Further east, II SS Panzer Corps drove the defenders north towards the village of Prokhorovka. Over the next four days, these two panzer corps inched their way north towards Oboyan and Prokhorovka in the face of bitter Soviet resistance sustained by freshly arrived reserves. Between 10 and 11 July, German forces successfully pierced the third Soviet defensive line in an attempt to outflank the Soviet units located further west around Oboyan. Sensing the danger in this success, the Soviets redeployed the Fifth Guards Tank Army to the area north of Prokhorovka.

THE GREATEST TANK BATTLE

On 12 July, the climax to *Citadel* occurred – the titanic clash of armour at Prokhorovka, into which the Soviets committed Fifth Guards Tank Army. With 800 Soviet tanks engaging 600 panzers, this action was the largest armoured battle of the war. For eight hours, the battle raged back and forth with the tanks throwing up vast clouds of dust that limited visibility to just a few yards.

The Soviets exploited these conditions, closing the range so that the Germans could not benefit from their lethal long-range guns. Tactically the battle was a draw, but strategically it was a German disaster: the Germans spent their armoured strength – whereas sizable Soviet armoured reserves remained available – and lost the initiative to the Red Army, an opportunity the latter then ruthlessly exploited.

Prokhorovka convinced Hitler that *Citadel* could not succeed and on 13 July he cancelled the offensive. Between 15 and 25 July, the German assault forces conducted a slow fighting withdrawal back to their starting positions in the face of ferocious Soviet attacks. On 12 July, moreover, the Soviets had also launched an offensive against the German units that protected the northern flank of Model's forces. Catching the Germans by surprise, the Soviets gradually drove them back 120km (80 miles).

Then, on 3 August, the Soviets attacked the German forces concentrated along the southern shoulder of the erstwhile Kursk salient. This new Soviet attack swiftly eliminated the German-held bulge to the south of the former salient. After securing rapid success with these two counterattacks, the Soviets escalated their operations into a general strategic counteroffensive across the entire centre and south of the Eastern Front. During the remainder of 1943, this general counteroffensive west drove the Germans back to the river Dnieper and beyond.

AFTERMATH

All things considered, *Citadel* was a dire German strategic defeat. Despite their huge concentration of force, all the Germans gained was an advance never deeper than 40km (25 miles) and through insignificant terrain, for the heavy price of 52,000 casualties and 850 AFVs. Indeed, all *Citadel* accomplished was to shatter the German strategic armoured reserves, thus making it easier for the Soviets to achieve rapid operational successes with their counterattacks. In fact, Kursk – rather than Stalingrad – was probably the key turning point of the war, which ensured Germany would be defeated in 1945.

THE CREW OF A SOVIET T-34 tank surrender to an SS soldier, presumably during the fighting on the southern side of the Kursk salient.

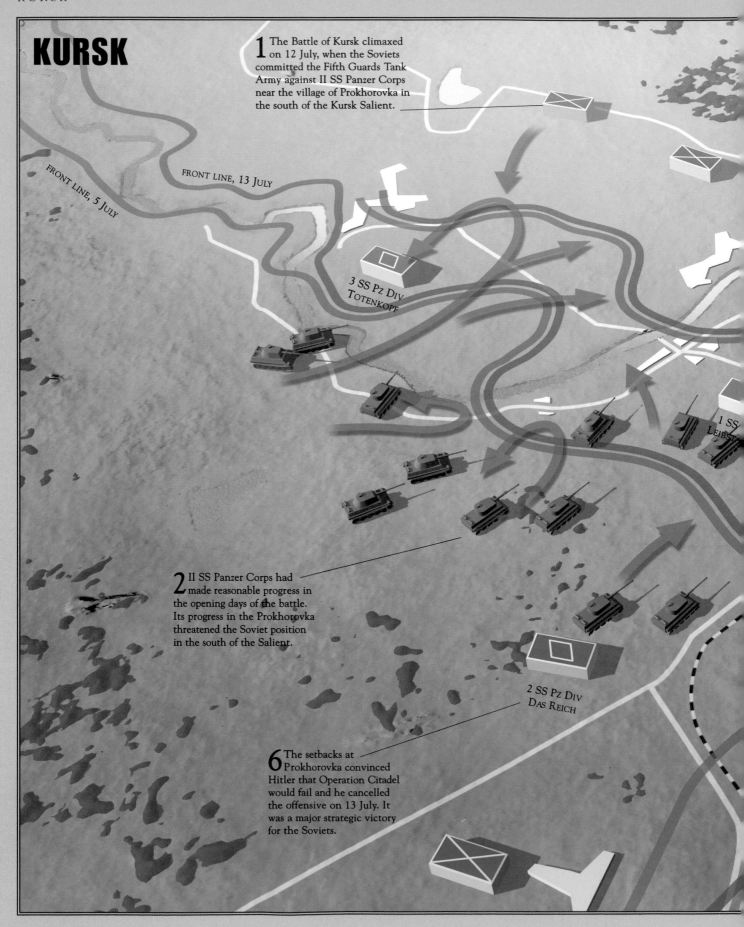

KURSK

1 The Battle of Kursk climaxed on 12 July, when the Soviets committed the Fifth Guards Tank Army against II SS Panzer Corps near the village of Prokhorovka in the south of the Kursk Salient.

FRONT LINE, 5 JULY

FRONT LINE, 13 JULY

3 SS Pz Div
TOTENKOPF

1 SS
LEIBST...

2 II SS Panzer Corps had made reasonable progress in the opening days of the battle. Its progress in the Prokhorovka threatened the Soviet position in the south of the Salient.

2 SS Pz Div
DAS REICH

6 The setbacks at Prokhorovka convinced Hitler that Operation Citadel would fail and he cancelled the offensive on 13 July. It was a major strategic victory for the Soviets.

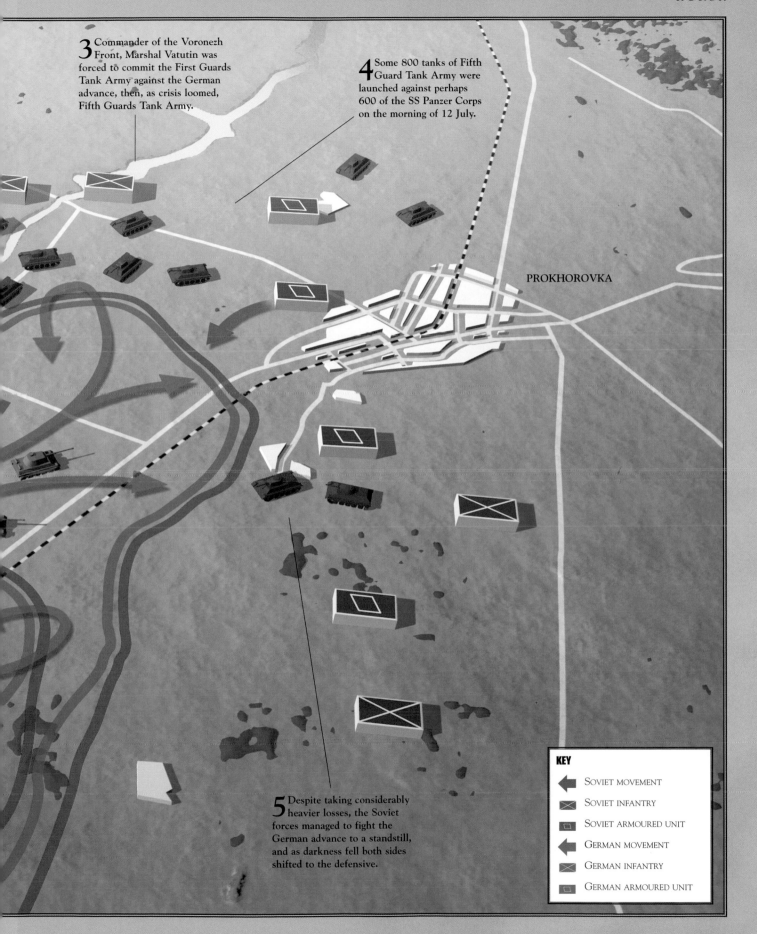

3 Commander of the Voronezh Front, Marshal Vatutin was forced to commit the First Guards Tank Army against the German advance, then, as crisis loomed, Fifth Guards Tank Army.

4 Some 800 tanks of Fifth Guard Tank Army were launched against perhaps 600 of the SS Panzer Corps on the morning of 12 July.

PROKHOROVKA

5 Despite taking considerably heavier losses, the Soviet forces managed to fight the German advance to a standstill, and as darkness fell both sides shifted to the defensive.

KEY

← SOVIET MOVEMENT

⊠ SOVIET INFANTRY

▭ SOVIET ARMOURED UNIT

← GERMAN MOVEMENT

⊠ GERMAN INFANTRY

◇ GERMAN ARMOURED UNIT

BATTLE OF IMPHAL AND KOHIMA 1944

The Battle of Imphal and the action at Kohima represented the high water mark of Japanese aspirations in Burma and India. However, after some initial successes, the defeated Japanese fell back into Burma and were subsequently driven back the way they had come.

T he Japanese advance in the early months of World War II seemed unstoppable. Allied forces were driven down the Malay Peninsula to the 'fortress island' of Singapore and forced to surrender there. Other formations were pushed back through Burma towards India. A determined rearguard action slowed the Japanese advance and the monsoon brought it to a halt.

This gave the Allies a chance to regroup and mount a defence, which the terrain favoured. The jungle and hills of the Burmese–Indian border region would

BATTLE OF IMPHAL FACTS

Who: British and Indian troops opposed by Japanese forces and elements of the anti-British Indian National Army.

What: Japanese forces encircled the city of Imphal but were driven off and then counterattacked.

Where: The city of Imphal, the capital of the state of Manipur in northeast India.

When: 8 March–3 July 1944

Why: The Japanese wished to invade India and 'liberate' it from the British. This was their last chance of launching a major land invasion against British India, since their military resources were being rapidly used up against the United States in the Pacific.

Outcome: The Japanese were decisively defeated and never again threatened British India with invasion.

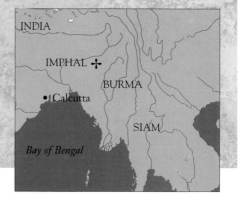

THE WIDE IRRAWADDY RIVER was a serious obstacle to the logistics services of armies operating in the region. This makeshift barge turns a disadvantage into an asset, using the river to transport a truck.

LIGHT UTILITY VEHICLES like these British Universal Carriers (Bren Carriers) were invaluable in keeping the supply lines open. As the name suggests, they could carry almost anything over rough terrain or on roads.

funnel an advance into corridors that could be defended with relative ease. The city of Imphal provided a base and logistics centre for the allies while the Japanese would have to operate at the end of a long supply line that ran through difficult terrain.

Breaking the Allied positions around Imphal would be a major undertaking, requiring resources that might be better used elsewhere. Thus the pressure dropped off considerably, allowing the Allies to build up their strength for an offensive back into Burma. Raids, including the famous exploits of the Chindits, were launched into Japanese territory.

This required some kind of countermeasure, and Japanese commanders decided that since it would require as much manpower to mount a proper defence of Burma as to drive the Allies out of Imphal, the offensive option was the most suitable.

THE JAPANESE ATTACK AT IMPHAL

Japanese forces in the region gained a new and aggressive commander, Lieutenant-General Masakazu Kawabe (1886–1965), who thought an attack on Imphal was practicable. There were several benefits to a victory there. As well as countering the Chindit raids, elimination of the logistics base at Imphal would cut off Allied supplies going

to Chinese Nationalist forces that were still fighting the Japanese to the North. More importantly, it would open the way to attack India.

India was extremely important to the British Empire, supplying large numbers of troops to the Imperial forces. However, there was a movement towards independence and the Japanese believed that India might be induced to break away, depriving the Allies of a vast amount of manpower. For this reason, the coming offensive was to include elements of the Indian National Army, a force raised from Indian prisoners taken by the Japanese during the Malaya campaign and who were willing to fight against the British in the name of Indian independence.

The Allies had occupied several forward positions in preparation for their own offensive into Burma. The Japanese plan was to encircle and eliminate these quickly before advancing on Imphal and driving off the defenders. This was by no means as easy as it sounded, since the attack would have to be made through difficult country at the end of a long supply chain. Some of the senior officers involved had grave doubts about the plan, especially the logistical elements.

Nevertheless the campaign opened on 8 March 1944, at which point the Allies began to withdraw their forward units. Some managed this without undue difficulty, but others had to fight their way out with the aid of the few available reserves. By the beginning of April, the Allies had pulled back to the Imphal plain and were receiving reinforcements by air.

Japanese troops then converged on Imphal along several roads. They were travelling light, having left much of their artillery and heavy equipment behind. One reason for this was the conviction that the terrain was unsuitable for tanks and so antitank weapons would not be needed. Ironically, it was exactly the same misconception that allowed Japanese tanks to do so much damage to the Allies in Malaya at the beginning of the war.

The Allies were using US-supplied M3 Lee light tanks, which could cope with the difficult terrain. Although far too light for anything

EXPECTING TO FIGHT ONLY INFANTRY, *the Japanese forces brought along anti-personnel support weapons like this light machinegun but left most of their antitank weaponry behind as they advanced on Imphal.*

but armoured reconnaissance elsewhere in the world, the Lees were more than capable of cutting up infantry, with little in the way of antitank equipment.

There were other serious problems too. The Japanese needed to capture Allied supplies or at least airfields suitable to fly them into before their supplies ran out. Inventive solutions, such as bringing herds of buffalo along behind the combat formations as rations 'on the hoof', had failed, and the situation was becoming serious. Foraging parties were able to obtain some supplies at a cost of diluting the combat effectiveness of the units involved.

Repeated attacks were put in against Imphal, but they grew steadily weaker and never really had a chance of success. Conversely, although the Allies were themselves getting short of supplies and ammunition their defence became increasingly aggressive, launching local counterattacks to harass the Japanese positions.

MERRILL'S MARAUDERS

Named after its commander, Brigadier-General Frank Merrill (1903–55), the 5307th Composite Unit (Provisional) became better known as Merrill's Marauders during its long-range raiding exploits in the China-Burma theatre.

After training with the highly successful Chindits, the all-volunteer Marauders embarked on a campaign of harassment deep within Japanese territory. Despite heavy casualties and sickness caused by the harsh jungle conditions, they were able to cut Japanese supply lines and inflict serious losses on their opponents in dozens of actions.

At the end of the war, every member of the Marauders was awarded the Bronze Star and the unit was honoured with a Distinguished Unit Citation for its contribution to the Burma campaign.

ABOVE: THE ROUGH TERRAIN of the Imphal region could in many places be crossed only on foot, and slowly at that. This severely restricted the offensive capabilities of both sides.

BELOW: WHERE THE TERRAIN was more open, light vehicles and tanks such as these Lee-Grants were able to operate. Lacking antitank weapons, the Japanese could do little about them.

The Allies were able to fly supplies into Imphal, as they had during the battle of the Admin Box a few months earlier. Where similar attempts had failed, such as the German 'air bridge' at Stalingrad, the position at Imphal was such that the besieging Japanese forces ran short before the Allies did.

OPERATIONS AGAINST KOHIMA

Meanwhile, the Japanese had tried for two weeks in early April to capture the Kohima ridge, which would allow them to control the main supply route into Imphal. The ridge was to have been seized early in the campaign, but stubborn defence by Allied troops encountered in the advance delayed the arrival of the Japanese at their objective. This bought time for a defence to be put in place.

The defenders at Kohima came under increasing pressure due to heavy shelling interspersed with infantry assaults. They held out in a shrinking perimeter, and by 17 April the situation was desperate. However, the position was relieved the next day by troops moving up from India. The attacks continued unabated, but the chances of success were ever decreasing.

By early May, more Allied troops had joined the fight at Kohima, and the Japanese, now very short of supplies, came under air attack as well as increasing bombardment. The ridge was partially cleared of Japanese defenders after a very stubborn fight, but as late as mid-May some high points were still stubbornly held.

However, with Allied troops across their supply line and almost out of ammunition, the starving Japanese were forced to pull back and leave the ridge to the Allies. Not that there was much left of it or the villages there – Kohima has been referred to as the Stalingrad of the East, and with good reason.

ABOVE: COOPERATION BETWEEN BRITISH *and Indian formations allowed the Allies to go over to the offensive after the Imphal-Kohima road was reopened. Field conferences like this one were essential to maintain coordination.*

At the end of May, the Japanese pulled back from Kohima entirely. Many units broke up, straggling east and south in search of food. They were unable to play any further part in the campaign. Meanwhile, with the road now open, the British began to push through to Imphal.

THE ALLIES COUNTERATTACK AT IMPHAL

Japanese attacks on Imphal itself wound down by 1 May. A siege continued, but there was no longer any real chance of a successful assault. As the Japanese supply situation worsened, the Allies were re-supplied by airdrops at both Imphal and Kohima. This was a difficult and hazardous undertaking, especially at Kohima, but it enabled the Allies to establish superiority over their weakening opponents.

This took time due to poor weather and the stubbornness of the Japanese troops. Even desperately short of food and ammunition, they were difficult to shift from their positions. Although the Japanese commanders on the spot knew they could not win this battle, a final effort was ordered. A few reinforcements had arrived and these allowed the assault to achieve some limited success. Nevertheless by 22 June the road through to Kohima was opened and the siege was effectively over.

The Japanese divisions around Imphal were at the end of their tether and more or less ignored orders from above to make a new assault. Bowing to the inevitable, the order was given for a retreat and on 3 July the divisions began pulling back. Many of these formations were debilitated by disease and starvation and were able to do little more than shamble eastwards, leaving their remaining heavy equipment and artillery behind.

AFTERMATH

The ill-advised advance on Imphal was the turning point of the campaign. From then on the Japanese were on the defensive and were steadily pushed back. For the Allies, the dark days of shambolic retreat were long over and they returned to Burma confident that they could take on and beat the Imperial Japanese Army.

ABOVE: INDIAN TROOPS WAIT IN A CLEARING. *The thick vegetation was a serious obstacle to troop movements and tended to funnel units into predictable lines of advance.*

BATTLE OF IMPHAL AND KOHIMA

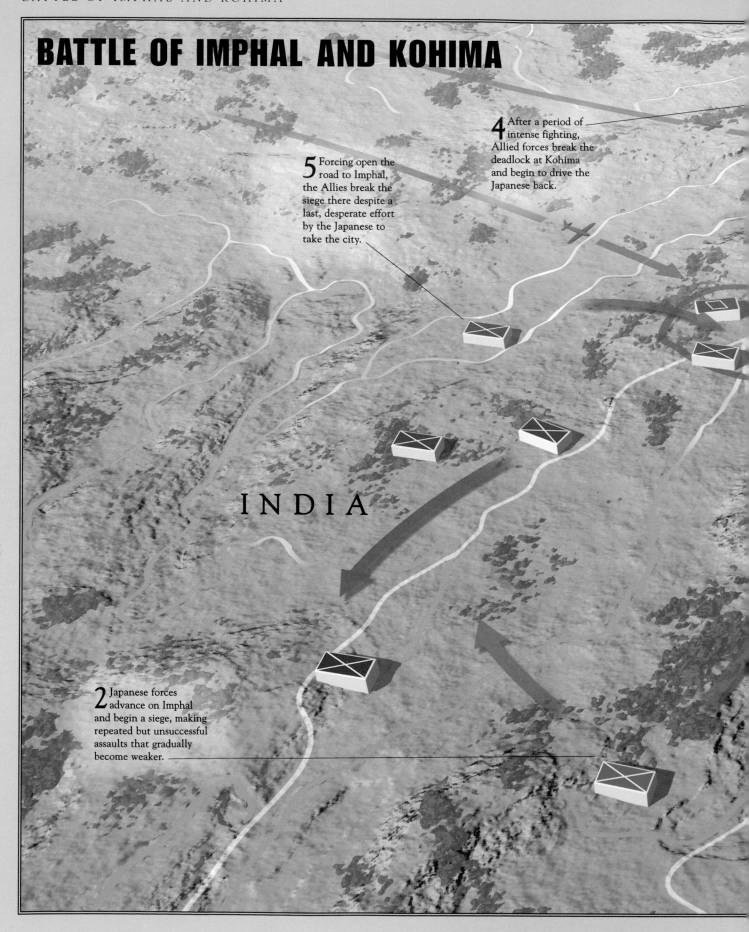

4 After a period of intense fighting, Allied forces break the deadlock at Kohima and begin to drive the Japanese back.

5 Forcing open the road to Imphal, the Allies break the siege there despite a last, desperate effort by the Japanese to take the city.

INDIA

2 Japanese forces advance on Imphal and begin a siege, making repeated but unsuccessful assaults that gradually become weaker.

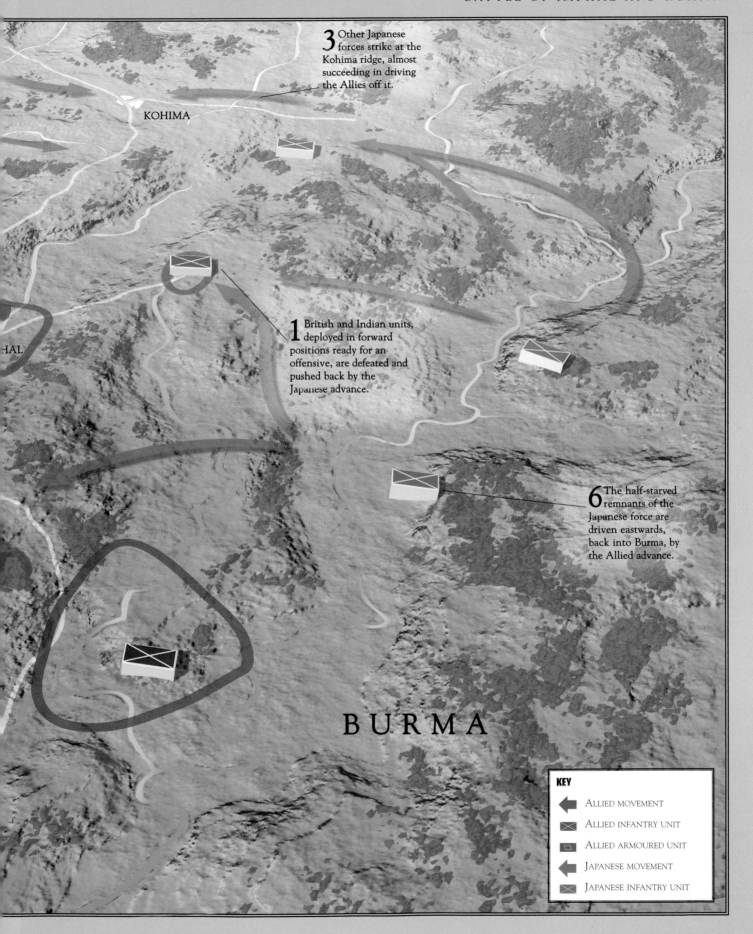

3 Other Japanese forces strike at the Kohima ridge, almost succeeding in driving the Allies off it.

KOHIMA

1 British and Indian units, deployed in forward positions ready for an offensive, are defeated and pushed back by the Japanese advance.

HAL

6 The half-starved remnants of the Japanese force are driven eastwards, back into Burma, by the Allied advance.

B U R M A

KEY

← ALLIED MOVEMENT

⊠ ALLIED INFANTRY UNIT

▱ ALLIED ARMOURED UNIT

← JAPANESE MOVEMENT

⊠ JAPANESE INFANTRY UNIT

MONTE CASSINO 1944

The Battles of Monte Cassino between January and May 1944 represented something of an anomaly in the conduct of the war in Europe. In an unusually static period of warfare, the Allies took five months and four separate battles to break through the German Gustav Line, anchored around the position at Monte Cassino.

It cost the Allies – including the fighting at Anzio – 105,000 casualties and the Germans at least 80,000. Despite the breakthrough, the opportunity to destroy the Germans in Italy was missed and the slog up Italy would continue for another year.

Italy surrendered to the Allies on 8 September 1943. The British Eighth Army had already crossed the Straits of Messina five days before, and on 9 September the Fifth Army, a mixed US-British force, landed at Salerno. The near successes of the German counterattack against the Salerno beachhead

MONTE CASSINO FACTS

Who: II US Corps and II New Zealand Corps of General Mark Clark's (1896–1984) Fifth Army and subsequently General Oliver Leese's (1884–1978) British Eighth Army under overall command of General Harold Alexander (1891–1969) faced Lieutenant-General Fridolin von Senger und Etterlin's (1891–1963) XIV Panzer Corps.

What: A series of offensives against the Gustav Line, a German defensive line anchored around the imposing position of Monte Cassino.

Where: The area surrounding Monte Cassino and the nearby town, just over 100km (62 miles) south of Rome.

When: 24 January–18 May 1944

Why: Cassino controlled the mouth of the Liri Valley and thus the most straightforward route to Rome.

Outcome: Despite the efforts of Allied forces, the Germans held their position through the first three costly attritional battles, before the Gustav Line was finally broken across the front in May 1944.

GERMAN PARATROOPERS OF *the 1st Paratroop Division man an MG 42 in the ruins of the monastery. The Allied bombing did little more than create even more defensible positions and legitimize the German occupation of the building.*

157

convinced Hitler to follow the advice of Field Marshal Albert Kesselring (1885–1960) and resist the Allied advance as far south as possible. He also issued orders for the construction of the Gustav Line 160km (100 miles) south of Rome. This stretched from the Adriatic to the Tyrrhenian sea.

The key to the position was the entrance of the Liri valley, which offered the most obvious route to Rome. Monte Cassino dominated the approach, overlooking the rivers that crossed the mouth of the valley. The Germans built pillboxes and dugouts across the Liri, established positions in the surrounding mountains, fortified the town of Cassino and flooded the rivers. It was probably the most formidable defensive position in Europe.

ANZIO LANDINGS

Operation *Shingle*, a planned landing at Anzio behind the Gustav Line, forced the Fifth Army to push on to draw the German reserves from the Anzio area. General Mark Clark (1896–1984), the Fifth Army commander, launched the French Expeditionary Corps (FEC) against the German positions north of Cassino while the British X Corps

attempted to cross the river Garigliano to the west in mid-January. Neither operation was wholly successful, although they did draw the Germans south.

Then Clark committed US II Corps against the Cassino position. The 36th Division had two regiments destroyed trying to cross the Gari river between 20 and 22 January. The Anzio landings took place virtually unopposed on 22 January. Clark knew the Germans would throw everything available at the beachhead, so he committed his final division, the 34th Red Bull, north of Cassino to maintain the pressure. The 34th attacked on the night of 24 January. It took them three days to establish themselves in strength across the Rapido river.

On 29 January, the division pushed into the high ground behind the monastery and managed to secure a foothold in the outskirts of the town. It then inched its way across the Cassino massif before the attack petered out on 12 February. Despite the extraordinary efforts of the US infantry, the town and monastery remained in German hands. Aware

THE DOMINATING POSITION of the monastery at Monte Cassino is clear in this photograph taken prior to the bombing of 15 February 1944. Castle Hill sits in front of the monastery, while the town of Cassino nestles around its base.

that the Germans still intended to counterattack at Anzio, the Allies attacked again using II New Zealand Corps, made up of 2nd New Zealand and 4th Indian Divisions under Lieutenant-General Bernard Freyberg (1889–1963). The 4th Indian took over US 34th Division's positions, finding that the key piece of terrain, Point 593, had been retaken by the Germans. Much to the disgust of the divisional commander, Francis Tuker (1894–1967), Freyberg ordered a direct assault on the monastery.

Despite misgivings, the Allied commander in Italy, General Harold Alexander (1891–1969), authorized the bombing of the monastery. On the morning of 15 February, more than 250 bombers destroyed the abbey. However, due to an appalling lack of coordination, the lead formation of 4th Indian Division was unable to attack until the night of 16–17 February, 36 hours later, by which time German paratroopers had occupied the ruins. Despite strenuous efforts, 4th Indian Division failed to capture either Point 593 or the monastery over the next three days. On 17 February, the New Zealanders attacked the town from the east, managing to seize the railway station, but they were unable to advance further.

GERMAN COUNTERATTACK

Despite the efforts against Cassino, the Germans launched a massive attack on the Anzio beachhead. Still desperate to maintain pressure on the Gustav Line, Alexander ordered Freyberg to attack again. This time 4th Indian Division would attack the monastery on a slightly different axis,

RIGHT: A GERMAN 150mm (6IN) S-FH 18 artillery piece in action. Most German artillery at Cassino was located in the Liri valley. As the Germans held most of the high ground, they could bring observed fire on the whole battlefield.

INDIAN SOLDIER

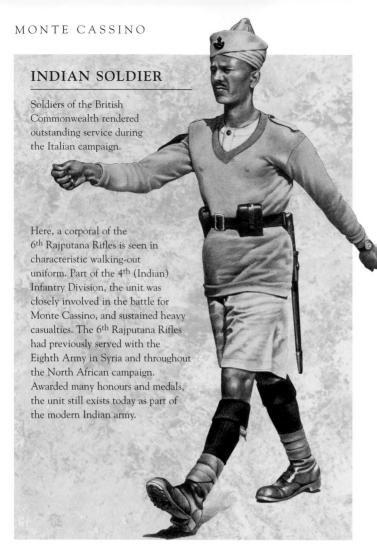

Soldiers of the British Commonwealth rendered outstanding service during the Italian campaign.

Here, a corporal of the 6th Rajputana Rifles is seen in characteristic walking-out uniform. Part of the 4th (Indian) Infantry Division, the unit was closely involved in the battle for Monte Cassino, and sustained heavy casualties. The 6th Rajputana Rifles had previously served with the Eighth Army in Syria and throughout the North African campaign. Awarded many honours and medals, the unit still exists today as part of the modern Indian army.

above the town through Castle Hill, while the New Zealanders attacked the town from the north. After air raids and a massive bombardment, the two divisions attacked on the morning of March 15 and managed to seize the railway station, but were unable to advance further.

Again the German paratroopers put up fierce resistance, and even though the New Zealanders managed to clear most of the town and 4th Indian Division took Castle and Hangman's Hills, the Allies were not able to gain complete control of Cassino or capture the monastery. Having achieved very little, Freyberg called off the offensive.

EIGHTH ARMY TAKES OVER

As the weather improved, the Allies reorganized their forces and Cassino became the responsibility of the Eighth Army. Alexander's chief-of-staff, General John Harding (1896–1989), was the driving force behind Operation *Diadem*, the fourth battle of Cassino. He organized a coordinated offensive across the front. In the west, US II Corps would drive up the coastal plain towards Anzio, where US VI Corps had been reinforced and was ready to break out from the beachhead.

The FEC would attack through the Aurunci mountains and break into the Liri valley behind the Gustav Line. The British XIII Corps would attack up the mouth of the Liri with Canadian I Corps ready to exploit up the valley. The Polish

US ARTILLERY MEN demonstrating a massive 240mm (9.5in) M-1 Howitzer to British troops. The largest piece of field artillery in the US armoury, the M-1 was also used by the British Eighth Army at Cassino.

RIGHT: A NORTH AFRICAN GOUMIER of the 2nd Moroccan Division of the French Expeditionary Corps. The achievements of these formidable troops in the Aurunci mountains were critical to Allied success in the fourth battle.

II Corps would attack Cassino, while British X Corps would conduct minor operations north of the town.

MONASTERY CAPTURED

Diadem opened at 11.00 p.m. on 11 May. The main thrust up the Liri by XIII Corps made slow progress, as did US II Corps on the coast. The French, however, achieved excellent results, threatening to turn the German flank.

The Poles took terrible losses up on the Cassino massif, but managed to seize Point 593 and the high ground around the monastery by 17 May. The Poles entered the abbey the following day to find it abandoned.

Threatened by Allied success in the valley, the Germans withdrew north. Alexander ordered VI Corps to break out of Anzio and cut off the German retreat. The German Tenth Army faced being trapped and destroyed. However, in an act of gross insubordination and military stupidity, Clark countermanded Alexander's order and turned US VI Corps towards Rome, which fell to him on 4 June. Much to his astonishment, Kesselring was able to extricate his forces and regroup on a defensive line north of Rome. The chance for a decisive victory had been lost.

The conduct of the Allied offensives round Cassino was uninspired and costly, but the vulnerability of the Anzio beachhead and the psychological importance of the monastery necessitated action. The chance to redeem the campaign was lost with Clark's vainglorious decision to capture Rome rather than defeat the enemy.

BELOW: ALLIED TRAFFIC MOVES through the town of Cassino in the aftermath of the fourth battle. The ravages of four months of bitter fighting are evident.

MONTE CASSINO

CEPRANO

6 The combination of threats, particularly from the FEC, forced the German Tenth Army into retreat. On 23 May, the US VI Corps was ordered to breakout of the Anzio beachhead.

XIV Pz Corps

ITRI

GERMAN LINE, 18 MAY

FORMIA

GUSTAV LINE

GAETA

1 Operation *Diadem* was a fully coordinated Army Group offensive along the entire Gustav Line. This time, there was no piece-meal commitment of limited resources.

MEDITERRANEAN SEA

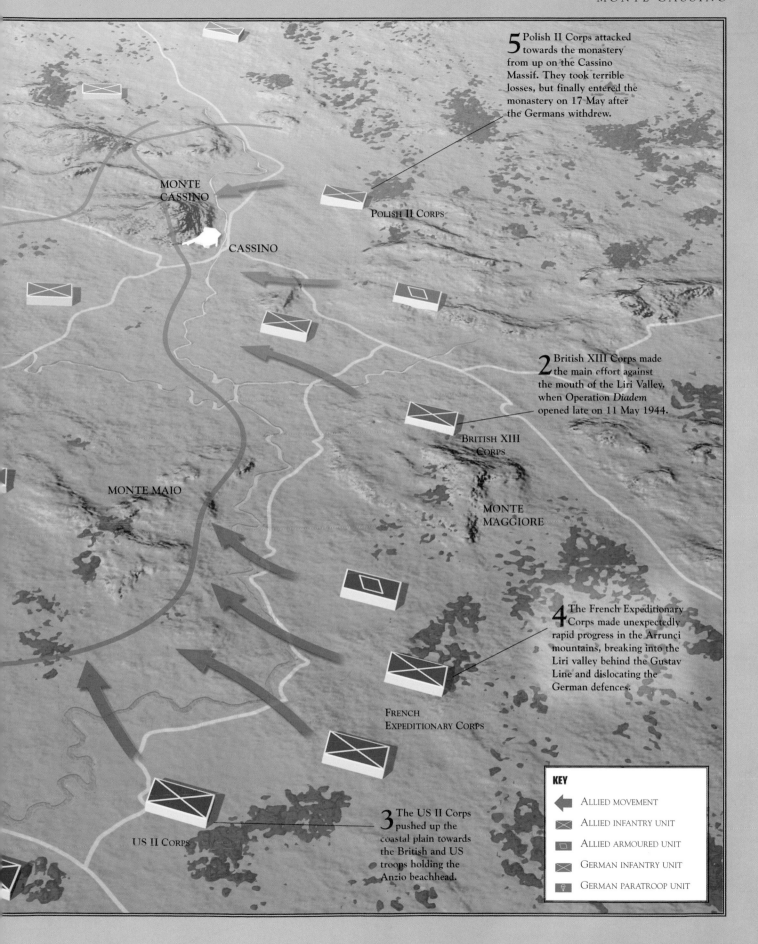

5 Polish II Corps attacked towards the monastery from up on the Cassino Massif. They took terrible losses, but finally entered the monastery on 17 May after the Germans withdrew.

POLISH II CORPS

MONTE CASSINO

CASSINO

2 British XIII Corps made the main effort against the mouth of the Liri Valley, when Operation *Diadem* opened late on 11 May 1944.

BRITISH XIII CORPS

MONTE MAIO

MONTE MAGGIORE

4 The French Expeditionary Corps made unexpectedly rapid progress in the Arrunci mountains, breaking into the Liri valley behind the Gustav Line and dislocating the German defences.

FRENCH EXPEDITIONARY CORPS

3 The US II Corps pushed up the coastal plain towards the British and US troops holding the Anzio beachhead.

US II CORPS

KEY

← ALLIED MOVEMENT

ALLIED INFANTRY UNIT

ALLIED ARMOURED UNIT

GERMAN INFANTRY UNIT

GERMAN PARATROOP UNIT

ALLIED VICTORY

Despite the tipping of the balance against the Axis countries, the nature of the regimes meant that they would fight to the bitter end. Thus the Allies had to fight their way across Europe and the Pacific towards the heartlands of Germany and Japan.

Although there were great and impressive military achievements from the Allies, such as the Normandy landings in June 1944 and the Soviet summer offensive the same year, the determination and remarkable resilience of the German and Japanese forces meant that the final campaigns would be extremely hard fought. Bitter defensive battles were fought at Monte Cassino and Iwo Jima, and the Allies suffered setbacks with the failed airborne operation at Arnhem in the autumn of 1944 and the surprise German offensive in the Ardennes in December of the same year. The final battles, for the island of Okinawa and the city of Berlin, proved costly outcomes to the most bloody war in world history.

THE END OF THE REICH: *as Soviet IS-2 tanks rumble along a Berlin street, refugees emerge from the cellars of gutted buildings, carrying their belongings with them. This photograph was taken in late April 1945, just days before the surrender of Germany.*

NORMANDY LANDINGS

1944

D-Day – the Allied landings on the Normandy coast of German-occupied France 6 June 1944 – was one of the most climactic days of World War II. Ever since 1943, the Western Allies had prepared for this operation, codenamed Neptune/Overlord. On D-Day, the Allies landed 160,000 US, British and Canadian forces (plus a small French contingent) to establish beachheads in Normandy.

With the 'Second Front' successfully established, the German Reich would subsequently find itself locked into a three-front war of attrition that would eventually overwhelm it. As Supreme Allied Commander, the US General Dwight 'Ike' Eisenhower (1890–1969) exercised overall control over the

NORMANDY LANDINGS FACTS

Who: Supreme Allied Commander General Dwight Eisenhower (1890–1969) commanded the US, British and Canadian forces of General Bernard Montgomery's (1887–1976) Twenty-First Army Group, which faced Field Marshal Erwin Rommel's (1891–1944) Army Group B.

What : The largest amphibious operation in history, marking the Western Allies return to North West Europe.

Where: The Baie de la Seine in Normandy, France.

When: 6 June 1944

Why: The British and Americans had long intended to return to Northern Europe, and

Normandy provided suitable beaches within range of land-based air cover.

Outcome: The Allies successfully established themselves ashore, thus opening the Second Front and marking a crucial turning point in the war.

BRITISH INFANTRY gather on Sword Beach in preparation for the push inland. British troops were meant to push on to the strategically important town of Caen in the first day, and did make significant inroads.

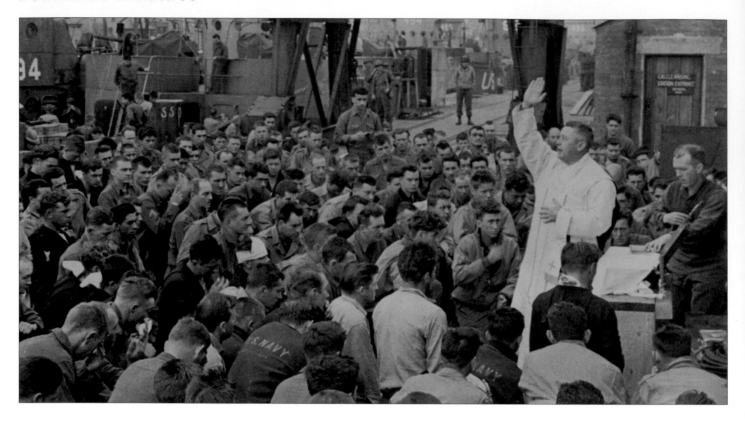

invasion while below him came the three British service chiefs: Admiral Bertram Ramsay (1883–1945), Air Chief Marshal Trafford Leigh-Mallory (1892–1944), and General Bernard Montgomery (1887–1976). Field-Marshal Erwin Rommel's (1891–1944) Army Group B controlled the German forces that opposed the D-Day landings.

NAVAL ARMADA

The D-Day plan began with the night-time passage across the Channel of a naval armada laden with Allied troops, to anchor opposite the five designated invasion beaches: in the east, the three Anglo-Canadian sectors – 'Sword', 'Juno' and 'Gold' and in the west the two US beaches, 'Omaha' and 'Utah'. Shortly before this, three Allied airborne divisions would land to secure the invasion's eastern and western flanks. Finally, after heavy aerial and naval bombardments, the assault forces would land on these five beaches. After these initial assaults had established small beachheads, follow-up forces would advance inland so that by the end of D-Day Allied forces would have captured Bayeux and consolidated the four eastern beachheads and the British airborne zone into a single salient.

BAD WEATHER

D-Day was slated to begin on 5 June, but bad weather forced Eisenhower to postpone the invasion. It nevertheless went ahead on the 6th despite the continuing rough seas. However, the launching of the invasion in bad weather enabled the Allies to surprise the Germans, whose slow

A PRIEST ADMINISTERS a blessing to US sailors and soldiers on 4 June 1944. Operation Overlord was scheduled to begin on 5 June, but was delayed by bad weather.

reactions let slip their best chance of defeating the invaders. On 5 June, 6939 vessels assembled off the coast of southern England and that evening headed south towards the Normandy coast. Next, from 11.30 p.m., 1100 Allied transport planes transported 17,000 airborne troops to Normandy. In the early hours of 6 June, British airborne forces landed northeast of Caen and seized key locations to protect the invasion's eastern flank. Simultaneously two US airborne divisions landed in the marshes behind 'Utah' to delay German ripostes against the invasion's western flank.

While local German forces concluded that these airborne landings were the start of the invasion, higher German authorities remained convinced that they were a diversion prior to the main Allied attack in the Pas de Calais. As these airborne operations unfolded, the naval armada weighed anchor off the Normandy coast. As dawn approached, the Allies commenced naval and aerial bombardments of the German coastal defences.

BEACH ASSAULTS

Next, between 6.30 a.m. and 7.45 a.m, the Allied amphibious assaults commenced on the five designated beaches. At the eastern beach, 'Sword', the British 3rd Division commenced its assault at 7.15 a.m.; here the assault force, as at the other beaches, comprised a combination of infantry, commando and specialized armoured units. Over

SHERMAN 'FLAIL' TANK

The Sherman Crab was one of a number of specialized armoured vehicles used during the D-Day landings. The Crab mounted a flail – a set of heavy chains suspended on a rotating drum in front of the tank – that was used to clear a path through a minefield. The method was first used, aboard a Matilda tank, at El Alamein. The Crab, mounted on the standard Allied medium tank the M4 Sherman, could clear a lane about 3.3m (11 ft) wide at the speed of 2km/h (1.2mph). The chains would need replacing after several detonations.

the next two hours, the British forces fought their way off the beach and captured the fiercely defended German strongpoint at La Brèche. Meanwhile, other Allied units fought their way east into the fringes of Ouistreham and advanced 3.2km (2 miles) inland to capture Hermanville. All morning, follow-up forces landed on 'Sword' beach,

which became increasingly narrow as the tide rose. The resulting traffic jam prevented the supporting armour from moving inland, but eventually the British spearheads renewed their drive inland despite this lack of armour.

FOUR PATHFINDER OFFICERS of British 6th Airborne Division synchronize their watches in front of a Dakota C-47, before take-off at RAF Harwell.

LEFT: AMERICAN TROOPS from the 1st Infantry Division, the 'Big Red One', board landing craft in preparation for Normandy landings.

Meanwhile, at 7.45 a.m., 3rd Canadian Infantry Division commenced its assault on 'Juno'. In the face of fierce enemy resistance, it took over two hours to secure the first exits from the beach. Over the rest of the morning, British and Canadian units advanced through St-Aubin and Courseulles to create a defensive line 6.4km (4 miles) inland. Further west, the British 50th (Northumbrian) Infantry Division had commenced its assault on 'Gold' at 7.30 a.m. Here the preliminary bombardments suppressed German resistance and thus the spearheads established an initial beachhead despite their lack of armour, delayed by the heavy seas.

On the western flank, however, the German strongpoint of le Hamel had escaped much of the recent bombardment. British forces battled for many hours against intense enemy resistance to capture le Hamel. While this action raged, other British units both pushed inland and drove 6.4km (4 miles) west to seize Port-en-Bessin, narrowing the 14.5km (9-mile) gap that existed between 'Gold' and 'Omaha'.

BLOOD BATH AT OMAHA BEACH

The assault of 1st and 29th US Infantry Divisions on 'Omaha' commenced at 6.30 a.m. Even before this time, things had gone awry, with the fire support proving less effective than planned. The heavily loaded infantry that managed to struggle through the neck-high water to the shore then encountered murderous enemy fire that inflicted terrible casualties; Allied intelligence had failed to detect the recent

BELOW: THE SCALE OF OPERATION OVERLORD is clear here in this picture of beached landing craft and supply ships on Omaha Beach in the aftermath of the fighting.

ABOVE: WOUNDED MEN OF the US 3rd battalion, 16th Infantry Regiment pause to smoke and eat after capturing Omaha Beach on 6 June 1944.

reinforcement of the German defences here. Throughout the morning, US troops strove to fight their way off the beach and into the bluffs beyond, yet by midday the US foothold on enemy-occupied soil still remained precarious.

THE OTHER BEACHES

This stood in stark contrast to the less costly assault mounted at 'Utah', located along the southeast corner of the Cotentin Peninsula. Here, at 6.30 a.m., the 4th US Infantry Division commenced its assault after accurate naval gunfire had smashed the relatively weak German defences; the enemy believed that the marshes located behind 'Utah' would persuade the Allies not to land there. In the face of moderate resistance, the Americans soon advanced inland to close with the perimeter held by the US airborne forces.

Over the rest of D-Day, the Allies advanced further inland from these seven separate amphibious/airborne assaults, to create four larger beachheads. In the west, British units linked up with the airborne forces located east of the Orne. However, a German armoured counterattack north prevented the forces landed at 'Sword' from linking up with those landed on 'Juno'. Meanwhile, in the latter sector Canadian forces had linked up with British forces landed on 'Gold'. Further west at 'Omaha', US forces had secured a tenuous 1.6km (1-mile) deep foothold on French soil but at

the price of more than 2000 casualties, while at 'Utah' US forces had linked up with their airborne comrades.

By midnight on 6 June 1944, the 159,000 Allied troops ashore had established four sizable beachheads. While the Allied invasion front remained vulnerable to German counterattack, D-Day's success now made it virtually impossible for the enemy to throw the invaders back into the sea. The establishment of the 'Second Front' on 6 June 1944 represented a crucial step forwards on the Allied march to victory over Nazi Germany, which was finally realized on 8 May 1945.

RIGHT: A PARATROOPER SERGEANT of US 101st Airborne Division. He carries .30 M1A1 Carbine with a folding stock, a weapon specifically designed for paratroopers.

D-DAY

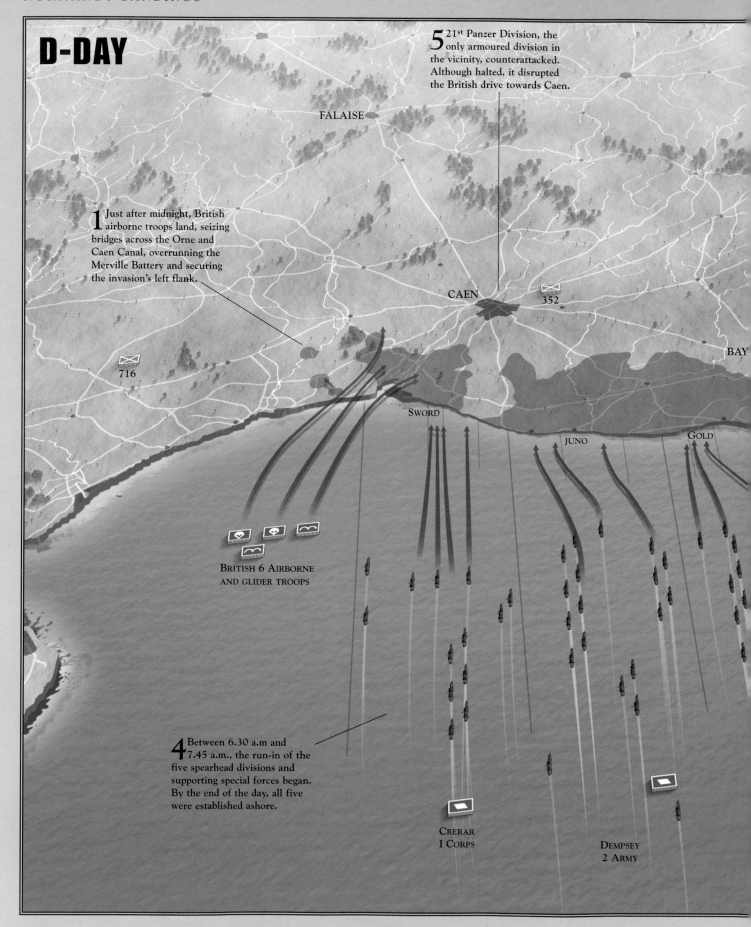

5 21st Panzer Division, the only armoured division in the vicinity, counterattacked. Although halted, it disrupted the British drive towards Caen.

FALAISE

1 Just after midnight, British airborne troops land, seizing bridges across the Orne and Caen Canal, overrunning the Merville Battery and securing the invasion's left flank.

CAEN

352

716

BAY

SWORD

JUNO

GOLD

BRITISH 6 AIRBORNE AND GLIDER TROOPS

4 Between 6.30 a.m and 7.45 a.m., the run-in of the five spearhead divisions and supporting special forces began. By the end of the day, all five were established ashore.

CRERAR
I CORPS

DEMPSEY
2 ARMY

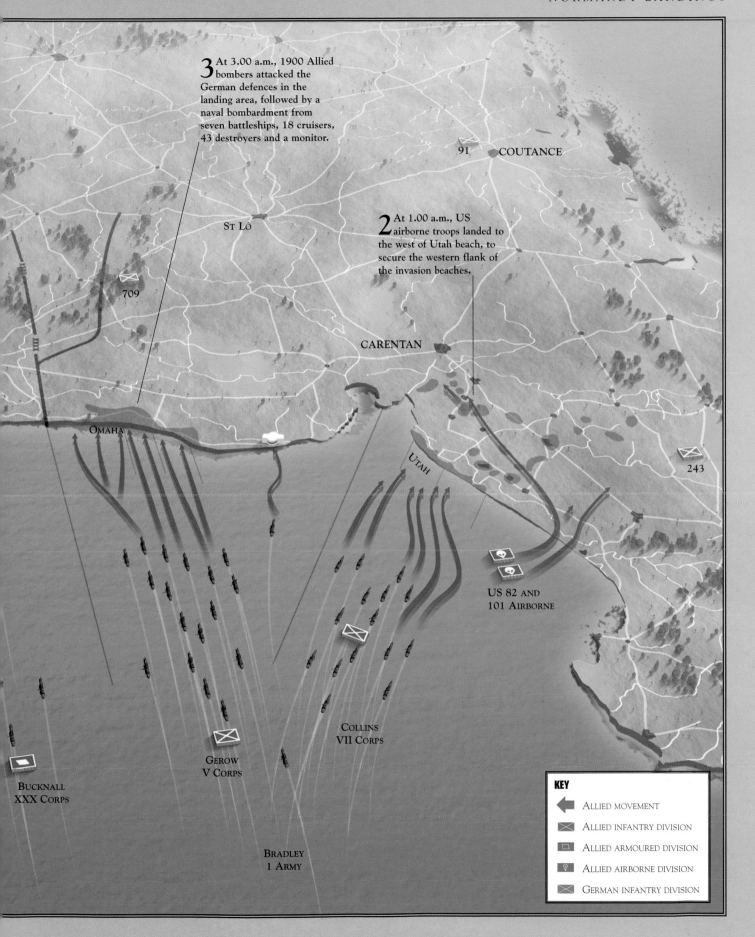

3 At 3.00 a.m., 1900 Allied bombers attacked the German defences in the landing area, followed by a naval bombardment from seven battleships, 18 cruisers, 43 destroyers and a monitor.

91   COUTANCE

2 At 1.00 a.m., US airborne troops landed to the west of Utah beach, to secure the western flank of the invasion beaches.

ST LÔ

709

CARENTAN

243

OMAHA

UTAH

US 82 AND
101 AIRBORNE

COLLINS
VII CORPS

GEROW
V CORPS

BUCKNALL
XXX CORPS

BRADLEY
1 ARMY

KEY

⬅ ALLIED MOVEMENT

✉ ALLIED INFANTRY DIVISION

▭ ALLIED ARMOURED DIVISION

▽ ALLIED AIRBORNE DIVISION

✉ GERMAN INFANTRY DIVISION

BREAKOUT FROM NORMANDY
1944

During late July and August 1944, the Western Allies successfully broke the stalemate that had emerged in the Battle for Normandy and subsequently translated this into a decisive strategic victory that saw the German forces expelled from the region.

The development of such a stalemate was far removed from Allied plans. Their expectations were that once the D-Day landings had established a beachhead subsequent operations would quickly force the Germans to withdraw behind the river Seine, where the decisive battle would ensue. Hitler, however, ordered his forces to prevent the Allies advancing inland, forcing the latter Allies to mount continual attacks against fierce resistance that turned the campaign into a bitter six-week attritional struggle.

BREAKOUT FROM NORMANDY FACTS

Who: Twenty-First Army Group and from 1 August 1944 US Twelfth Army Group commanded by Lieutenant-General Omar Bradley (1893–1981) under land commander General Bernard Montgomery faced Field Marshal Günther von Kluge (1882–1944) until 18 August, then field Marshal Walther Model's (1891–1945) Army Group B.

What: A series of Allied offensives that finally cracked the German line in Normandy and allowed the Allied forces to break out of the bridgehead.

Where: Normandy, France

When: 25 July–30 August 1944

Why: Rather than withdraw to behind the River Seine once the Allies established

their beachhead, German forces were ordered to hold their ground by Hitler, leading to a six-week attritional struggle.

Outcome: The German position in Normandy was broken and the Allies crossed the Seine, liberated Paris on 25 August and embarked on a rapid advance westwards across France towards Germany. It was a decisive strategic victory.

BRITISH MEDICS *recover a wounded comrade and carry him to a Jeep, somewhere in Normandy, July 1944.*

These grinding battles began to bear fruit in mid-July as Allied numerical superiority wore down the Germans. In mid-July, General Bernard Montgomery (1887–1976) launched Operation *Goodwood*, an armoured assault to outflank Caen from the east. While the operation failed to achieve its objectives, it did facilitate the success of the subsequent US offensive – Operation *Cobra* – initiated on 25 July. To sustain their fierce defensive stands against *Goodwood*, the Germans had to divert most of their logistical supplies to the eastern sector of the front. Consequently, the German forces defending the Saint-Lô front were starved of vital logistical supplies just prior to *Cobra*, and their ensuing shortages of fuel and ammunition made it easier for the Americans to secure success.

WAR OF ATTRITION

On 25 July, General Omar Bradley's (1893–1981) First US Army initiated *Cobra*, a massed break-in operation preceded by massive aerial and artillery bombardments. Once these infantry forces had torn a hole in the German line, the Americans aimed to insert three mobile divisions that would advance through the enemy's rear areas to the coast near Coutances, thus cutting off sizable enemy forces. The heavy bombing strike so weakened the defending German forces that VII US Corps drove forwards 3.2km (2 miles) during that first day. Over the

A BRITISH SECTION MOVES up a sunken lane in Normandy. The close nature of the Normandy bocage is well illustrated here.

next 48 hours, US audacity turned this break-in into a decisive breakout by securing a 27.4km (17-mile) advance. By 29 July, the Americans had ripped asunder the German front and so Bradley now widened the scope of *Cobra*. Between 29 and 31 July, US forces crossed the Sélune river at Pontaubault, thus rounding the base of the Cotentin peninsula and opening the gateway for further advances west into Brittany, south towards the Loire and east towards the Seine.

On 30 July, to widen this breach, Montgomery launched an improvised British offensive from Caumont towards Vire, codenamed *Bluecoat*. By 1 August, therefore, the grinding attritional battle of Normandy had been transformed by *Cobra* into a rapid campaign of mobile warfare. The growing US influence on the campaign was now underscored when Bradley's Twelfth US Army Group became operational and assumed command of the First Army and General George Patton's (1885–1945) Third Army.

GERMAN COUNTERATTACK

On 2 August, Hitler reacted to the US breakout by attempting to stuff the genie back into the bottle: he ordered Army Group B to mount a hasty counterattack against the

weak western flank of the breakout. By retaking Avranches, this would isolate the US forces located south of the penetration. During the night 6–7 August, a hastily assembled mobile force attacked down the narrow corridor between the Sée and Sélune rivers towards Mortain. Unsurprisingly, after some initial success this German riposte was halted. This failure now presented the Allies with a strategic opportunity to encircle and destroy the German forces in Normandy, either in the Argentan–Falaise area or via a larger envelopment along the Seine.

In early August, US forces were surging west against feeble enemy resistance, thus outflanking the still cohesive German line against the British around Caen. With this deep US advance into their rear areas, the only feasible German strategy was to withdraw behind the river Seine – but Hitler insisted that his forces stood and fought where they were.

ADVANCE TO FALAISE

By early August, given the scale of recent US success, it had become crucial for the British and Canadian forces bogged down near Caen to advance south towards Falaise. This

LEFT: A TIGER TANK of the SS Schwere Panzerabteilung 101 moves through a Normandy town on 10 June 1944.

BELOW: A US INFANTRY SECTION lies prone on the edge of a field. The time of year meant that the corn in Normandy was often chest high.

ABOVE: A MIXTURE OF *jubilant American GIs and French civilians aboard what appears to be a tracked German AFV.*

advance would assist the British attacks being executed further west to widen the breach in the enemy lines created by *Cobra*. Thus between 7 and 8 August General Guy Simonds' (1903–1974) II Canadian Corps commenced Operation *Totalize*, its drive on Falaise. By using a novel night-infiltration attack, supported by strategic bombers, *Totalize* secured significant initial success. However, determined German resistance slowed Simonds' armour and so on 11 August he halted the attack.

Meanwhile, between 8 and 13 August US forces had raced northwest deep into the German rear to reach Alençon, just 32km (20 miles) away from Simonds' spearheads. If the two forces could link up in the Falaise–Argentan area, the German Seventh Army would be caught in a huge pocket. This led Simonds on 14 August to mount an improvised offensive towards Falaise, codenamed *Tractable*. On 15 August, however, bitter German resistance stymied Simonds' advance before it could secure the key high ground north of Falaise.

SEINE BRIDGEHEAD

But by then the Americans had halted their advance north from Alençon, partly due to supply shortages and fears about friendly fire from Simonds' forces. Instead, Bradley divided his forces and directed US V Corps to race eastwards to the Seine. Incredibly, by 19 August, this corps had secured a

bridgehead across the Seine at Mantes-Gassicourt. Despite the US halt at Alençon, the Falaise pocket was nevertheless well-formed by 16 August with the Germans holding just a precarious 16km (10-mile) wide neck around Trun.

FALAISE BREAKOUT

Between 16 and 19 August, Simonds' armour thrust southeast towards Trun and linked up with the Americans to close the pocket. This weak Allied blocking position could not withstand the ensuing German breakout, for as the battered remnants of Seventh Army desperately fought their way out of the pocket through these blocking positions, SS armour also attacked the latter from outside the pocket. These attacks enabled some 40,000 German troops to escape, albeit without their heavy equipment. With Seventh Army no longer cohesive and with the Americans racing into the interior of France, the Germans now had no choice but to withdraw back to the Seine.

Even before the Falaise pocket had been closed, Montgomery had initiated his own offensive towards the Seine, reflecting his desire to enact the 'long' rather than 'short' envelopment. By 21 August, four corps had struck northeast towards the Upper Seine north of Paris, seeking to

ABOVE: A FRENCH RESISTANCE *fighter armed with a sten submachine gun and an American officer crouch behind a car during a gun fight in a French city.*

catch up with the US advance. However, between 21 and 30 August, the battered remnants of Army Group B mounted a controlled withdrawal back to the northern bank of the Seine. At Vernon on 26 August, the first British bridgehead was established across the river. Just four days later, all German resistance south of the Upper Seine had ceased and with this the Normandy campaign ended. By this

ON 20 JUNE 1944, US troops pause for a break outside a small French café during their advance inland.

juncture, Paris had fallen and the Americans had raced north beyond the Seine and east into the interior of France. The Allies had won the Battle of Normandy and now their thoughts turned to advancing into the German Reich itself.

TIGERS IN NORMANDY

The PzKpfw VI Tiger Mark I heavy tank entered service in late 1942. The appearance of the Soviet T-34 spurred the production of the Tiger, mounting the formidable 88mm (3.46in) gun and extremely thick armour. It was automotively less impressive.

Nonetheless the Tiger – deployed in heavy tank battalions at the corps and army level – was the scourge of Allied tank crews in Normandy. It could deal with any of the British and US tanks deployed and was virtually invulnerable to the Sherman's 75mm (2.95in) gun from the front. It achieved massive tactical success on occasion, but there were never enough available to make a difference.

BREAKOUT FROM NORMANDY

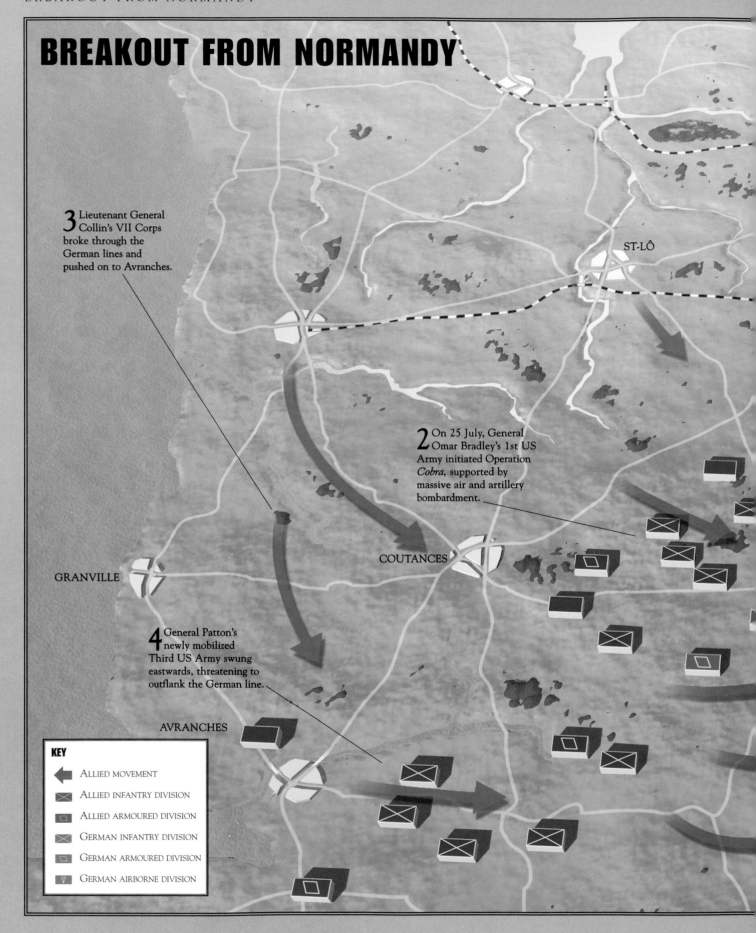

3 Lieutenant General Collin's VII Corps broke through the German lines and pushed on to Avranches.

ST-LÔ

2 On 25 July, General Omar Bradley's 1st US Army initiated Operation *Cobra*, supported by massive air and artillery bombardment.

COUTANCES

GRANVILLE

4 General Patton's newly mobilized Third US Army swung eastwards, threatening to outflank the German line.

AVRANCHES

KEY

◄ ALLIED MOVEMENT

ALLIED INFANTRY DIVISION

ALLIED ARMOURED DIVISION

GERMAN INFANTRY DIVISION

GERMAN ARMOURED DIVISION

GERMAN AIRBORNE DIVISION

BAYEUX

CAEN

FALAISE

1 On 18 July, Operation *Goodwood* began, sucking in the German reserves. It was followed by *Totalize* on 7 August, fixing the Germans in the area.

5 Hitler ordered a counterattack against Mortain, which opened on 7 August. It did little more than push the remaining German armour deeper into the pocket now forming.

6 The US forces made rapid progress to the south and finally linked up with British and Canadian forces on 19 August, sealing the Falaise pocket at last.

PHILIPPINE SEA 1944

Rising like the mythical phoenix from the devastation of Pearl Harbor, the United States Navy had become a veritable juggernaut by the spring of 1944. In support of amphibious operations, which had wrested key bases and outposts from the Japanese in the Gilbert and Marshall Islands, the US Pacific Fleet was poised to accomplish another primary mission – the destruction of the Imperial Japanese Navy.

During 30 months of fighting, the grand strategy for victory in the Pacific – Island Hopping – had carried the US armed forces across vast expanses of ocean. On 15 June 1944, amphibious landings were conducted on the island of Saipan in the Marianas, an archipelago that lay in the path of the American advance towards the Philippines. The capture of Saipan, along with the islands of Guam and Tinian, would disrupt Japanese supply efforts to the far reaches of the Empire, while providing bases from which long-range US bombers could regularly attack the Japanese home islands.

PHILIPPINE SEA: FACTS

Who: Admiral Soemu Toyoda (1885–1957), commander of the Japanese Combined Fleet, and Admiral Jisaburo Ozawa (1886–1966), commander of the First Mobile Fleet, versus Admiral Raymond Spruance (1886–1969), commander of the US Fifth Fleet, and Admiral Marc Mitscher (1887–1947), commander of Task Force 58.

What: The Japanese committed the majority of their air power against the US fleet.

Where: The Philippine Sea in the Central Pacific.

When: 19–20 June 1944

Why: The Japanese hoped to stem the tide of the US advance across the Pacific.

Outcome: A decisive victory for the US Navy resulted in the virtual annihilation of Japanese carrier air power.

A DAMAGED US NAVY Curtiss SB2C Helldiver dive bomber is inspected by officers and crewmen on the flight deck of an aircraft carrier. The Helldiver replaced the ageing Douglas SBD Dauntless.

ABOVE: A TWO-SEAT CARRIER-based dive bomber, the Curtiss SB2C Helldiver proved to be highly successful during the Pacific War. The Helldiver was also heavily armed with machine guns and 20mm (0.78in) cannon.

ABOVE: ADMIRAL CHESTER W. NIMITZ served as the US Navy Commander-in-Chief in the Pacific. Nimitz assumed command days after Pearl Harbor and led the revitalized fighting force to victory.

Anticipating dire consequences if the Americans succeeded, Admiral Soemu Toyoda (1885–1957), Commander-in-Chief of the Japanese Combined Fleet, set in motion operation A-Go, a desperate gambit. Toyoda dispatched Admiral Jisaburo Ozawa (1886–1966) and the First Mobile Fleet to the waters of the Philippine Sea to confront the US naval armada, which was screening the Saipan invasion force and fully expecting such a response from the Japanese.

Ozawa hoped to utilize the one advantage his aircraft still possessed, that of greater range than the American planes, and to leverage land-based air power in the Philippines and surrounding islands to hit the Americans decisively before they could bring their overwhelming superiority to bear. Under his command was a still potentially lethal assemblage of five fleet and four light aircraft carriers, five battleships, 11 heavy cruisers, two light cruisers, 28 destroyers and more than 500 aircraft. The force included the super battleships *Yamato* and *Musashi*, each displacing 71,400 tonnes (78705 tons), the largest warships of their kind ever built.

Admiral Raymond Spruance (1886–1969), commander of the US Fifth Fleet, was in overall command of a striking force built around the core of Task Force 58, led by Admiral Marc Mitscher (1887–1947). Organized into four battle groups, Task Force 58 included a complement of seven large fleet carriers, eight light carriers, seven battleships, 21 cruisers, 69 destroyers and nearly 1000 aircraft.

Although the US naval contingent was quite capable of potent offensive action, Spruance realized that his mission was twofold. Not only was he to engage the Japanese when and where practical but he was also charged with protecting the Saipan invasion beaches and support shipping. Therefore he determined to conduct a defensive operation rather than concentrate wholly on annihilating Ozawa.

In retrospect, Ozawa's effort appears doomed from the start. Warned by Naval Intelligence and a cordon of picket submarines that the Japanese were on the move, Spruance was well prepared for the coming engagement. He did not have long to wait.

TURKEY SHOOT

On the morning of 19 June 1944, Ozawa launched 69 planes against the Americans, 45 of which were soon shot down. A follow-up strike of 127 planes met a similar fate, 98 of them splashing into the sea under the guns of US Grumman F6F Hellcat fighters. During four raids against Task Force 58, the Japanese managed to inflict only slight damage on one US carrier and two battleships. The slaughter of planes and pilots was so thoroughly one-sided that the action came to be known as the 'Great Marianas Turkey Shoot'. In effect, Spruance was allowing what remained of Japan's carrier air power to dash itself against the rocks of his formidable air defences.

Compounding Ozawa's troubles, the newest aircraft carrier in the Japanese fleet and the admiral's flagship, *Taiho*, was struck by a torpedo from the submarine USS *Albacore* on 19 June. The damage had not been fatal, but early in the afternoon a young officer ordered the ship's ventilation

system to be turned on to clear fumes from ruptured fuel lines, and the *Taiho* quickly became a floating bomb. A spark ignited the fumes, causing a catastrophic explosion, and the carrier slid beneath the waves within an hour. Furthermore, just after noon the submarine USS *Cavalla* slammed three torpedoes into the aircraft carrier *Shokaku*. Hours later, the ship was shattered by a massive internal explosion and sank.

COME RETRIBUTION

US search planes hunted the Japanese warships throughout the next day, but it was late when Ozawa's force was finally discovered. Mitscher, aware that the enemy ships were steaming at the outermost range of his planes and his returning pilots would probably have to land on decks in gathering darkness, quickly turned his carriers into the wind and launched 240 aircraft.

The sun was low in the West when the US planes found their target. Sweeping in to attack, they seriously damaged the carrier *Zuikaku*, the lone surviving veteran of the Pearl Harbor attack 30 months before. The light carriers *Ryuho* and

A HEAVILY ARMED VERSION of the North American B-25 Mitchell medium bomber, with .50-cal. machine guns mounted in its nose, strafes a Japanese patrol craft off the Philippines in July 1944.

Junyo were hit by bombs and the light carrier *Hiyo* was sunk. As combat operations ebbed, the most formidable foe faced by the Americans during the Battle of the Philippine Sea turned out to be darkness. Numerous accidents occurred as planes with nearly empty fuel tanks attempted to land on their carriers. Other pilots were forced to ditch in the open sea and await rescue. Courageously, Mitscher risked attack by enemy submarines in ordering his ships to turn on their lights and fire star shells to assist the returning pilots. Eighty-two planes were lost, but the majority of the downed airmen were plucked from the water the next day.

AIR POWER ON THE WANE

The Battle of the Philippine Sea resulted in the destruction of Japanese carrier air power. When the fighting was over, Ozawa had only 35 aircraft remaining. He had lost three

AIRCRAFT BURN AS DAMAGE control parties attempt to contain the flames aboard a US aircraft carrier that has been struck by a Japanese kamikaze. Another stricken carrier is visible in the distance.

carriers and more than 400 planes over two disastrous days. More than 200 land-based planes had been shot down or destroyed on the ground as well. The victory had cost the Americans 130 aircraft and relatively few casualties. Some historians have criticized Spruance for failing to completely

destroy Ozawa's fleet and deliver the decisive blow against the Japanese navy. However, given his dual responsibilities, it must be concluded that Spruance accomplished both to the best of his ability.

In October, the Battle of Leyte Gulf, the last great naval engagement of the Pacific War, would settle the issue once and for all. After the Philippine Sea, however, the final defeat of Japan was a foregone conclusion.

PHILIPPINE SEA

2 Launched from the Philippines, Japanese land-based aircraft augment the carrier planes. Four major raids are attempted throughout the day on 19 June 1944.

1 Hoping to utilize the greater range of his carrier-based aircraft, Admiral Ozawa launches a series of airstrikes against the US fleet in the Philippine Sea.

OZAWA FLEET

4 *Taiho*, the newest aircraft carrier in the Japanese fleet and Ozawa's flagship, is torpedoed by the submarine USS *Albacore* and later explodes.

5 The Japanese are further shaken as three torpedoes from the submarine USS *Cavalla* sink the aircraft carrier *Shokaku* shortly after noon on 19 June.

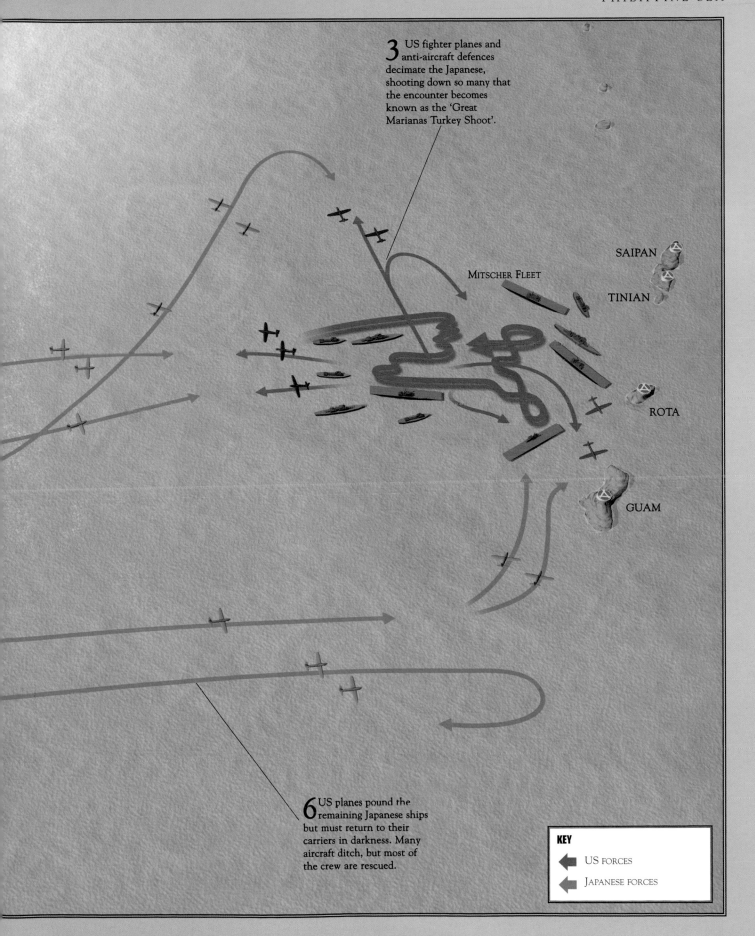

3 US fighter planes and anti-aircraft defences decimate the Japanese, shooting down so many that the encounter becomes known as the 'Great Marianas Turkey Shoot'.

MITSCHER FLEET

SAIPAN

TINIAN

ROTA

GUAM

6 US planes pound the remaining Japanese ships but must return to their carriers in darkness. Many aircraft ditch, but most of the crew are rescued.

KEY

⬅ US FORCES

⬅ JAPANESE FORCES

WARSAW RISING

1944

As the war moved towards its conclusion, the Allies agreed to divide Europe into spheres of influence. This was not acceptable to the Polish people, who wanted once again to be a free and sovereign nation. To demonstrate their independence, the Poles planned an uprising to liberate their capital before the advancing Red Army arrived.

Poland was one of the earliest victims of Nazi aggression, invaded in September 1939. The nation's army resisted as best it could, but defeat was inevitable even before the Soviet invasion from the other direction. However, this was not the end of Polish resistance. Free Polish forces were an important part of the war while resistance networks at home did all they could to further the Allied cause.

WARSAW RISING FACTS

Who: More than 40,000 Polish irregulars versus German occupying forces of roughly 25,000 troops.

What: The Uprising began on 1 August 1944 as part of a nationwide rebellion. It was intended to last for only a few days until the Soviet Army reached the city. However, it developed into a long urban guerrilla campaign against the occupiers.

Where: Warsaw, Poland.

When: August–October 1944.

Why: The Poles sought to re-establish their sovereignty after four years of Nazi-German occupation.

Outcome: The uprising was ultimately put down with great losses on both sides. It is estimated that more than 200,000 civilians died in the fighting, while 700,000 were expelled from the city.

IN AUGUST 1944, Polish volunteers equipped with whatever weapons they could obtain seized much of Warsaw from the German occupation forces, beginning a long and bitter struggle for the city.

MEN OF THE *Dirlewanger Brigade, a formation supposedly intended to rehabilitate criminals by military service. The brigade's career of atrocities reached its peak during the Warsaw Rising.*

Once the tide of the war had turned and German forces began the long retreat out of Russia, it became obvious that Poland was going to be 'liberated' by the Soviet Union, which meant inevitably falling into its sphere of influence. Indeed a pro-Soviet government was being readied for installation as soon as the Red Army pushed the Germans out. The Poles did not welcome this prospect. They wanted a free and independent state and that meant doing more than waiting for one foreign army to leave and another to arrive. The plan, named Operation *Tempest*, called for orchestrated risings in several cities and a campaign of attacks in various regions of the country.

This would hopefully drive the German occupiers out before the Red Army arrived and also assist the Allied cause by distracting German attention. Once the capital was liberated, members of the Polish government would come out of hiding and assume control.

No one had any illusions that there would not be bloodshed when the rising took place, but the Poles were willing to make the sacrifice. They had been fighting a hidden war for the entire occupation, hampering German efforts in Russia by disrupting the logistics chain running eastwards.

The largest resistance organization was named *Armia Krajowa* (Home Army). It had over 400,000 members, who were armed with weapons dropped by the Allies or obtained

from German sources – by theft, capture or sometimes black market purchase. In addition, there were stocks of weaponry concealed in the last days of freedom when it became apparent that the German advance could not be halted.

Thus there was no shortage of willing and experienced fighters available for the operation. The resistance forces had been fighting this kind of guerrilla war for years, albeit on a smaller scale. Now they saw their opportunity to win a decisive victory.

THE RISING

In July 1944, the Red Army was advancing on Warsaw and it seemed obvious that the battle for the city would soon begin if the German garrison did not retreat. This was unlikely as the city was a major logistics and transport centre and was also politically significant.

Plans were made to use Polish labour to construct fortifications around the city and a demand was made for men to come forward to do the work. Suspicious of the motives behind the order, the population largely refused to obey it. This increased tensions between the population and the occupiers even further and prompted the Home Army commanders to move up their timetable. The order was given to launch the rising on 1 August 1944.

The Home Army had about 45,000 members in Warsaw at the time of the rising, under General Antoni Chrusciel (1895–1960). About half of these personnel were equipped for combat, though it was necessary to get weapons to many of them just before the rising started.

ABOVE: FLAMETHROWERS PROVED VERY EFFECTIVE *in the urban fighting for Warsaw. Their use was acceptable to a regime that did not care about damage to the city – indeed, much of it was deliberately destroyed.*

Organizing such a large-scale operation was difficult, especially within an enemy-held city, and it was not possible to conceal from the occupiers that something was going on. The garrison and internal security forces, including SS troops and secret police, were alerted and able to prepare to an extent. The original plan had been for the first strikes to be made at night and by surprise. Instead, the Home Army had to attack alert troops in daylight. Success was mixed: in some areas, objectives were quickly overwhelmed where in others the attacks were met with intense machine-gun and small-arms fire and repelled.

There were about 11,000 German troops in the city under the overall command of Lieutenant-General Reiner Stahel. About half were regulars; the rest were mostly from the *Luftwaffe*. There were also more than 5000 SS personnel in the area under the command of Colonel Paul Giebel. Cooperation between these units was patchy at times and there was no coherent strategy for dealing with the uprising.

The result was a very confused situation with groups from both sides cut off from their allies by territory held by the enemy. Barricades were erected and control over captured areas consolidated, and gradually the insurgents took

RIGHT: HITLER TOOK A *personal interest in the battle for Warsaw, allocating large resources and condoning the harsh measures used to suppress the insurgency.*

ABOVE: A GERMAN OFFICER *directs his men during street fighting in Warsaw. In this sort of close-quarters battle, effective junior leadership was of paramount importance; in a fluid situation higher command could not react quickly enough.*

control of more and more of the city. By 4 August, most of Warsaw was under Polish control. All that was necessary was to hang on until the Red Army arrived.

GERMAN COUNTERMEASURES

Even as the Poles were reaching the high watermark of their uprising, an organized response began to unfold. German reinforcements came up, and all forces were placed under a single commander, General Erich von dem Bach (1899–1972), an SS officer who formulated plans to retake the city.

A spearhead of combat troops drove into the city, establishing a line behind which the streets were under firm German control. Here the SS and Gestapo were free to operate as they wished. There was no pretence of justice or justification – civilians were simply rounded up behind the German line and shot.

The massacre was intended to break the will of the population and bring the insurgency to an end without having to dig the Poles out house by house. In this, it failed. Resistance became ever more determined, partly from outrage and partly from the feeling that to surrender was a death sentence anyway.

Once it became apparent that reprisals were not the answer, a different approach was used. Instead of simply executing captured resistance fighters, some were accorded the status of prisoners of war and fairly treated in the hope that this would make it seem that it was worth surrendering. This also had little effect.

STREET FIGHTING

The uprising had been intended as a short campaign to end with the Red Army arriving at the city limits. Yet the Red Army remained strangely inactive, suddenly unable or perhaps unwilling to make much progress in its advance. Thus the Poles were forced to fight on.

The arrival of tanks on 7 August did not shift the balance much. The insurgents had prepared obstacles and barricades, and although some ground was lost the situation had stabilized by 9 August. The fighting reached a climax between 9 and 18 August, with large-scale urban combat raging across wide areas of the city.

By 2 September, the tide had turned. Under air attack and bombardment by distant artillery to which they had no reply, the Poles had to pull out of the old town, using the sewers to avoid detection. The fighting went on elsewhere, the German forces grinding their way through the city in a manner not dissimilar to the urban hell of Stalingrad.

THE SOVIETS APPROACH

By the middle of September, the advance units of the Red Army had almost reached the Vistula and were pushing the Germans back once again. Although Soviet forces seemed unwilling to help the insurgents, Free Polish units fighting with them moved into the city and joined their countrymen. They were not given support by their Soviet comrades in arms, however, and were badly defeated.

The Free Polish commander, General Zygmunt Berling (1896–1980), was relieved of command by his Soviet allies and the remainder of the Soviet army halted short of

LEFT: THE RED ARMY *had significant forces nearby and could perhaps have come to the aid of the insurgents, but did not. Instead, weapons like this Su-152 self-propelled gun stood idle while the battle raged.*

Warsaw and stayed there. There were solid tactical reasons – the Soviets were closely engaged with German armoured battle groups at the time – but there was more to it than this.

Although the Soviets had been calling for a Polish uprising for months, Stalin did not desire the Warsaw insurgency to succeed. He wanted Poland under Soviet control, not independent, and the insurgents had risen in the name of the pro-West government-in-exile based in London. By waiting until the rising was crushed and then moving in, he ensured that Poland would fall under the sway of Moscow.

Stalin also refused to allow the Western Allies to use Soviet airbases to fly supplies in to the insurgents. Some drops were

THESE WOUNDED POLISH insurgents were captured at the end of the uprising, and stood a good chance of being treated as prisoners of war. Earlier on, captured personnel were simply shot.

still made, but they had to fly out of distant bases and were not effective. Soviet troops at times fired on Allied aircraft making supply runs, though a re-supply mission was eventually permitted. By then, it was too late: the insurgents had been ground down to the point where they could no longer resist.

On 2 October 1944, General Tadeusz Bor-Komorowski (1895–1966), Chrusciel's superior in the Home Army, surrendered what was left of the forces in Warsaw after receiving a promise that the insurgents would be treated as regular combatants in accordance with the relevant conventions. The civilian population was also to be spared reprisals.

THE DESTRUCTION OF WARSAW

Some of the insurgents did not turn themselves in but tried to fade out of sight among the population. Of those who did surrender, some were treated as any other prisoners of war and sent west to camps in Germany. Of the remainder, some were sent to concentration camps, some to labour projects and most dispersed and released. None was allowed to remain in the city.

The city was then systematically destroyed by fire and explosives. Some houses escaped but all public and historic buildings were deliberately targeted. The Red Army finally entered Warsaw in mid-January 1945, by which time very little remained of the city.

A CITY DESTROYED

About a quarter of Warsaw was destroyed in the fighting that resulted from the uprising. After the Polish surrender, the population was driven out and an attempt was made to burn or demolish the remainder of the city. In fact, 85 per cent of Warsaw was destroyed in this manner, with special emphasis put on cultural buildings, from churches and schools to monuments and the university.

The city was rebuilt after the war, and considerable effort was put into recreating the historic city centre, which is now a World Heritage Site. In 2004, a ceremony was held to mark the 50th anniversary of the uprising, though it was suggested that the Russian delegation should observe from the far bank of the Vistula.

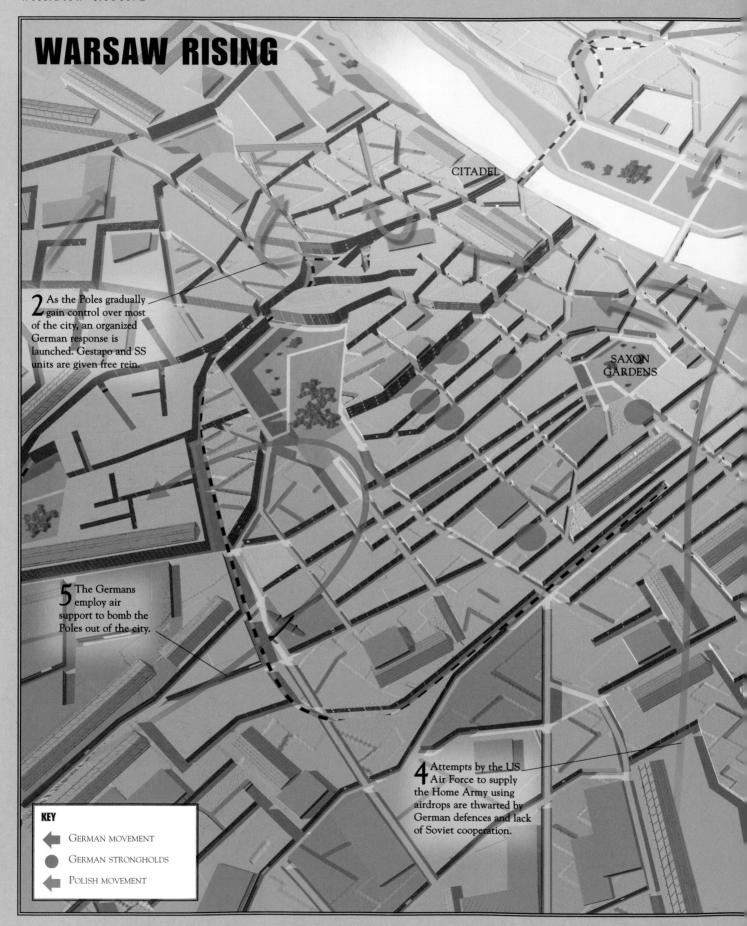

WARSAW RISING

CITADEL

SAXON GARDENS

2 As the Poles gradually gain control over most of the city, an organized German response is launched. Gestapo and SS units are given free rein.

5 The Germans employ air support to bomb the Poles out of the city.

4 Attempts by the US Air Force to supply the Home Army using airdrops are thwarted by German defences and lack of Soviet cooperation.

KEY

← GERMAN MOVEMENT

● GERMAN STRONGHOLDS

← POLISH MOVEMENT

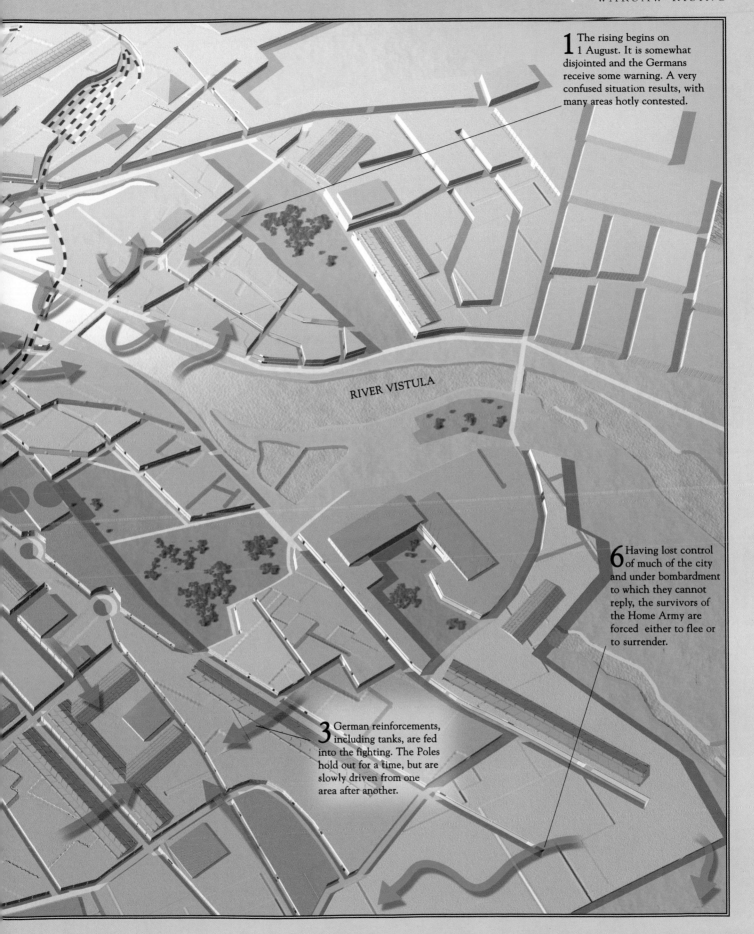

1 The rising begins on 1 August. It is somewhat disjointed and the Germans receive some warning. A very confused situation results, with many areas hotly contested.

RIVER VISTULA

6 Having lost control of much of the city and under bombardment to which they cannot reply, the survivors of the Home Army are forced either to flee or to surrender.

3 German reinforcements, including tanks, are fed into the fighting. The Poles hold out for a time, but are slowly driven from one area after another.

OPERATION 'MARKET GARDEN' 1944

Operations 'Market' and 'Garden' were complementary halves of a daring plan to seize strategic bridges with airborne troops, then rush ground forces up and across them. Had it succeeded, Market Garden might have shortened the war by a year.

The Siegfried Line, or Westwall, was a chain of fortifications facing France, constructed before the war. Rather than a solid line, it was a deeply defended zone covered by minefields, pillboxes, bunkers and antitank obstacles, all covered by artillery in protected emplacements. Entrenched in such positions, even third-line troops could inflict serious casualties.

In the summer of 1944, it was obvious that if the Allies were forced to assault the Siegfried Line they would suffer serious casualties. An alternative line of attack, into the heavily defended Ruhr, would be equally costly. So the Allies

OPERATION 'MARKET GARDEN' FACTS

Who: Allied airborne and ground forces, including the British 1st Airborne Division and Polish Brigade, opposed by German armoured and infantry units.

What: Although at first the advance was a success, German resistance was heavier than expected.

Where: The Netherlands, near the town of Arnhem, on the River Rhine.

When: 17–25 September 1944

Why: The Allies wanted to get across the Rhine quickly, bypassing major German defences and trapping large numbers of German forces in the Netherlands.

Outcome: The operation was a failure, prolonging the war in Northwest Europe by at least a few months.

PARATROOPS AND GLIDERBORNE *infantry land at Arnhem. Putting troops in a glider required less training than creating paratroops, though it was scarcely less dangerous. Glider troops were also less prone to being scattered.*

199

sought an alternative and found one that, with luck and daring, might be workable.

The plan was relatively simple. Attacking by surprise, the Allies would seize strategic bridges over the rivers Maas, Waal and Lower Rhine, enabling the establishment of a bridgehead behind the enemy's main defended zone and the most formidable natural obstacles. The only problem was that the first bridge might indeed be taken by *coup de main*, perhaps by light armoured forces racing up to grab it, but by the time the assault force got across and reached the next bridge, they might find it to be blown or strongly held.

The answer was for all the bridges to be captured at the same time, by paratroops and glider-borne infantry who would defend their objective until relieved by the rapidly advancing armoured spearhead. The airborne component was codenamed *Market* and the armoured advance *Garden*, but in reality neither had any point without the other. It was the whole, Operation *Market Garden*, that mattered. It was a bold plan – perhaps a little too bold. One Allied officer, feeling that the Allies were about to overextend themselves remarked, 'I think we're going a bridge too far'. But it was all

BRITISH PARATROOPERS EN ROUTE to Arnhem. Just getting onto the ground was a dangerous business; 'jump casualties' from enemy fire or a bad landing were inevitable on any operation.

or nothing – there was no point in grabbing just some of the bridges. *Market Garden* had to succeed completely or not at all.

The most serious threat to the operation was not the enemy but poor planning. Perhaps as a result of complacency following the success of the Normandy landings, much was taken for granted. As a result, re-supply operations came unstuck and cooperation between units failed. Sometimes this was due to problems with radios but just as often to a lack of good communications procedures.

OPENING MOVES

The operation began with paratroop landings by British, American and Free Polish units. RAF concerns about the air defences in the Arnhem region meant that the paras were dropped at a distance from their objectives, requiring a forced march and giving the enemy time to react to the threat.

This might not have been too serious but for two facts. Firstly, II SS Panzer Corps was in the region, rebuilding its strength after taking a battering in Normandy. This was an experienced and well-equipped unit that retained its offensive spirit. Secondly, Field-Marshal Walter Model (1891–1945) was in the immediate vicinity. Model had gained a well-deserved reputation as an excellent commander on the Eastern Front, where he staved off defeat again and again by scraping a battle group together from whatever was to hand and improvising a brilliant battle plan. Now, that experience came to the fore.

Model gave orders to prevent the paras from reaching their objectives, then went to his headquarters and began organizing a response to the overall situation. By this time, he knew that Allied armour was smashing its way towards him and that paratroops had landed along its projected route. It was not at all difficult to determine what the Allies were attempting.

Model's fast response meant that very few of the paras assigned to take the Arnhem bridges reached the town at all. Elements of 2nd battalion, the Parachute Regiment under Lieutenant-Colonel John Frost (1912–1993), along with an assortment of troops gathered along the way, were able to reach the north end of the bridge and hang on there, but this was the limit of the paras' success. Model assigned part of his force to contain the paras and began gathering everything else he could find to halt the armoured attack coming his way.

THE ALLIES ADVANCE

Although some of the airborne troops were still in England, unable to take off due to fog, the advance went ahead. There were several minor waterways to cross and plans had been laid to set up temporary bridges if necessary, but in the event the Allies were able to overrun what defenders there were and to gain control of the permanent bridges.

However, there were two waterways that could not be bridged: at Nijmegen and Arnhem the Allies had to cross

ABOVE: ALTHOUGH PARATROOPERS jumped in quick succession, a 'stick' could become widely separated if there was much wind. Paradrop operations always began confused, with lost personnel hoping to rejoin their units later.

BELOW: THE SDKFZ 251/22 mounted a heavy antitank gun on a proven half-track truck chassis. These vehicles were effectively used as mobile tank destroyers by SS troops fighting at Arnhem.

arms of the Rhine. There was no way for combat engineers to create a temporary crossing of such wide rivers. Here the bridges would have to be taken and that meant getting there while the paras still had control of the bridges.

Despite this, the ground assault had been delayed, waiting for confirmation that the airborne operation was a success. As a result, resistance along the roads towards the bridges firmed up and the advance fell behind schedule. Nightfall forced a stop and by the time the armoured spearhead reached Nijmegen an organized defence was in place. Attempts to break through were met by fire from 88mm (3.46in) antitank guns and repelled.

The original plan had called for all the bridges to be in Allied hands within 48 hours. However, by this time the ground forces were still trying to get on to the Nijmegen bridge while the airborne forces were fighting sporadic and scattered actions all over the countryside. Some were successful and more paras reached Arnhem, but overall the chances of success were diminishing fast.

Frost's paras were still clinging to the end of the Arnhem bridge, incidentally denying its use to the enemy, but they were under ferocious pressure from artillery and tanks. The Allies had to get across the Waal at Nijmegen and start making some headway before it was too late.

BELOW: A KAMPFGRUPPE OF German infantry advances. In such a confused situation, an attack could come from anywhere and it was not always possible to tell whether a contact was a couple of lost paras or a major force.

ABOVE: THE ROAD BRIDGE at Arnhem. Although the paratroopers were not able to capture the whole bridge, they held one end of it long enough to deny its use to a German counterattack.

The solution was daring and aggressive: US airborne troops would make an assault crossing in small boats and then storm the far end of the bridge. While their attack distracted the defenders' attention, the armoured forces would advance across at full speed.

The crossing was extremely difficult even without the intense enemy fire that came from the bank. Many paddles were missing from the boats so the troops used rifle butts and helmets to crawl slowly across the wide river. Even with assistance from tank guns and aircraft, many boats were riddled, yet somehow the paras got across and launched an attack up the bank.

As the assault boat crews took them back across to pick up more paras, those that had survived the crossing fell on the defenders and drove them from the banks. In a very confused action, where aggression counted for more than anything else, the armoured troops charged on to the bridges from one end while the paras attacked the other.

During the advance, the German commander on the spot tried to detonate previously laid demolition charges, which failed to work. The likely explanation is that a member of the Dutch Resistance cut the wires during the fighting. After the bridge was made safe, the armoured forces were able to advance across it.

The Allies were finally across the Waal and only 18km (11 miles) from where Frost and his paras were holding one end of the Arnhem bridge. A rapid advance might have been in order but the Allied force was tired and disorganized. It was not possible to put together a sufficient force to break through and achieve anything at Arnhem.

A BRIDGE TOO FAR

The situation was still very fluid, with German forces coming in from the flanks and at times cutting the Allied line of communications. Model's forces at Arnhem were gaining strength and Frost had finally been overrun.

It was clear that an assault was very unlikely to succeed. Worse, Model had managed to get some panzers across the river (using an alternate route since Frost's paras denied him the use of the bridge until it was too late) and was advancing down the road to Nijmegen.

An Allied armoured thrust up the Arnhem road was unable to break through and attacks along other axes ran into heavy resistance. The operation had obviously failed and it was time to salvage all they could. As many paras as possible were brought across the river in assault boats during the night of 25/26 September.

AFTERMATH

The goal of getting across the Rhine quickly and without fighting through heavy defences had not been achieved. A combination of mischance, poor planning and the determination of the enemy robbed the operation of success.

ABOVE: MAN-PORTABLE MORTARS were the only artillery available to the lightly equipped paratroopers. They were effective in close-range urban fighting, but ammunition was limited by what could be carried.

As a result, the allies were forced to fight their way in 'though the front door' and took heavy casualties as a result. The damage in still-occupied territory caused by the extra months of war was also considerable.

ABOVE: ALTHOUGH GOOD TACTICS and use of cover could improve the odds, it was also possible to be in the wrong place at the wrong time. This German soldier may have made a mistake or simply been unlucky.

OPERATION 'MARKET GARDEN'

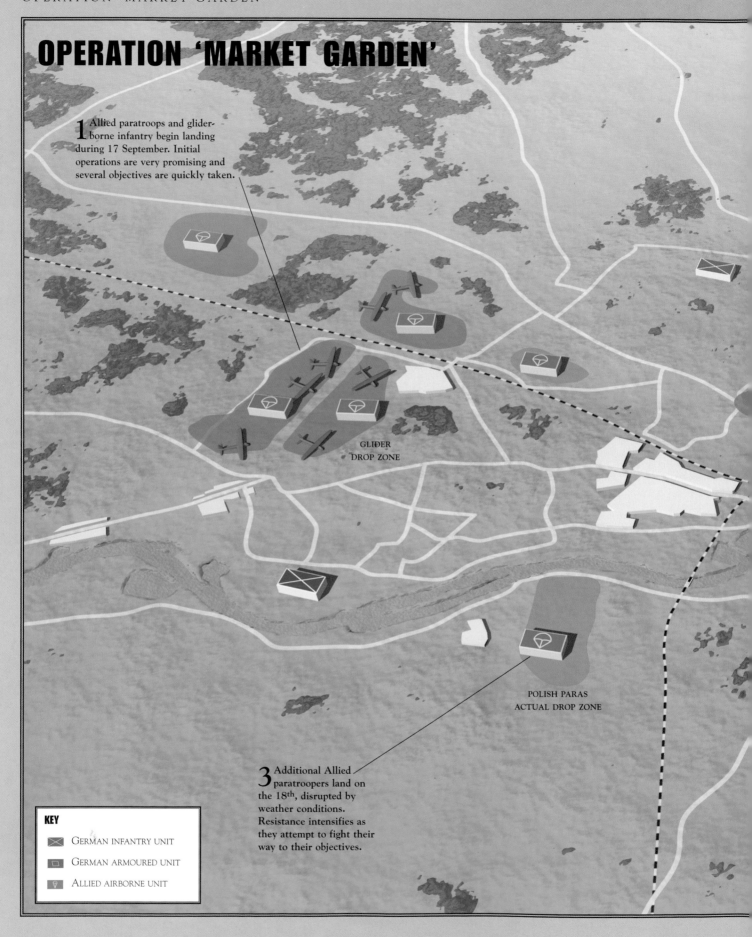

1 Allied paratroops and glider-borne infantry begin landing during 17 September. Initial operations are very promising and several objectives are quickly taken.

GLIDER
DROP ZONE

POLISH PARAS
ACTUAL DROP ZONE

3 Additional Allied paratroopers land on the 18th, disrupted by weather conditions. Resistance intensifies as they attempt to fight their way to their objectives.

KEY

⊠ GERMAN INFANTRY UNIT

▭ GERMAN ARMOURED UNIT

▽ ALLIED AIRBORNE UNIT

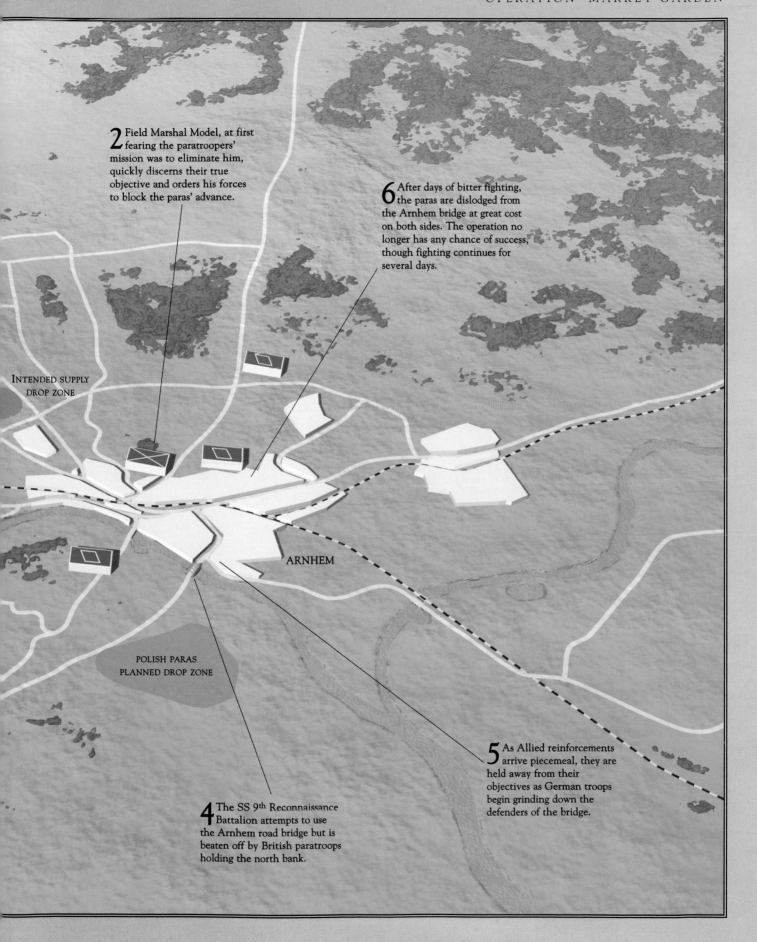

2 Field Marshal Model, at first fearing the paratroopers' mission was to eliminate him, quickly discerns their true objective and orders his forces to block the paras' advance.

6 After days of bitter fighting, the paras are dislodged from the Arnhem bridge at great cost on both sides. The operation no longer has any chance of success, though fighting continues for several days.

INTENDED SUPPLY DROP ZONE

ARNHEM

POLISH PARAS PLANNED DROP ZONE

5 As Allied reinforcements arrive piecemeal, they are held away from their objectives as German troops begin grinding down the defenders of the bridge.

4 The SS 9th Reconnaissance Battalion attempts to use the Arnhem road bridge but is beaten off by British paratroops holding the north bank.

BATTLE OF THE BULGE

DVD TRACK 8

1944–45

At 5.30 a.m. on the morning of 16 December 1944, the thunder of hundreds of German guns shattered the stillness of the Ardennes, a relatively quiet sector of the Allied lines on the German frontier. It was the beginning of Operation Wacht am Rhein (Watch on the Rhine), a last gamble by Adolf Hitler in the West.

The *Führer's* objective was to force a wedge between the Allied Twelfth and Twenty-First Army Groups with a fast-moving armoured thrust that would drive across the river Meuse and on to the vital Belgian port city of Antwerp. Hitler also hoped subsequently to shift forces to meet a coming offensive in the East, where the Soviet Red Army was poised to strike across the river Vistula into

BATTLE OF THE BULGE FACTS

Who: German forces under the command of *Führer* Adolf Hitler (1889–1945) and his generals versus Allied forces under General Dwight Eisenhower (1890–1969).

What: Hitler hoped to divide Allied army groups in the West, drive to the port of Antwerp and change the course of the war.

Where: The front lines in Belgium, France and Luxembourg.

When: 16 December 1944 to 15 January 1945

Why: Hitler sought to divide the Western Allies and gain time to confront the coming Soviet offensive along the river Vistula in the East.

Outcome: The battle resulted in a disastrous defeat for Nazi Germany. Less than four months later, World War II in Europe was over.

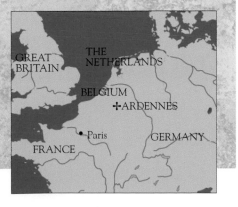

HALTED MOMENTARILY ALONG *an icy road in Belgium, German Panzer V 'Panther' tanks spearhead the German Ardennes offensive. With its large gun, the Panther was one of the best tanks of World War II.*

ABOVE: CAPTURED DURING THE opening phase of the Battle of the Bulge, American prisoners are marched by their German captors towards an uncertain fate. SS soldiers were guilty of atrocities during the fighting.

the heart of Germany. Bypassing Field-Marshal Gerd von Rundstedt (1875–1953), his commander in the West, Hitler instructed three armies – Sixth Panzer under SS General Josef 'Sepp' Dietrich (1892–1966) to the north, Fifth Panzer commanded by General Hasso von Manteuffel (1897–1978) in the centre and Seventh Army under General Erich

Brandenberger (1892–1955) further south – to strike on a 97km (60-mile) front from Monschau, Germany, to the town of Echternach in Luxembourg.

THE STORM BREAKS

For months, Hitler had mulled over his plan. Finally, with 275,000 troops, hundreds of tanks and nearly 2000 artillery pieces, he launched his attack against a sector of the line that Allied commanders had considered virtually inactive. Warning signs of a pending offensive had been ignored and when the Germans jumped off, numerous American units were taken completely by surprise. However, pockets of stiff resistance formed along Elsenborn Ridge, particularly by troops of the 99th Division.

These determined efforts slowed Dietrich to a crawl until a shift of troops to the south outflanked some defensive positions along the Schnee Eifel, a cluster of hamlets and tree-covered hills in front of the high ground. Thousands of US soldiers were scooped up as prisoners. The untested troops of the 106th Infantry Division found themselves cut off in the Schnee Eifel, and on 19 December two entire regiments surrendered – but the Americans on Elsenborn Ridge stood their ground.

Dietrich's armoured spearhead, commanded by SS Colonel Joachim Peiper (1915–1976), pushed hard for several key bridges over the Meuse and other waterways, which would facilitate rapid crossings. In the process, however, the Germans were held up by groups of US combat engineers, one of which disabled Peiper's lead tank and blocked access to a bridge across the Amblève river at the town of Stavelot. Other bridges were blown up nearly in the Germans' faces by the engineers. Enraged by the delays, Peiper was also plagued by a shortage of fuel. His force, which originally numbered 4000, was eventually surrounded and only around 800 managed to escape. Peiper and his command gained lasting infamy in the fight, which would

BELOW: THE GERMAN TIGER II or King Tiger tank combined a high velocity 88mm (3.46in) cannon and sloped armour in a formidable fighting vehicle. The horizontal lines of anti-mine zimmerit coating are faintly visible.

RIGHT: SOLDIERS FROM KAMPFGRUPPE PEIPER on the road to Malmédy. In the background is a SdKfz 251 half-track armoured personnel carrier.

come to be known as the Battle of the Bulge. One of his units was guilty of murdering 85 captured Americans in a field near Malmedy in one of the most publicized atrocities of World War II.

As Allied troops held Elsenborn Ridge, the north shoulder of the great bulge began to form. Brandenberg's thrust ran into the veteran 9th Armoured and 4th Infantry Divisions of the US Army and made little or no progress along the southern edge of the offensive. In the centre, Manteuffel's tanks came closest to reaching the Meuse near Dinant, roughly 80km (50 miles) from their start line. A heroic stand by elements of the US 7th Armoured Division at the town of St Vith delayed the Germans for six days. The town did not fall until 23 December and British Field-Marshal Bernard Montgomery (1887–1976), placed in command of forces north of the bulge, used the time to consolidate his defences.

BELOW: AS THE TIDE of the fighting in the Ardennes begins to turn in late December 1944, American infantrymen proceed through some abandoned, snow-covered buildings towards German positions.

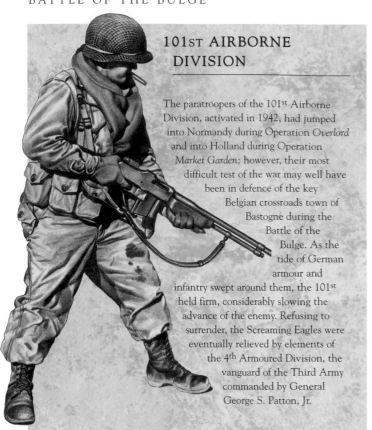

101ST AIRBORNE DIVISION

The paratroopers of the 101st Airborne Division, activated in 1942, had jumped into Normandy during Operation *Overlord* and into Holland during Operation *Market Garden*; however, their most difficult test of the war may well have been in defence of the key Belgian crossroads town of Bastogne during the Battle of the Bulge. As the tide of German armour and infantry swept around them, the 101st held firm, considerably slowing the advance of the enemy. Refusing to surrender, the Screaming Eagles were eventually relieved by elements of the 4th Armoured Division, the vanguard of the Third Army commanded by General George S. Patton, Jr.

'NUTS!'

Southwest of St Vith, the Belgian crossroads town of Bastogne proved critical to the outcome of the Battle of the Bulge. Continued possession of Bastogne by the Americans would deny the Germans use of a key road network and slow their advance considerably. On 17 December, the vanguard of Manteuffel's forces reached the outskirts of the town. Unable to capture it by direct assault, the Germans bypassed Bastogne, which was defended by the lightly armed 101st Airborne Division and elements of other units.

The encircled paratroopers held on by their fingernails, but when heavy German forces drew the noose tighter on 22 December they were invited to surrender. The ranking US officer in the embattled town was Major-General Anthony McAuliffe (1897–1983), and his famous reply to the German ultimatum was simply, 'Nuts!'.

Although he was in dire straits, McAuliffe did have reason to hope. Foul weather, which had benefited the Germans, had begun to clear the previous day and allowed an airdrop of desperately needed supplies. Of even greater importance, relief for the beleaguered defenders of Bastogne was already on the way.

BARRICADES NOW OPEN, *American troops move through a village in Belgium that shows signs of heavy fighting, late December 1944.*

Americans in the Ardennes, and his gamble had reached the brink of success. In the end, a lack of fuel, unexpectedly stiff resistance and clearing weather had conspired to bring about a crushing defeat.

The offensive had cost the *Führer* dearly. More than 120,000 Germans had been killed, wounded or taken prisoner during a month of hard fighting. Scores of tanks and other armoured vehicles had been destroyed or abandoned. American casualties totalled nearly 80,000, with about 8500 dead, 46,000 wounded and more than 20,000 captured. Both sides had suffered terribly. For the Allies, the losses could be made good. For the Germans, they could not.

PATTON PIVOTS

On 20 December, under orders from the Supreme Allied Commander, General Dwight Eisenhower (1890–1969), elements of General George Patton's (1885–1945) Third Army disengaged from their own offensive in the Saar, wheeled 90° to the north and began slashing towards the surrounded town, which appeared on maps as an American island in a sea of German tanks and troops. Hardly stopping to rest or eat, the men of Third Army penetrated the German perimeter. Patton's spearhead, the 4th Armoured Division, made contact with the 101st Airborne on the day after Christmas.

The relief of Bastogne sealed the fate of the German offensive, while heroic defensive efforts at Elsenborn Ridge, St Vith and elsewhere had contained the German thrust within a week. Soon the great bulge began to resemble a gigantic Allied pincer movement rather than a tremendous German threat. As 1944 ebbed away, so too did Hitler's dream of ultimate victory in the West. By 15 January 1945, Allied forces had converged on the city of Houffalize, Belgium, effectively reducing the German salient.

IRREPLACEABLE LOSSES

With the failure of Operation *Watch* on the Rhine and the commencement of the Red Army winter offensive in the East on 12 January 1945, the endgame of World War II in Europe had begun. In two months, the Allies would be across the Rhine, the last imposing natural barrier to their advance. Soon the Soviets would be fighting in the suburbs of Berlin. Hitler had diverted precious troops and matériel from the Eastern Front for the all-out effort against the

RIGHT: MAJOR-GENERAL ANTHONY MCAULIFFE, *acting commander of the* 101st *Airborne Division at Bastogne, issued the famous reply of 'NUTS!' to a German demand for surrender during the Battle of the Bulge.*

BATTLE OF THE BULGE

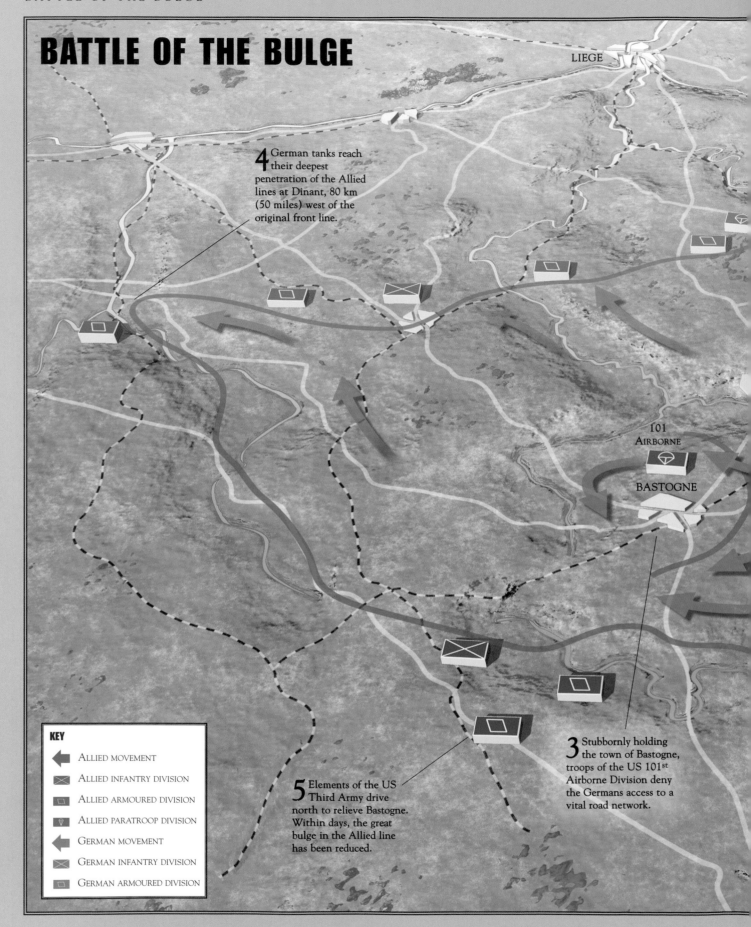

LIEGE

4 German tanks reach their deepest penetration of the Allied lines at Dinant, 80 km (50 miles) west of the original front line.

101 AIRBORNE

BASTOGNE

3 Stubbornly holding the town of Bastogne, troops of the US 101st Airborne Division deny the Germans access to a vital road network.

5 Elements of the US Third Army drive north to relieve Bastogne. Within days, the great bulge in the Allied line has been reduced.

KEY

⬅ ALLIED MOVEMENT

▥ ALLIED INFANTRY DIVISION

▢ ALLIED ARMOURED DIVISION

▽ ALLIED PARATROOP DIVISION

⬅ GERMAN MOVEMENT

▧ GERMAN INFANTRY DIVISION

▢ GERMAN ARMOURED DIVISION

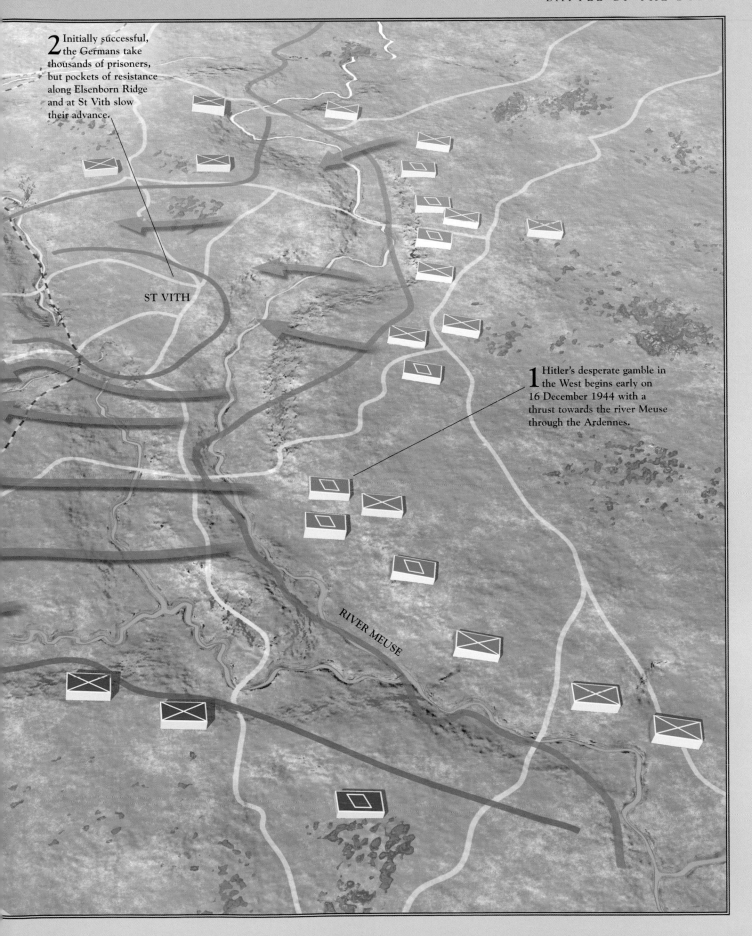

2 Initially successful, the Germans take thousands of prisoners, but pockets of resistance along Elsenborn Ridge and at St Vith slow their advance.

ST VITH

1 Hitler's desperate gamble in the West begins early on 16 December 1944 with a thrust towards the river Meuse through the Ardennes.

RIVER MEUSE

IWO JIMA

1945

The island road to Tokyo was long and bloody for the US military. Although the United States had seized the initiative in the Pacific, it was clear throughout the campaign that the Japanese were resourceful and tenacious foes – willing to fight to the death. As the war entered its fourth year, American planners had become resigned to the fact that final victory would necessitate an invasion of the Japanese home islands.

Such an undertaking would require extensive logistical preparation and suitable staging areas were needed. Already, long-range bombers were being deployed to rain death and destruction on Japanese cities. Crippled bombers returning to distant bases in the Marianas needed a safe haven to land. Aboard each bomber was a crew of 10–14 men.

The island of Iwo Jima in the Volcanoes Group seemed to fill both requirements. Situated only 1062km (660 miles) south of Tokyo, the Japanese had already constructed airfields there. Although taking the island promised to be a

IWO JIMA FACTS

Who: Japanese troops under Lieutenant-General Tadamichi Kuribayashi (1891–1945) versus US Marines under Lieutenant-General Holland M. Smith (1882–1967).

What: US Marines attempted to capture the island in the Volcanoes Group.

Where: The island of Iwo Jima in the Pacific Ocean, less than 1127km (700 miles) from the Japanese home islands.

When: 19 February to 26 March 1945

Why: Iwo Jima could provide a staging area for future operations and a safe haven for crippled bombers returning from raids on Japanese cities.

Outcome: US Marines captured Iwo Jima after more than a month of savage fighting. Over 20,000 Japanese soldiers were killed and just a few hundred captured. American forces suffered almost 7000 killed and 19,000 wounded.

CAPTURED BY PHOTOGRAPHER Joe Rosenthal, this image of US Marines and a Navy corpsman raising the US flag on Mount Suribachi at Iwo Jima is perhaps the most enduring of World War II. In fact, the flag had been raised earlier that day but the action was restaged for the camera.

IN THIS AERIAL VIEW of the American landings at Iwo Jima, assault craft approach the black, volcanic sand beaches. The Japanese waited for the landing areas to choke with men and equipment before opening fire.

LVT-4 'WATER BUFFALO'

At the landings on Iwo Jima, the LVT-4 (Landing Vehicle Tracked) was the latest in a series of amphibious assault vehicles deployed in the Pacific during operations against the Japanese. Thousands of LVT variants were produced during the war.

Based upon an initial design by Donald Roebling in 1935, the LVT demonstrated its worth during the landings at Tarawa in November 1943, and was improved with greater armour protection and both .50-cal. and .30-cal. Browning machine guns.

difficult affair, Admiral Chester Nimitz (1885–1966), Commander-in-Chief of the Pacific Fleet, authorized Operation *Detachment* to commence in February 1945, with US Marine Major-General Holland Smith (1882–1967) in command of the offensive against Iwo Jima.

SULPHUR ISLAND

Shaped like a pork chop, Iwo Jima is scarcely 8km (5 miles) long and 7.2km (4.5 miles) across at its widest point. At the southern tip, the 170m (550-ft) Mount Suribachi rises to dominate most of the island. Despite its relatively diminutive stature, Iwo Jima had been turned into a fortress by more than 25,000 Japanese troops and a large contingent of Korean labourers under the command of Lieutenant-General Tadamichi Kuribayashi (1891–1945).

Across the island the Japanese had constructed a labyrinth of pillboxes, bunkers, machine-gun nests, artillery emplacements and spider holes large enough only for a single soldier. Many of the Japanese guns were positioned with interlocking fields of fire, their positions reinforced with steel, concrete, coconut logs and heaps of sand to absorb the shock waves of American pre-invasion bombardment. The Japanese had also honeycombed Mount Suribachi itself with tunnels and artillery and machine-gun emplacements near the mouths of caves.

The US plan was straightforward: the 4th and 5th Marine Divisions with the 3rd Division in reserve, more than 40,000 strong, were to assault beaches on the southern end of Iwo Jima. From there, they would isolate and capture Mount Suribachi, fight their way across the island, take the airfields and subdue pockets of Japanese resistance.

TO THE SUMMIT OF SURIBACHI

On the morning of 19 February 1945, US Marines hit the beach on Iwo Jima. For 20 minutes, there was virtually no reaction from the Japanese defenders. Kuribayashi, who had instructed his soldiers to kill 10 Americans before sacrificing themselves for the emperor, had also told his men to hold their fire until the invasion beaches were choked with American troops and landing craft. With a thunderous crash, the eerie silence was broken. Japanese bullets and shells rained down on the Americans and inflicted heavy

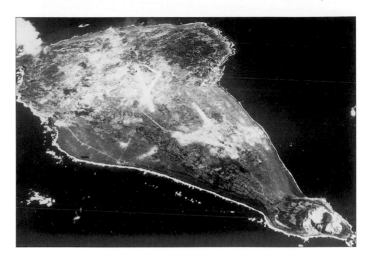

ABOVE: SHAPED LIKE A pork chop, the island of Iwo Jima is dominated by the 170m (550-ft) Mount Suribachi. Control of its airstrips saved the lives of thousands of American airmen.

BELOW: GRUMMAN F4F WILDCAT fighter planes prepare to take off on a support mission from the deck of the escort carrier USS Makin. US air superiority was complete by this stage in the war.

WARY OF JAPANESE SNIPERS *and well camouflaged machine gun nests, a US Marine shouts to a comrade. After more than a month of bitter fighting, Iwo Jima was declared secure.*

casualties. To make matters worse, the black volcanic sand of the island made footing difficult and impeded the progress of tracked vehicles.

Nevertheless, the Marines braved withering enemy fire and managed to cut off Mount Suribachi on the first day. Subsequently they fought their way to the base of the extinct volcano and began an arduous climb. Although the high ground was far from secure, on 23 February a patrol worked its way to the top of Mount Suribachi and triumphantly raised a small US flag amid exploding Japanese grenades and sniper fire.

Hours later a second, much larger flag was located and carried to the summit. It was the raising of this flag which Associated Press photographer Joe Rosenthal captured on film. At the sight of the banner, Americans fighting and even dying across Iwo Jima lifted a collective cheer. Naval vessels offshore sounded their horns and claxons. Rosenthal's frame became one of the enduring images of the twentieth century and made instant celebrities of the group of six flag raisers, three of whom did not survive the battle for Iwo Jima to learn of their newfound fame. The image became the focus of a war bond tour across the United States and inspired the US Marine Corps Memorial in Washington DC.

YARD BY TERRIBLE YARD

In spite of this great boost to morale, more than a month of difficult fighting lay ahead for the Americans, whose numbers continued to grow on this small spit of land. Tanks were called upon regularly to fire point blank into Japanese fortifications. Individual acts of heroism occurred everywhere, and 26 Marines were awarded the Congressional Medal of Honor for their courage.

Progress was measured in yards, and otherwise nondescript locales earned lasting nicknames such as Bloody Gorge, the Amphitheater, Turkey Knob and the Meat Grinder. Marines crawled forward to fling grenades and satchel charges into the firing slits of Japanese bunkers or the mouths of caves. Flamethrowers burned defenders alive, routing them out of their defensive positions or immolating them where they stood. Some caves were sealed with explosives or bulldozers, burying their enemy occupants alive. Several times, the Japanese hurled themselves against well-entrenched Marines in suicidal banzai charges and died to the last man.

By 27 February, the two completed airstrips were in US hands and a third, which was under construction, had been taken as well. On 4 March, with the battle for the island still raging, the first four-engine Boeing B-29 Superfortress bomber made an emergency landing on Iwo Jima. During the remainder of the war, more than 2200 such landings were made and the estimated number of airmen saved topped 24,000. Fighters soon began flying escort missions with the big bombers as well.

IN THE MOUNTAIN'S SHADOW

Not until 26 March, after 36 days of combat, was Iwo Jima finally declared secure. The Japanese garrison on the island was virtually wiped out during the fighting. The Marines captured only 216 prisoners and some 3000 holdouts were still being eliminated months later. Although Kuribayashi's

body was never found, he was reported either to have committed suicide or to have been killed while leading a final desperate banzai charge. The Americans lost more than 6800 dead and 17,000 wounded at Iwo Jima, but the objectives of Operation *Detachment* had been achieved. Just days after the official end of the Iwo Jima battle, Marines and troops of the US Army landed on the island of Okinawa, moving another step closer to the home islands of Japan.

Iwo Jima stands as an epic of heroism and sacrifice by the men of the US Marine Corps. 'The raising of that flag on Suribachi means a Marine Corps for the next 500 years,' noted Secretary of the Navy James Forrestal (1892–1949). Admiral Nimitz captured the essence of the struggle, stating that at Iwo Jima 'uncommon valour was a common virtue'.

A US MARINE uses a flamethrower to silence a Japanese bunker on Iwo Jima. The island's fanatical defenders usually fought to the death, preferring even suicide to surrender.

IWO JIMA

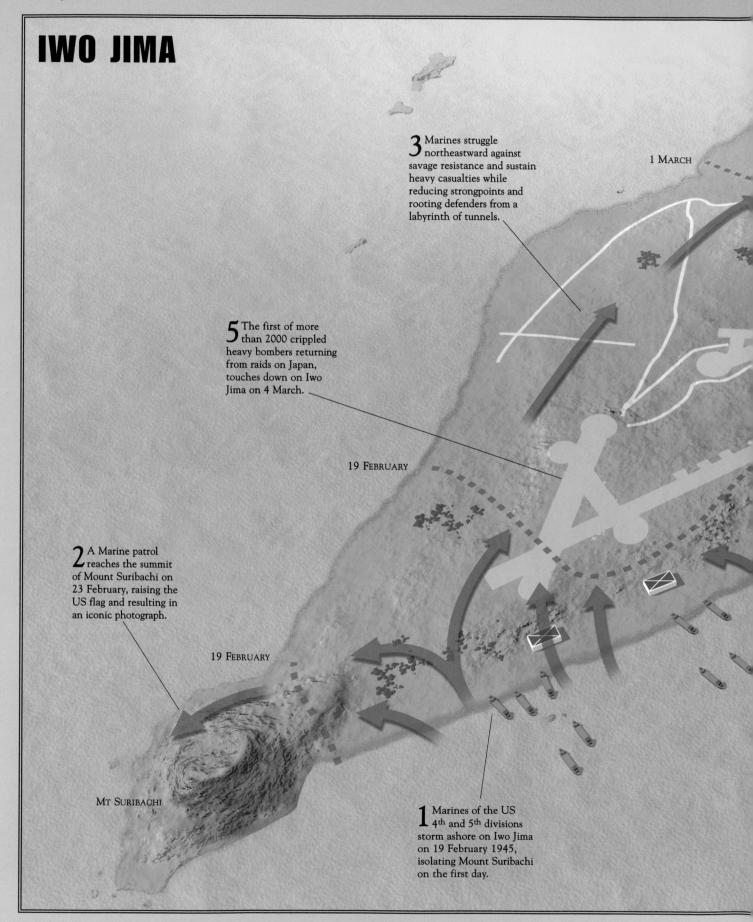

3 Marines struggle northeastward against savage resistance and sustain heavy casualties while reducing strongpoints and rooting defenders from a labyrinth of tunnels.

1 MARCH

5 The first of more than 2000 crippled heavy bombers returning from raids on Japan, touches down on Iwo Jima on 4 March.

19 FEBRUARY

2 A Marine patrol reaches the summit of Mount Suribachi on 23 February, raising the US flag and resulting in an iconic photograph.

19 FEBRUARY

MT SURIBACHI

1 Marines of the US 4th and 5th divisions storm ashore on Iwo Jima on 19 February 1945, isolating Mount Suribachi on the first day.

6 Following 36 days of harrowing combat, Iwo Jima is declared secure on 26 March. US casualties exceed 17,000. The Japanese garrison is virtually annihilated.

9 MARCH

4 Using flamethrowers and explosive charges, the Marines seal some enemy positions with bulldozers. Three airfields constructed by the Japanese are captured by 27 February.

KEY

US MOVEMENT

US MARINES

JAPANESE FORCES

BATTLE FOR BERLIN

1945

By the end of 1944, it was clear that Germany was losing the war. Two Red Army Fronts, commanded by Marshal Ivan Konev (1897–1973) and Marshal Georgy Zhukov (1896–1974), were advancing rapidly across western Poland. Further north, the 2nd Belorussian Front under Marshal Konstantin Rokossovsky (1896–1968) pushed into the Baltic states.

Here Colonel-General Gotthard Heinrici's (1886–1971) under-equipped Army Group Vistula was the sole barrier between Berlin and the Soviets. On the western front, German forces had smarted from the failed offensive in the Ardennes. By 3 April, Anglo-American forces had completed their encirclement of the Ruhr and prisoners were being taken at the rate of 15,000–20,000 a day.

BATTLE FOR BERLIN FACTS

Who: Red Army forces ordered by Stalin to capture Berlin, led by Marshal Ivan Konev (1897–1973) and Marshal Georgy Zhukov (1896–1974), versus Hitler's designated defender of Berlin, General Karl Weidling (1891–1955)

What: Victory was eventually assured for the Soviet Union as German forces, overwhelmed by sheer weight of men and armour, were encircled by eight Soviet armies smashing their way through Berlin.

Where: The Soviet Army's final offensive broke across the Oder and after vicious street-by-street fighting took the *Reich's* capital itself.

When: Between 16 April 1945 and 2 May 1945.

Why: The Allies believed that only with the successful assault on Berlin and defeat of the forces controlling it could the war be brought to a final, irreversible conclusion.

Outcome: Nazism was effectively defeated, leaving Berliners to count the cost. The daunting task of rebuilding a shattered Europe lay ahead.

LARGE ARTILLERY PIECES such as this tractor-borne 152mm (6.5in) gun formed a significant arm of Red Army forces shattering Berlin, along with assault guns, infantry and support troops.

LEFT: RED ARMY SOLDIERS *were involved in a week of street fighting in Berlin before finally destroying any effective German resistance. By 27 April, the capital's garrison was confined to a narrow 16km (10-mile) corridor.*

assured that the Red Army would never reach Germany, soon realized that the enemy was edging into the city suburbs. Amid the rumble of Soviet guns, people of all ages were mustered to build fortifications. Houses and blocks of flats were transformed into concrete strong points. On Sunday 15 April, Adolf Hitler, confined to his bunker beneath the Chancellery garden, issued the last of his directives, which was given an optimistic gloss: 'The enemy will be greeted by massive artillery fire. Gaps in our infantry will have been made good by countless new units … The Bolshevik … must and shall bleed to death before the capital of the German *Reich* … ', The prospect of new units was the *Führer's* delusion. Manpower ranged from 15-year-old Hitler Youth personnel to men in their seventies. So-called 'infantry' consisted of 60,000 untrained, exhausted *Volkssturm* (Home Guardsmen) whose average ammunition supply was around five rounds per rifle and these, along with such machine guns as there were, had largely been salvaged from occupied countries.

At 3 a.m. Berlin time the next day, three red flares shot into the sky and the artillery opened fire. The sky was full of searchlight beams boring into dense smoke and boiling dust. Although many of the pontoon bridges had not been completed, Red Army infantry north and south of the bridgehead situated near the town of Kustrin, which had expected the arrival of assault boats, plunged into the river Oder, their log boats supporting guns and rafts heavy with supplies.

BRIDGEHEAD ATTACK

The troops of Zhukov's First Belorussian Front had been ordered by Stalin to make the attack on Berlin from the bridgehead. At the Seelow Heights, situated some 90km

By then, Berlin was an outnumbered fortress city: one million men were concentrated in the sector with 10,400 guns and mortars, 1500 tanks and assault guns and 3300 aircraft. The Soviets had 2,500,000 men, more than 42,000 guns and mortars, more than 6200 tanks and self-propelled guns and 8300 aircraft. Berliners, who had been

BELOW: THE T34/85, *part of the 4000-strong Soviet armada of tanks approaching Berlin, was a later variant on the USSR's highly effective leviathan, armed with enlarged turret and armament. By the war's end, the T-34 was accounting for around 70 per cent of Soviet tank production.*

30 APRIL 1945: Soviet infantrymen battle their way into the still defended Reichstag, fixing an improvised flag to one of its columns. The event was later restaged for cameras.

(60 miles) east of Berlin and overlooking the western flood plain of the Oder, reception was fierce and the Soviets were held off until late on 17 April. This was in contrast with Konev, who had crossed the Neisse to the south across open terrain more favourable to tanks and made rapid progress. Stalin ordered Konev to turn two of his tank armies northwards to aid Zhukov. The breakthrough to the Berlin suburbs was achieved on 19 April.

The next day was the *Führer's* birthday, marked by barrages of exploding artillery shells and the deafening howls of multi-barrelled rocket launchers. But still there were forces desperately fighting to hold their positions before the city. Ninth Army under General Theodor Busse had originally been given the task of blocking the Soviets' direct route to Berlin, while General Hasso von Manteuffel's 3rd Panzer Army had been positioned further north. Although von Manteuffel had some success and managed to hang on briefly, it was clear by 21 April that Busse's forces were on the point of total collapse. An appeal went out to Lieutenant-General Hans Krebs of the High Command of the Army Chief of Staff, that Busse should withdraw or face total destruction. The reply was predictable: Ninth Army was to stay where it was and hold on to its positions.

HOPES OF RESCUE

Hitler next seized on the presence of SS *Obergruppenführer* Felix Steiner's III SS *Germanische* Corps, situated in the area of Eberswalde to the north of Berlin. Steiner's Corps was directed to attack forthwith on von Manteuffel's flank, drive south to cut off the Soviet assault and re-establish contact between the Third and Ninth Armies. But there were no experienced troops available to Steiner. What Hitler called Army Group Steiner was mostly sweepings from the *Luftwaffe* personnel, local *Volkssturm* and assorted police. In no way could they challenge the strength of Rokossovsky's and Zhukov's fronts. Von Manteuffel was heard to comment, 'We have an army of ghosts'.

ABOVE: ON 20 APRIL, HIS 56TH BIRTHDAY, Hitler in the Berlin Chancellery garden makes his last photographed appearance, awarding decorations to Hitler Youth, the youngest of whom was 12.

BELOW: RED ARMY ARMOUR passes through the suburbs of Berlin following the surrender of the city, May 1945.

Frantically clutching at straws, Hitler next pinned his hopes on the Twelfth Army of General Walther Wenck, which was to be rushed from the Western Front. Wenck was ordered to disengage from the Americans to his west and attack to the east, linking up with Busse and together attacking the Soviets surrounding Berlin. Sole resources were raw recruits; there were no battle-worthy tanks. On 23 April, Hitler received a blunt report from General Karl Weidling, Battle Commandant of Berlin, that there was only sufficient ammunition for two days' fighting. Nevertheless, Weidling hung on with such forces as he possessed while the Soviet stranglehold grew tight around the city, now a few blocks from the bunker. There Hitler, rapidly declining in health and lost in his delusions, kept saying, "Where is Wenck? Where is Wenck?" But by now Wenck, a realist and severely disillusioned, was seeking to bring remnants of his own army and of Ninth Army, together with as many civilian refugees as possible, safely across the Elbe into US Army-occupied territory. By 30 April, Berlin was a raging inferno throughout. For the Soviets, there was a prime objective: the capture of the iconic *Reichstag*, still heavily defended by its garrison. Even so, by early afternoon the Soviet Red victory banner was flying from the dome.

UNCONDITIONAL SURRENDER

Later that same day Hans Krebs, a Russian speaker, was dispatched under a white flag to meet the Red Army's General Vasily Chuikov to discuss surrender terms and to

MARSHAL GEORGY ZHUKOV

A man of peasant background, Georgy Zhukov emerged as the most outstanding military figure in the Red Army during World War II. He was created First Deputy Supreme Commander-in-Chief Soviet Armed Forces in August 1942, serving in the post throughout the conflict. Responsible for the attack that relieved Stalingrad, he went on to coordinate the First and Second Belorussian Fronts in the 1944 summer offensive, and he commanded the First Belorussian Front in the final assault on Germany and capture of Berlin, becoming Commander-in-Chief of Soviet occupation forces. In 1955–57, he served as Soviet Minister of Defence, but had long incurred Stalin's jealousy, and was dismissed and disgraced for allegedly challenging the Communist Party leadership of the Armed Forces. Partly rehabilitated under Khrushchev, he died in June 1974, his ashes buried in the Kremlin wall with full military honours.

THE BERLIN POPULACE faces the reality of defeat, with hardly a building left intact. Here, women and children pass by the Brandenburg Gate.

inform him that Hitler and his new spouse Eva Braun had committed suicide. Chuikov made it clear that the Soviets would not accept anything but unconditional surrender. Meanwhile, Soviet military action would be unremitting. Krebs also killed himself and his body was later found in the bunker. It was left to Weidling, the last commander of the Berlin defence zone, formally to surrender the city to the Soviets at 1.00 p.m. on 2 May. By 4.00 a.m., the fighting was over. Figures for the number of dead during the battle could never be calculated precisely, but it is generally thought that up to 100,000 German troops lost their lives and a likely equal number of civilians. Around the same number of Soviet soldiers died. Berlin, in effect, had to be recreated.

AFTERMATH

Defeat heralded a long period of decline for much of Germany. With the ending of the Nazi dictatorship, East Germany faced years of Communist oppression, economic misery and, for the ordinary citizen, many of the familiar trappings of dictatorship, notably the presence of the Stasi secret police, regarded by many as successors to the Gestapo. Not until 12 September 1990 was Germany formally reunified and many of the inequalities of the poor East and prosperous West consigned to history.

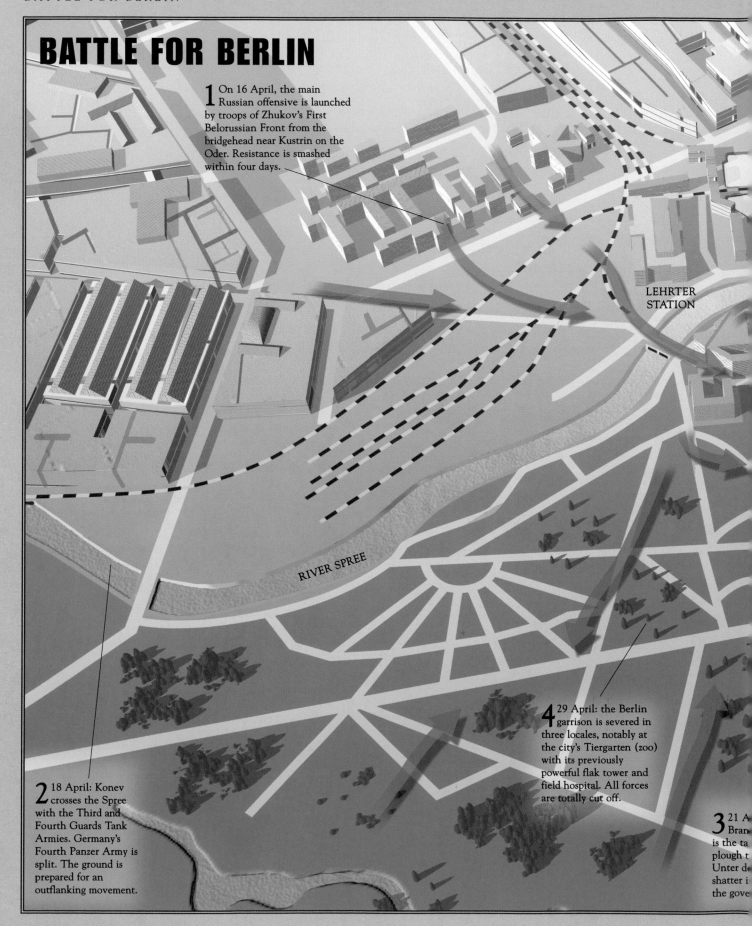

BATTLE FOR BERLIN

1 On 16 April, the main Russian offensive is launched by troops of Zhukov's First Belorussian Front from the bridgehead near Kustrin on the Oder. Resistance is smashed within four days.

LEHRTER STATION

RIVER SPREE

4 29 April: the Berlin garrison is severed in three locales, notably at the city's Tiergarten (zoo) with its previously powerful flak tower and field hospital. All forces are totally cut off.

2 18 April: Konev crosses the Spree with the Third and Fourth Guards Tank Armies. Germany's Fourth Panzer Army is split. The ground is prepared for an outflanking movement.

3 21 A Bran is the ta plough t Unter de shatter i the gove

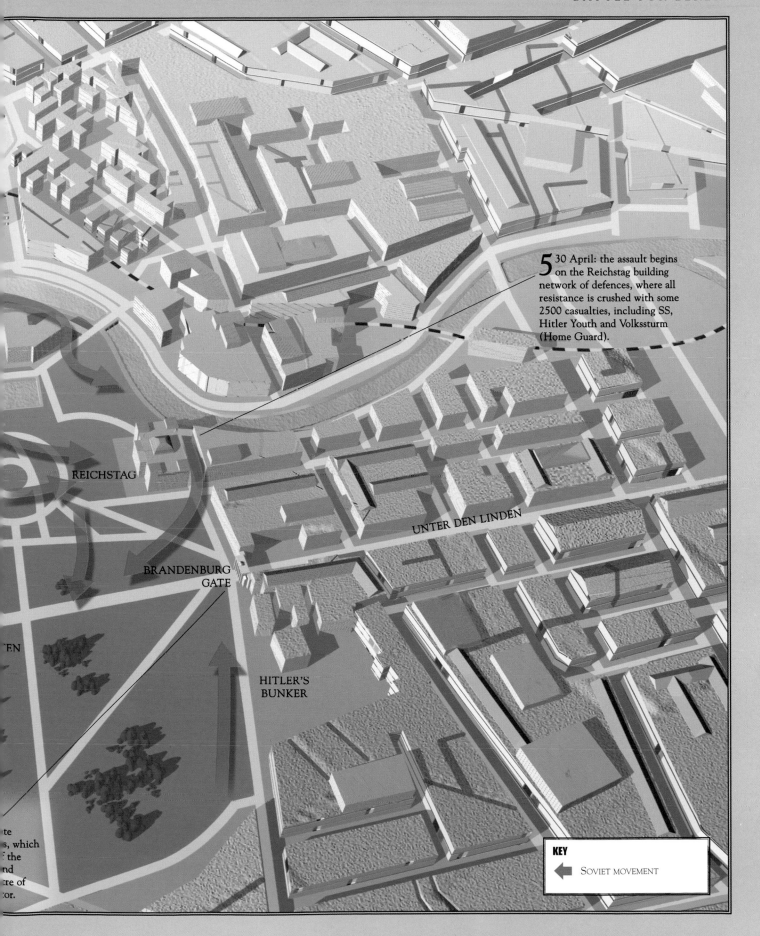

5 30 April: the assault begins on the Reichstag building network of defences, where all resistance is crushed with some 2500 casualties, including SS, Hitler Youth and Volkssturm (Home Guard).

REICHSTAG

UNTER DEN LINDEN

BRANDENBURG
GATE

'EN

HITLER'S
BUNKER

te
s, which
f the
nd
re of
or.

KEY

◄ SOVIET MOVEMENT

OKINAWA 1945

The Allies' amphibious invasion of Okinawa was a massive undertaking, against heavy and determined resistance. Japanese forces on the island were aware that they faced overwhelming opposition and were determined to exact as high a price as they could from the invaders.

The war in the Pacific was characterized by 'island-hopping' operations, which allowed the Allies to steadily encroach on the Japanese islands. Where possible, garrisons cut off by the Allied advance were bypassed and allowed to wither on the vine. Without amphibious transport, they were no threat and, lacking re-supply, would eventually become incapable of combat.

However, some objectives simply had to be taken. Okinawa was one – it was needed as a staging post for the final assault on Japan. This was obvious to the Japanese as well as the Allies and preparations were put in place well in advance. As the Japanese perimeter out in the Pacific gradually collapsed inwards, fortifications were dug and plans were laid to make the assault on Okinawa as expensive as possible.

OKINAWA FACTS

Who: Allied (mainly US) forces numbering 548,000 soldiers and 1300 ships, versus 100,000 Japanese ground, air and naval forces.

What: The Allies launched the largest amphibious operation of the Pacific campaign.

Where: Okinawa, in the Pacific Ocean

When: 1 April–21 June 1945

Why: The island was to be used as a staging point for the invasion of the Japanese homeland.

Outcome: The Allies captured Okinawa and 90 per cent of the buildings on the island were completely destroyed. Okinawa provided a fleet anchorage, troop staging areas and airfields in close proximity to Japan, allowing the Allies to prepare for the invasion of Japan.

US LANDING CRAFT bring stores ashore on 13 April 1945, during the battle for Okinawa. The packed horizon gives an indication of the size of the naval armada involved in the operation.

ABOVE: AIR SUPPORT FOR THE NAVAL armada and the ground forces fighting on Okinawa was supplied by naval fighters and fighter-bombers, such as these F4U Corsairs, flying from more than 40 Allied aircraft carriers.

With near-total command of the sea, the Allies could land more or less anywhere they pleased. It was not possible to prevent a landing and unlikely that a counterattack could contain one. The Japanese assumed that the Allies would get ashore, though they did what they could to make this costly. The defences of the island were centred on a medieval castle whose position guaranteed that the Allies would have no easy avenue of attack and would have to fight through the well-prepared fortifications.

While some of the islands the Allies assaulted were garrisoned by small forces, often with little artillery or air defence equipment, Okinawa was defended by several divisions with good support and, critically, plenty of artillery. These belonged to the Thirty-Second Army under the

command of Lieutenant-General Mitsuru Ushijima (1887–1945), who had his headquarters in the medieval fortress of Shuri Castle in the south of the island. Defence of the northern sector was the responsibility of Colonel Takehido Udo.

The Allied ground commander was Lieutenant-General Simon Buckner Jr (1886–1945), commanding the US Tenth Army. Buckner had a marine and an infantry corps under his command, each of two divisions, plus an additional marine and two more army divisions as a reserve.

THE ALLIES ARRIVE

The first phase of the battle was the Allied effort to establish air and naval supremacy in the vicinity of Okinawa. Forces from Britain, Australia and New Zealand contributed here, though the ground forces were exclusively American.

Marines were landed on nearby islands from 26 March onwards, clearing opposition to create a safe anchorage. Meanwhile carrier-borne aircraft attacked airfields while the Japanese struck back with air attacks including hundreds of kamikaze aircraft. These sank several vessels and damaged others; the US Navy suffered its heaviest battle casualties of the war off Okinawa.

The Allies also faced naval attacks. By this time, the Imperial Japanese Navy was a skeleton of its former power, short of fuel and with few ships remaining. However, the super-battleship Yamato was available along with the light cruiser Yahagi and eight destroyers. There was only enough fuel for a one-way mission, so the Yamato was to attack the Allied fleet while her fuel remained, then beach herself on Okinawa, where her 450mm (18in) guns would join the defence.

RIGHT: THE US INVASION force moors off Okinawa, April 1945. The Americans committed more than half a million men and 1300 ships to capturing this small Japanese island.

THESE US MARINES' ARMAMENT includes rifles and carbines, which were handier for close-range combat in the jungles of the island. Semi-automatic operation allowed for a high rate of fire.

Yamato and her escorts sailed on 6 April under the command of Admiral Seiichi Ito (1890 1945), who had originally refused to carry out what he saw as a wasteful and hopeless gesture. Events proved him right.

Yamato was incredibly well protected, but the Allies had total air supremacy with large numbers of dive-bombers and torpedo aircraft available. The Yamato task force was sighted soon after leaving port. On 7 April, it came under intense air attack from more than 400 Allied planes. One by one, the escorts were sunk and the giant ship was hit by several bombs as well as ten torpedoes.

A battleship force was waiting in case Yamato somehow got through, but there was no need. After two hours of attack, the last Japanese battleship capsized and exploded, taking most of her crew with her. There was no further naval interference in the invasion.

THE ALLIES ADVANCE

US Marines began going ashore on Okinawa on 31 March 1945, when an advance force was put ashore. The main landings began the next day, assisted by diversionary operations to distract the enemy and slow their response.

USS *INTREPID*

Aircraft carriers were a vital weapon in attacking the islands of the Pacific, which were often out of range of land-based aircraft, and in defending the fleet against air attack. Although the Japanese naval air arm was irretrievably smashed by 1945, kamikaze aircraft and small-scale raids still posed a serious threat.

USS Intrepid, an Essex-class carrier, suffered a near miss and a hit from kamikaze aircraft while on station off Okinawa. Good damage control procedures kept her in action. She operated 90-100 fighters, dive bombers and torpedo bombers; her loss or withdrawal for repairs would have dented Allied air superiority, though not badly, as many other carriers were available.

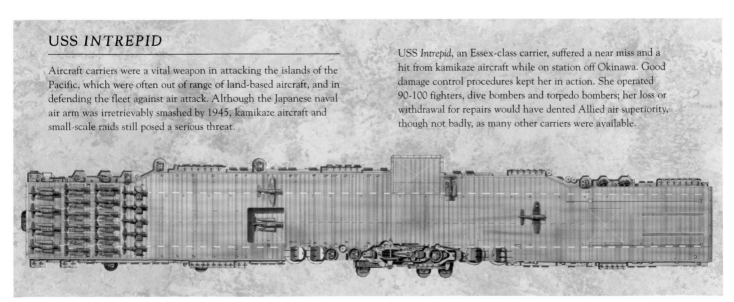

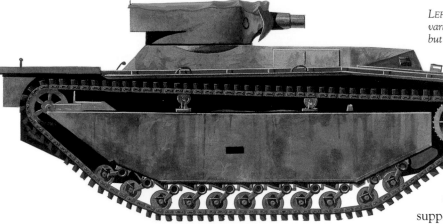

LEFT: THE LANDING VEHICLE (TRACKED) *is an armoured fire support variant designated LVT(A)-4. Its 75mm (2.95in) howitzer had a short range but could provide vital fire support for troops assaulting a defended island.*

The initial landings went well, largely because the defenders knew they could not be strong everywhere and had concentrated their forces where they would be most effective. Okinawa is a long, narrow island running broadly southwest–northeast with small peninsulas and a number of islands off the coast. The main Japanese force was concentrated in the southern end of the island and took some time to reduce. Defences were lighter to the north, and after clearing the immediate area the Allies were able to push northeast, driving the defenders steadily back.

The Allies made steady progress in the north, reaching the end of the island by 13 April, though the Motobu Peninsula and the island of Ie Shima were stubbornly held and not taken until 21 April. Pushing south was more of a problem: progress was slow and fiercely opposed by well dug-in Japanese troops. High ground, caves and artificial strongpoints had to be cleared by assault, resulting in hand-to-hand combat. Each was hotly contested and the Allies took heavy casualties as they pushed onwards.

After clearing what turned out to be a strong outpost line at Cactus Ridge, the advance became stalled for a time against the main Japanese line of resistance at Kakazu Ridge. Then from 12–14 April the Japanese counterattacked strongly.

Each assault was beaten off with heavy casualties on both sides and after this attempt the Japanese went back on the defensive.

On 19 April, the Allies made a renewed attempt to get the offensive moving. Under cover of diversionary operations and a huge artillery and naval bombardment, a powerful assault went in, supported by heavy air attack. However, the Japanese had ridden out the barrage in strong positions and were in good shape to resist the assault. Tanks – including flamethrowers – were of some assistance, but little headway was made.

Ushijima considered a counterattack but decided against it. His reserves were needed to counter a possible landing behind his lines by US 2nd Marine Division, which was making threatening movements by way of a diversion.

THE FIGHT FOR OKINAWA

The stalemate went on until the end of the month despite fresh US troops rotating into the line. On 4 May, the Japanese again counterattacked. The plan was ambitious and included an attempt to outflank US positions by amphibious operations. Despite determined efforts, the counterattack failed, and on 11 May Buckner went back over to the offensive. On 13 May US forces finally broke the Shuri defensive line. Infantry of the 96th Division and armoured supports ground their way into Japanese positions on Conical Hill as 6th Marine Division took Sugar Loaf Hill. With these key terrain features in US hands, the main Japanese line was compromised, but the monsoon weather made further advances difficult for a time.

The centre of the main line was Shuri Castle. With the flanks turned, the castle was exposed to attack and there was a chance to encircle the defenders. Major-General Pedro del Valle's (1893–1978) 1st Marine Division stormed the castle on 29 May. This not only broke the main defensive line but also greatly disheartened the Japanese forces on Okinawa, though they were able to fall back to a final position on the southern tip of the island.

The costly advance was then resumed, with the marines forced to dig fanatical defenders out of their positions. Many fought to the last or killed themselves to evade capture. Among them were Ushijima and his chief of staff, Lieutenant-General Isamu Cho. The remainder held their final line until 17 June, when the defence finally collapsed. This was a rare occasion on which significant numbers of Japanese troops surrendered. The

LEFT: *A US* MARINE FIRES *his Thompson submachinegun during the fighting on Wana Ridge. Heavy shelling has reduced the vegetation to tree stumps and tangles of fallen branches.*

RIGHT: A JAPANESE BOY CARRIES his baby sibling following the surrender of Okinawa. The civilian population suffered terribly, with an estimated 140,000 dying over the course of the three-month battle.

US Marines developed techniques to reduce casualties: for example, one method of clearing a cave involved the mouth being taken under heavy fire, after which a flamethrower tank approached and sprayed burning fuel into the interior, clearing any last defenders. However, despite such measures losses were very severe.

In the last days of the campaign, General Buckner was killed by enemy shellfire, making him the most senior US officer to be killed in action during the war. Heavy shellfire from both sides was a characteristic of the Okinawa campaign, which became known as the Typhoon of Steel.

The last organized resistance on Okinawa was the 24th Infantry Division, which was still fighting on 21 June. After this formation was broken, pockets of Japanese soldiers held out for another 10 days or so, but were mopped up one by one. The most senior Japanese officer captured alive was a major.

Many of those who survived tried to hide among the local population but were revealed by the Okinawans, who had no reason to shelter their enemies. Japanese soldiers had used Okinawan civilians as human shields or sent them to collect water under fire. In the closing stages of the battle, the Japanese encouraged locals to kill themselves rather than submit to the Allies.

AFTERMATH

Okinawa was firmly in Allied hands by the end of June. There was never any chance of the Japanese military holding the island. The defence was intended to delay the Allies as long as possible and to inflict as many casualties as possible. In this, the defence was a success. US forces suffered extremely heavy casualties, in part because of the refusal of Japanese troops to surrender even when surrounded and cut off. Once Okinawa was taken, it could be used as a base for the invasion of Japan itself. The nature of the resistance and the casualties incurred worried the Allies. An attack on the Japanese islands would be extremely costly. However, such a costly assault was made unnecessary by the use of atomic bombs in August 1945, which brought the war to an end.

BELOW: ALTHOUGH THE JAPANESE defence of Okinawa collapsed on 17 June, clearing out the last pockets of resistance took until the end of the month.

OKINAWA

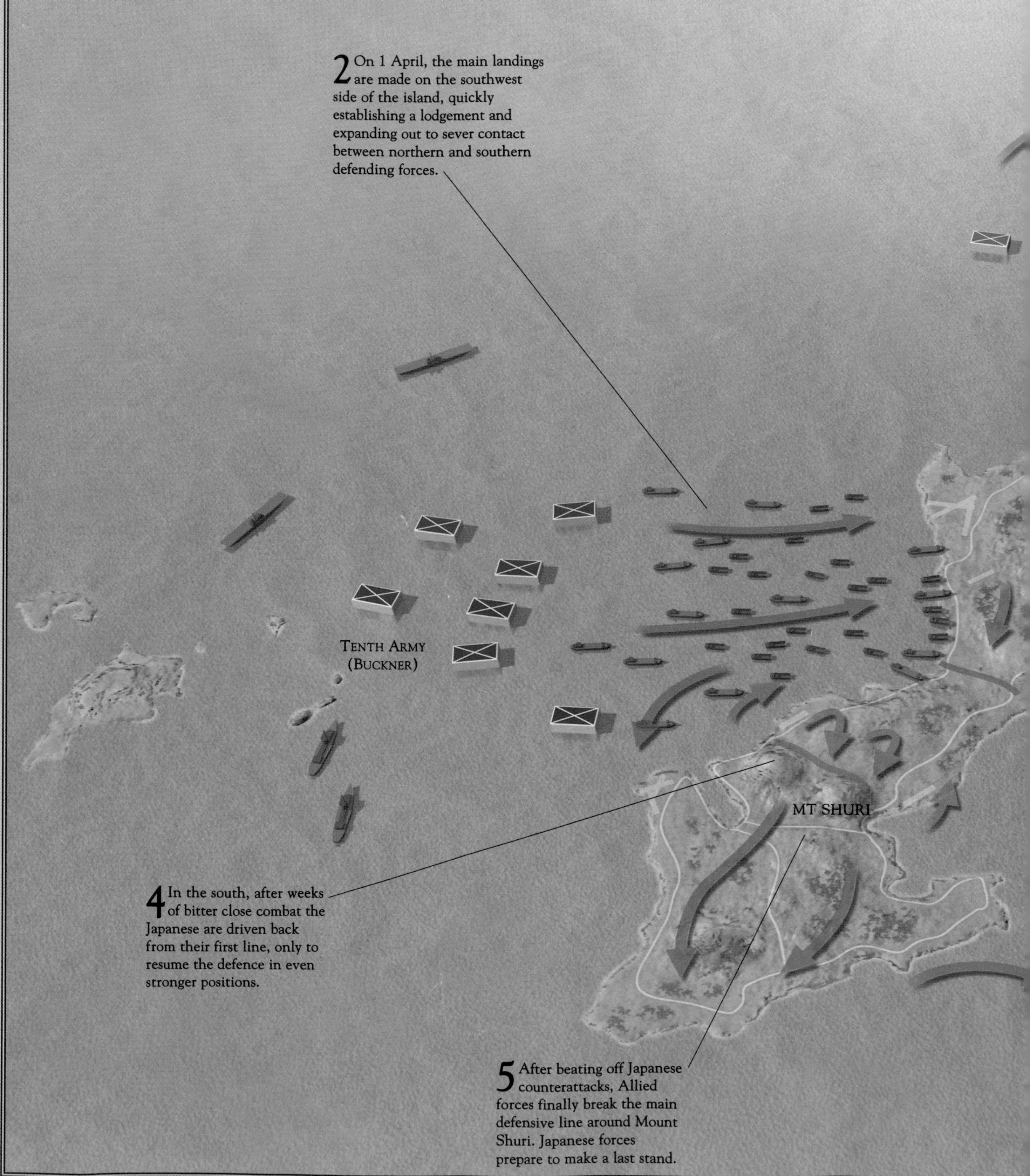

2 On 1 April, the main landings are made on the southwest side of the island, quickly establishing a lodgement and expanding out to sever contact between northern and southern defending forces.

TENTH ARMY
(BUCKNER)

4 In the south, after weeks of bitter close combat the Japanese are driven back from their first line, only to resume the defence in even stronger positions.

MT SHURI

5 After beating off Japanese counterattacks, Allied forces finally break the main defensive line around Mount Shuri. Japanese forces prepare to make a last stand.

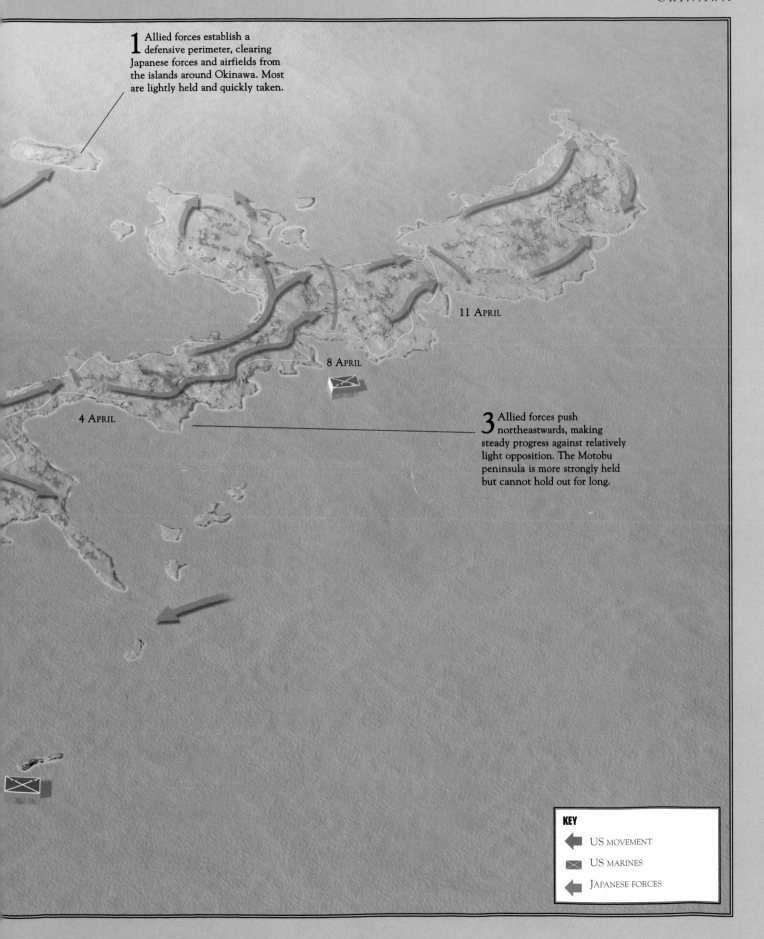

1 Allied forces establish a defensive perimeter, clearing Japanese forces and airfields from the islands around Okinawa. Most are lightly held and quickly taken.

11 APRIL

8 APRIL

4 APRIL

3 Allied forces push northeastwards, making steady progress against relatively light opposition. The Motobu peninsula is more strongly held but cannot hold out for long.

KEY

US MOVEMENT

US MARINES

JAPANESE FORCES

INDEX

Page numbers in *Italics* refer to illustrations: those in **bold** type refer to map illustrations with text.

1942

2 JANUARY British and Commonwealth forces in Malaya retreat in the face of Japanese forces.

8 FEBRUARY Red Army cuts off 90,000 German troops at Demyansk.

15 FEBRUARY Surrender of British and Commonwealth forces to the Japanese at Singapore.

24–29 OCTOBER British launch their big offensive at El Alamein, defeating Rommel's Africa Corps.

8 NOVEMBER Allied forces land unopposed in Vichy French North Africa.

24 DECEMBER German forces are encircled in Stalingrad.

1 FEBRUARY New Enigma cipher adopted by U-boat fleet, rendering communications traffic unreadable by British codebreakers.

7 FEBRUARY Supply convoys sail to Malta, carrying Spitfire fighters aboard aircraft carriers.

16 FEBRUARY U-boats launch a major anti-shipping offensive off the US eastern seaboard, sinking 71 ships during the remainder of the month. As a consequence, convoys are introduced.

7–8 MAY Battle of the Coral Sea.

4–5 JUNE Battle of Midway. All four Japanese aircraft carriers are sunk by the end of the 5 June.

12 NOVEMBER Battle for Guadalcanal begins.

19 FEBRUARY Japanese bomb Darwin, Australia.

5 APRIL Japanese bomb Colombo, Ceylon.

18 APRIL 'Doolittle raid' on Tokyo by US bombers.

30/31 MAY First 1000 bomber raid against Cologne, planned by new Air Chief Marshal Arthur 'Bomber' Harris.

25/26 JUNE Third and final 1000 bomber raid by RAF against Bremen.

10 AUGUST RAF's area bombing offensive threatened as Germans begin jamming the Gee navigation system.

12 JANUARY Japan declares war on Dutch East Indies.

25 JANUARY Siam declares war on Britain and US.

8 MARCH Japanese forces enters Siam, oil-rich Rangoon and land on Australian New Guinea.

9 MARCH Dutch East Indies surrender to Japan.

8 NOVEMBER Marshal Pétain secretly instructs the French High Commissioner in Algiers to open negotiations with the invading Allied forces of French North Africa.

11 NOVEMBER French forces in Morocco and Algeria sign armistice with the Allies; in retaliation, Germans occupy Vichy France.

1943

22 JANUARY German Sixth Army in Stalingrad cut in two: the final phase of the defeat of the Germans at Stalingrad begins.

1/2 FEBRUARY Japanese begin evacuation of Guadalcanal after Allied attack.

7 MAY Tunis falls to Allies.

5–12 JULY Germans launch Operation Citadel at Kursk in an attempt to gain the initiative on the Eastern Front. The operation is a failure.

3 SEPTEMBER Allied landings on mainland Italy begin.

6 NOVEMBER Soviets liberate Kiev.

27 DECEMBER In Italy, Eighth Army captures Ortona after fierce German resistance.

18 FEBRUARY US Navy bombards Japanese positions in the Aleutian Islands.

24 MAY Germany withdraws U-boats from North Atlantic after losing 33 U-boats in a month.

1 JULY Allies concentrate on attacking 'Milch Cow' refuelling U-Boats in Bay of Biscay.

10 JULY Allied landings in Sicily begin.

20 SEPTEMBER The Wolfpack U-boat campaign attacking Allied convoys reopens.

26 DECEMBER *Scharnhorst* sunk by British Home Fleet in last major gunnery duel in Royal Navy history.

18 FEBRUARY US Navy bombards Japanese positions in the Aleutian Islands.

17 MARCH The Axis powers now outnumbered in North Africa: while Britain and America have 3000 aircraft, the Axis powers have only 500.

13 MAY Sardinia bombarded by Allies from air for 14 days.

16/17 MAY RAF 617 Squadron carries out 'bouncing bomb' raids against German Ruhr dams.

17 AUGUST USAAF raid on Schweinfurt and Regensburg suffers heavy losses.

10 OCTOBER US Flying Fortresses begin attacks on Greece and Romanian oil fields.

9 MARCH Due to illness, Rommel is replaced as German commander-in-chief in North Africa.

18 APRIL Admiral Yamamoto, mastermind of the Pearl Harbor attack, is shot down and killed by American fighters.

25 JULY Mussolini arrested and deposed as Italian leader.

8 SEPTEMBER Italian surrender announced.

13 NOVEMBER Allies recognize Italy as a co-belligerent, formally accepting Italy's wish to change sides.

28 NOVEMBER–1 DECEMBER Tehran Summit between Churchill, Roosevelt and Stalin.